Pilgrimage Explored

YORK MEDIEVAL PRESS

York Medieval Press is published by the University of York's Centre for Medieval Studies in association with Boydell & Brewer Ltd. Our objective is the promotion of innovative scholarship and fresh criticism on medieval culture. We have a special commitment to interdisciplinary study, in line with the Centre's belief that the future of Medieval Studies lies in those areas in which its major constituent disciplines at once inform and challenge each other.

Editorial Board (1996–98):

Prof. A. J. Minnis (Chair; Dept of English & Related Literature)
Prof. M. O. H. Carver (Dept of Archaeology)
Dr C. R. E. Cubitt (Dept of History)
Dr E. C. Norton (Dept of Art History)
Prof. W. M. Ormrod (Dept of History)

All inquiries of an editorial kind, including suggestions for monographs and essay collections, should be addressed to: The Secretary, University of York, Centre for Medieval Studies, The King's Manor, York YO1 2EP (E-mail: LAH1@unix.york.ac.uk).

Previous publications of York Medieval Press:

God's Words, Women's Voices: The Discernment of Spirits in the Writing of Late-Medieval Women Visionaries, Rosalynn Voaden (1999)

York Studies in Medieval Theology:

Medieval Theology and the Natural Body, ed. Peter Biller and A. J. Minnis (1997)

Handling Sin: Confession in the Middle Ages, ed. Peter Biller and A. J. Minnis (1998)

Previous publications of The Centre for Medieval Studies:

Latin and Vernacular: Studies in Late-Medieval Texts and Manuscripts, ed. A. J. Minnis (1989) [Proceedings of the 1987 York Manuscripts Conference]

Regionalism in Late-Medieval Manuscripts and Texts: Essays celebrating the publication of 'A Linguistic Atlas of Late Mediaeval English', ed. Felicity Riddy (1991) [Proceedings of the 1989 York Manuscripts Conference]

Late-Medieval Religious Texts and their Transmission: Essays in Honour of A. I. Doyle, ed. A. J. Minnis (1994) [Proceedings of the 1991 York Manuscripts Conference]

Pilgrimage Explored

Edited by
J. STOPFORD

YORK MEDIEVAL PRESS

© Editor and Contributors 1999

All Rights Reserved. Except as permitted under current legislation no part of this work may be photocopied, stored in a retrieval system, published, performed in public, adapted, broadcast, transmitted, recorded or reproduced in any form or by any means, without the prior permission of the copyright owner

First published 1999

A York Medieval Press publication
in association with The Boydell Press
an imprint of Boydell & Brewer Ltd
PO Box 9   Woodbridge   Suffolk IP12 3DF   UK
website http://www.boydell.co.uk
and of Boydell & Brewer Inc.
PO Box 41026   Rochester   NY 14604–4126   USA
and with the
Centre for Medieval Studies, University of York

ISBN 0 9529734 3 X

A catalogue record for this book is available
from the British Library

Library of Congress Cataloging-in-Publication Data
Pilgrimage explored / edited by J. Stopford.
    p. cm.
    Includes bibliographical references.
    ISBN 0–9529734–3–X (alk. paper)
    1. Christian pilgrims and pilgrimages – Europe – History.
I. Stopford, J. (Jennie)
BV896.E85P56   1999
263'.041'09 – dc21   98–51451

This publication is printed on acid-free paper

Printed in Great Britain by
St Edmundsbury Press Ltd, Bury St Edmunds, Suffolk

CONTENTS

List of Illustrations   vii
Introduction   ix
List of Contributors   xvi
List of Abbreviations   xvii

1. Pilgrimage in Prehistoric Britain?   1
   Richard Bradley

2. Were there Christian Pilgrims before Constantine?   25
   E. D. Hunt

3. Sacred Journeying: Women's Correspondence and Pilgrimage in the Fourth and Eighth Centuries   41
   Julie Ann Smith

4. Patrons, Pilgrims and the Cult of Saints in the Medieval Kingdom of León   57
   Simon Barton

5. Jacques de Vitry and the Ideology of Pilgrimage   79
   Debra J. Birch

6. The Medieval Experience at the Shrine   95
   Ben Nilson

7. The Perils, or Otherwise, of Maritime Pilgrimage to Santiago de Compostela in the Fifteenth Century   123
   Wendy R. Childs

8. Pilgrimage and the Cult of St Katherine of Alexandria in Late Medieval England   145
   Katherine J. Lewis

9. Lifting the Veil on Pilgrim Badges   161
   A. M. Koldeweij

10. Pilgrimage to Walsingham and the Re Invention of the Middle Ages   189
    Simon Coleman and John Elsner

ILLUSTRATIONS

Chapter 1: *Pilgrimage in Prehistoric Britain?*

Fig. 1	The sites and regions considered in the text	2
Fig. 2	Concentration of monuments at Maes Howe	5
Fig. 3	Location of the Kilmartin monument complex	9
Fig. 4	Reconstruction of the stone structure at Stonehenge	11
Fig. 5	Outline plan of the timber circles at Woodhenge	14
Fig. 6	The occurrence of 'horned spirals' in Britain and Ireland	17

Chapter 4: *Patrons, Pilgrims and the Cult of Saints in León*

Map 1	Northern Spain	58

Chapter 6: *The Medieval Experience at the Shrine*

Fig. 1	The East End of Canterbury Cathedral	96
Plate 1	Detail of window from York Minster showing the life and miracles of St William of York	109

Chapter 7: *Perils, or Otherwise, of Maritime Pilgrimage*

Fig. 1	Routes between England and Galicia in the fourteenth and fifteenth centuries	124
Fig. 2	Ships licensed to carry pilgrims to Compostela, 1391–1448	130
Fig. 3	Pilgrims licensed to go to Compostela, 1391–1473	131
Fig. 4	Licences for pilgrims' ships, 1391–1473	134
Plate 1	Taking soundings in the mid-fifteenth century, as illustrated in the earliest surviving English treatise on sailing directions	140

Chapter 9: *Lifting the Veil on Pilgrim Badges*

Plate 1	Religious and secular badges excavated in the Netherlands, c. 1350–1525	169
Plate 2	St Roche with the angel	170
Plate 3	Hieronymus Bosch, lame beggar with a pilgrim sign	170
Plate 4	Pieter Brueghel the Younger, showing Flemish proverb	170
Plate 5	Badge showing crowned vulva as an archer on horseback	170

Plate 6	Phallus glass from Mainz, first half of sixteenth century	171
Plate 7	Phallus glass, first half of sixteenth century	171
Plate 8	Margin illustration from Johannis Andrea, *Novella in librum tertium Decretalium Gregorii IX*	172
Plate 9	Badge showing female smith forging a phallus	173
Plate 10	Badge showing vulva-pilgrim with phallus staff and rosary	173
Plate 11	Fragment of a badge showing vulva-pilgrim	173
Plate 12	Woodcut showing itinerant beggars	174
Plate 13	Cockle-shell, 1400–1450, pilgrim badge from Santiago de Compostela	174
Plate 14	Vera Icon badge from Rome	174
Plate 15	Badge: arrow	175
Plate 16	Pilgrim badge of the 'Engelweihe' at Einsiedeln	175
Plate 17	St Anne pilgrim badge from Düren	175
Plate 18	Fir-wood support with a pilgrim's sign	176
Plate 19	St Odilia pilgrim sign from Odilienberg (Alsace)	176
Plate 20	Records of trial	177–179
Plate 21	Pilgrim's horn	180
Plate 22	Beggar's badge of the city of Antwerp, 1565	180

Chapter 10: *Pilgrimage to Walsingham and the Re-Invention of the Middle Ages*

Plate 1	Statue of the Virgin and Child	197
Plate 2	Patten's tomb in the Anglican shrine church	202
Plate 3	View from the main door of the Anglican shrine church	205
Plate 4	The Augustinian Priory grounds during a Roman Catholic pilgrimage	211
Fig. 1	Map of Walsingham village centre	192

INTRODUCTION

The vast time scale and multi-cultural nature of pilgrimage have often been noted. It is a ritual which has been practised for thousands of years and has been a feature of every major religion and very many minor cults across the world. Less often stressed is the corollary that it is a ritual for which there is a great and continuing human need. Pilgrimage remains a popular practice today, and finds expression in both traditional religious and ostensibly secular spheres.

The papers of this volume, which are arranged in chronological order, seek to understand the nature and practice of pilgrimage at different times in what became the Christian world. Within this framework the three main themes are (1) the antiquity and duration of pilgrimage ritual, (2) the fluidity and adaptability of pilgrimage ideologies, and (3) aspects of the physical workings of pilgrimages (particularly in relation to the practicalities of the journey and practices at the shrine). The approaches taken incorporate several disciplines, including anthropology, archaeology, art history, literature and classical and medieval history.

The timespan of these papers, from prehistory to the early twentieth century, provides an opportunity for making comparisons between the attitudes of pilgrims at different times. In Chapter 1, Richard Bradley proposes that pilgrimage ritual was relevant in Neolithic Britain, about five thousand years ago, when people in this area are first known to have lived in a socially stratified society, built monuments and expressed concern about their own mortality. Subsequent chapters consider pilgrimage in early Christian times, during the Middle Ages and in the recent past. The volume concludes with a discussion by Simon Coleman and John Elsner of the creation of a modern Anglican shrine in the 1930s at Walsingham, Norfolk.

A wide range of pilgrim ideologies are analysed. The influence of the Bible on the nature of Christian pilgrimage is emphasised by David Hunt in relation to pilgrims of the second and third centuries (Chapter 2). He finds that the scholarly interests of early Christians who made journeys to holy places were inextricably linked with religious devotion. The surviving letters of women pilgrims of the fourth and eighth centuries are studied as a corpus for the first time by Julie Ann Smith (Chapter 3). She distinguishes between those women who travelled to holy places and then returned to their homes or religious communities, and those who journeyed to holy places but remained there for the rest of their lives. For this second group, re-location was a stage on the road to heaven. Their journeys were an embracement of death, bringing closer the attainment of a heavenly afterlife. The idea of pilgrimage as a metaphor for a

Introduction

journey through life was a theme of Christian writers of the fourth and sixth centuries which was subsequently taken up and developed in *c.* 1200 by Jacques de Vitry, bishop, cardinal, and perhaps the most famous preacher of his day. In a study comparing two of his sermons, Debra Birch presents an ideal of pilgrimage from the perspective of a leading early thirteenth century churchman (Chapter 5). Jacques de Vitry stressed the importance of pilgrimage as a penitential act, with suffering and hardship in this life rewarded by salvation in the next. The success of sermons like these is illustrated in Simon Barton's colourful study of religious devotion in the north of Spain, between the eighth and twelfth centuries (Chapter 4). Pilgrimage became an accepted form of penance at a time when acts of penance, in the hope of salvation, were at the heart of much pious activity. However, some pilgrimages had a specific relevance to particular sectors of society. Katherine Lewis' study is concerned with adaptations of the cult of St Katherine of Alexandria in England in the thirteenth to fifteenth centuries (Chapter 8). She shows how the devotion of genteel women to this saint was associated with aspirations toward a feminine ideal, while pilgrimage to the saint's shrine by women of lower status was a direct appeal for the provision of a good husband. Antiquarian records of folklore suggest that this popular aspect of the cult of St Katherine continued into the nineteenth century.

Several of the papers illustrate how invocations of the past were used to support ideological changes. All Christian pilgrimages involve reference to the past, recalling previous lives and events which are believed to be applicable in the present. Consequently, historical re-inventions and the adoption of so-called traditional observances can be particularly powerful forces for change in this sphere. Ideas about the practice of pilgrimage in one era become directly relevant to its practice in another. John Elsner and Simon Coleman's paper shows how modern perceptions of the medieval world, and its material remnants – in this case stones from pre-Reformation monasteries – played a crucial role in the successful establishment of a twentieth-century shrine (Chapter 10). This seems to echo some of the factors which determined the success or otherwise of shrines set up between the eighth and twelfth centuries in the Spanish kingdom of León, as discussed by Simon Barton. The story of the beginnings of the shrine of St James at Compostela, for example, includes the discovery of a Roman tomb and the invocation of an antique past in which St James had preached the gospel in Spain; something for which there is now, at least, no evidence. The adoption and re-enactment of past observances in a reconstituted form is also apparent in the pilgrimages to hill-top chapels dedicated to St Katherine in post-medieval England. Katherine Lewis suggests that these were mimetic pilgrimages, imitations of earlier 'traditional' medieval pilgrimages to St Katherine's burial place on Mt Sinai in the Holy Land.

The physical workings of some aspects of medieval Christian pilgrimage, and the complex interaction of spiritual, corporeal and economic forces, are

Introduction

addressed by Ben Nilson and Wendy Childs. Ben Nilson describes the activities and behaviour of pilgrims in England once they had reached an important shrine (Chapter 6). There appears to have been continuity in many aspects of the conduct of pilgrims at shrines between the twelfth and fifteenth centuries, although the nature of the sources makes identifying change difficult. Ben Nilson finds that viewings of the shrine became more controlled in the late Middle Ages, with a relative freedom of behaviour and access in the twelfth and thirteenth centuries giving way to more sober and orchestrated procedures in the fourteenth and fifteenth centuries. The route taken by pilgrims once they entered a great church may have been ordained by tradition, as also were the amounts and types of offerings made there, although money once left on altars or shrines was often in later times deposited in strong boxes. Continuity in physical practices at shrines may have disguised changes in ideology.

Wendy Childs discusses the practicalities of sea travel to Santiago de Compostela by English pilgrims in the fifteenth century (Chapter 7). The dangers and difficulties of sea travel in the late Middle Ages are often stressed in modern representations of medieval life. Wendy Childs suggests that, despite the undoubted risks and hardships, the longer sea routes between ports in England and northern Spain became increasingly popular among ordinary people in the first half of the fifteenth century. Using literary sources and records of licences permitting overseas travel, she shows that journeys by sea were often far quicker and cheaper than those by land. For the seamen, the routes were familiar and the pilgrims were a profitable cargo. Analysis of the sale of travel licences suggests that English ship owners took on a new role in the fifteenth century, offering what amounted to 'package tours' to pilgrims travelling to Compostela. This is something previously thought to be the preserve of the Venetians transporting pilgrims to the Holy Land. Simon Barton's paper also illustrates how closely pilgrimage was entwined in worldly, as well as spiritual, politics and economics (Chapter 4). The creation of a successful shrine or promotion of a popular cult, the support of religious institutions or provision of roads, bridges and other infrastructure necessary for pilgrimage, could accrue substantial material benefits to the donor.

Other ways in which pilgrimage spilled into, or merged with, secular life in the Middle Ages are discussed by Jos Koldeweij, who reviews the current state of study of pilgrim and other late medieval badges (Chapter 9). Recent finds of large numbers of both secular and religious badges in similar archaeological contexts in the Netherlands lead him to suggest that fewer distinctions were made between supposedly religious and supposedly secular badges in the fifteenth and sixteenth centuries than has been thought to be the case. This lack of distinction between religious and secular badges is also demonstrated by the apparently indiscriminate use of both types as identifiers among criminal and dissident fraternities of the time. It may also be apparent in the regular occurrence of both secular and religious badges with strong sexual imagery. Jos Koldeweij proposes that the interpretation of badges as amulets, objects

Introduction

which bring good luck, is equally applicable to pilgrim badges and to badges with no religious iconography.

This volume illustrates or comments upon some of the theoretical and methodological issues facing those working in multi-disciplinary areas. Our understanding of the nature of Christian pilgrimage has been strongly influenced by anthropological studies, in particular the pioneering work of Victor Turner (and subsequently Victor and Edith Turner) in the 1970s. The Turners attempted to form generalisations about Christian pilgrimage and identify what distinguished it from other kinds of ritual practice.[1] More recently, many of these generalisations have been rejected, particularly the idea of *communitas*, in which people, as pilgrims, were thought to shed the hierarchies and constraints of their daily lives, becoming part of an egalitarian and unstructured society. As expressed by John Eade and Michael Sallnow, the Turners' work is now seen as one possible view of a particular kind of pilgrimage, rather than as an explanation of pilgrimages in general.[2] Papers in the Eade and Sallnow volume show how deconstruction of the Turners' thesis has opened the way for a host of particularist studies of Christian pilgrimages, emphasising distinctions and differences in ideology, ritual and context.

Such particularist anthropological studies, which stress the diversity of human thought and behaviour, can be valuable to those in other disciplines. They can, for instance, broaden expectations of historical and archaeological data, hopefully leading to more convincing identifications and interpretations of that evidence. However the deconstruction of general models, such as those proposed by the Turners, also raises a number of problems. Deconstruction, which involves the breakdown of concepts into their constituent elements, often attempts to restrict the validity of broad based definitions. Occasionally, too, such work appears to deride the subject being explored, as if explanation and understanding can better be achieved through diminishing the subject. Multi-disciplinary studies, on the other hand, thrive on a plurality of meanings, succeeding best where connections are made between different facets of a topic so that previously unacknowledged aspects are highlighted. In this volume, for instance, rather than attempting to restrict the validity of the concept of pilgrimage, the chapters explore some of the means by which pilgrimage has retained its vitality, relevance and identity over a long period of time. Taken together, they suggest that the continued success of Christian pilgrimage has often been achieved through the combination of a fluid ideology, open to diverse and personalised adaptation, alongside an adherence to supposedly traditional observances and material assemblages.

---

1   V. Turner, *The Ritual Process: Structure and Anti-Structure* (London, 1969); V. Turner and E. Turner, *Image and Pilgrimage in Christian Culture: Anthropological Perspectives* (Oxford, 1978).
2   J. Eade and M. J. Sallnow (ed.), *Contesting the Sacred: the Anthropology of Christian Pilgrimage* (London, 1991).

Introduction

A variety of approaches to the sources are illustrated here. In Chapter 1, Richard Bradley uses comparisons between historically attested pilgrimage practices and the archaeological evidence of prehistoric sites and objects to argue for the existence of pilgrimage in prehistory. The attendant problems of imposing the interpretations of one discipline on the data of another are recognised by the author. In order to mitigate such difficulties he emphasises the importance of noting the discrepancies, as well as the similarities, which are identified through these comparisons. In Chapter 2 the tendency of recent studies to censor the existence of pilgrimage in some spheres, denying its applicability to early Christians, is rejected by David Hunt. He argues strongly from the textual evidence of the period for a devotional quest as a driving force in early Christian expeditions in the Holy Land. He makes the important point that differences between pilgrims in a variety of historical contexts do not necessarily validate the status of some or invalidate that of others.

Other contributors find ideas introduced by the Turners in the 1970s useful in interpretations of historical data. In Chapter 3, Julie Ann Smith extends the Turners' discussion of spatial liminality to explain some aspects of the nature of pilgrimage among women in the fourth and eighth centuries. In Chapter 10, Simon Coleman and John Elsner expand on views published by the Turners which emphasised the influence of the physical setting of pilgrimage sites on pilgrim behaviour. They suggest that the importance of the material culture of pilgrimage may be under-estimated in anthropological studies and that future work in this area might benefit by taking archaeological evidence and interpretation into greater account. Although, as noted above, it would now be widely accepted that the Turners' model does not provide an over-arching description of Christian pilgrimage, the expression of their views in generalised theoretical terms does mean that those ideas are available for use with other data, providing a basis for inter-disciplinary studies.

The potential for further work in some more specific areas is suggested by several of the papers. Better understanding of the use of pilgim badges will doubtless be much assisted by the international database now being created at the Catholic University of Nijmegen. It is hoped that the database will encourage more detailed recording of the archaeological contexts of finds. This would provide some independent dating evidence for particular types of badges and a log of their associations could begin.

Future work will, no doubt, also involve continued assessment of the numbers of medieval pilgrims. These are generally thought to be high, particularly from the twelfth century, but estimates vary widely. Given suitable sources, Ben Nilson's method of assessing the numbers of pilgrims visiting particular shrines might be adapted elsewhere. The figures analysed here suggest that overall numbers of pilgrims at established English shrines in the fourteenth and fifteenth centuries were not as great as might have been expected. This topic could also be addressed in a comparison of the documentary and archaeological evidence for the provision for pilgrims at some sites.

Introduction

Discrepancies in one's perception of the numbers of medieval pilgrims are, for example, provoked by the hospital of Santa Cristina at Somport, high up on one of the passes through the Pyrenees. This was described in the twelfth-century *Book of St James* as one of the three great 'columns' which God had established for the support of the poor (the other two being those of Jerusalem and Mont-Joux; see Simon Barton, p. 74). Such a celebrated institution, intended to cater for pilgrims on the hardest part of their journey in an area where they could be snowed up for days, might be expected to be of substantial size. Yet this is not borne out by the dimensions of the apsidal-ended church at Santa Cristina, still visible on the ground although now flanked by a ski resort, which are only about 16m. by 5m. There has as yet been little investigation of the physical remains of sites providing services to pilgrims and the lack of adequate recording of standing buildings along the Compostela route prior to the recent conservation programme funded by the European Union is a matter for regret.

It is hoped that this volume will lead to a reconsideration of conservation and heritage management policy in relation to pilgrimage sites. The significance of stones from pre-Reformation monastic sites is discussed by Simon Coleman and John Elsner in relation to Walsingham in Chapter 10. Stones from medieval religious sites are regularly sought by religious and charitable foundations today. A recent trawl through the archive relating to Whitby Abbey, North Yorkshire, shows that requests for pieces of stone from that site were received by Ministry of Works officials, and more recently by English Heritage inspectors and civic authorities, in a small but steady trickle throughout much of the twentieth century.[3] The requests were often from institutions dedicated to St Hilda, founder of the seventh-century monastery at Whitby. The stones were seen as a source of inspiration, providing a physical connection or bond with St Hilda's work and ideals, and were often to be built into the fabric of places which referred to women and to learning. Requests in the 1920s and 30s seem to have been granted, and stones went out to a woman sailing for New Zealand to join a Melanesian mission and to churches or religious communities in Ontario, Canada, and London and Sheffield in England. In the 1950s, however, a request from Mt Wellington, New Zealand, was refused on the grounds of administrative difficulties. A fundamental lack of understanding of the modern-day significance of such remains was demonstrated in 1962 when a church in Mornington, New Zealand, was refused in the following terms: 'We understand that the stone you saw is quite plain and has no carving on it, nor is it even moulded. We do not therefore see that such a stone would have any significance for the purpose you have in mind.' Responses to requests made in the 1960s on behalf of the Whitby American Montessori Center, Connecticut, St Hilda's Church in Auckland, New Zealand, and St Hilda's College of the University of Melbourne are not recorded in the archive.

[3] PRO, London, WORKS14/1169 37404; WORKS14/2669 37404.

Introduction

A more sympathetic hearing has been given to some similar requests in recent times but more detailed consideration should be given to the gamut of issues which arise in relation to these applications.

The continued importance of pilgrimage means that this volume, while about the past, is directly relevant to the present. Historical studies impact upon people's lives in the modern world by providing ideas and formats from which contemporary pilgrimages are sometimes constructed. It would appear also that historical, archaeological and anthropological studies have a role to play in explaining and demonstrating the significance of the physical remains of past pilgrimage sites, so as to inform future conservation and curatorial policies.

The lectures published here were given in the York Medieval Seminars programme for 1996. They were delivered either at the Centre for Medieval Studies, University of York, UK, or at the 31st International Congress on Medieval Studies, held 9–12 May, 1996, University of Western Michigan, Kalamazoo, USA. The contribution from Professor Dr Koldeweij was requested following the Medieval Europe 1997 conference held at Brugge, Belgium.

Jennifer Stopford, Department of Archaeology, University of York

CONTRIBUTORS

Richard Bradley
Department of Archaeology, University of Reading

E. D. Hunt
Department of Classics and Ancient History, University of Durham

Julie Ann Smith
Department of History, Massey University, New Zealand.

Simon Barton
Department of Spanish, University of Exeter

Debra J. Birch
Institute of Historical Research, University of London

Ben Nilson
Department of History, Okanagan University College, Canada

Wendy R. Childs
School of History, University of Leeds

Katherine J. Lewis
Centre for Medieval Studies, University of York

A. M. Koldeweij
Department of Art History, University of Nijmegen, Nederland

Simon Coleman
Department of Anthropology, University of Durham

John Elsner
Courtauld Institute of Art, London

ABBREVIATIONS

AASS	*Acta Sanctorum Bollandiana*, ed. J. Bollandus *et al.*, 61 vols. (Antwerp, 1643–)
AHN	Archivo Histórico Nacional
CUL, MS EDC	Cambridge University Library, Ely Dean and Chapter
DDCA	Durham Dean and Chapter Archives
EETS ES	Early English Text Society Extra Series
EETS OS	Early English Text Society Original Series
EETS SS	Early English Text Society Supplementary Series
LCA, D&C	Lincoln County Archive, Dean and Chapter
MGH.SS	*Monumenta Germaniae Historica, Scriptores*, 30 vols. (Leipzig, 1826–1934)
PL	*Patrologiae cursus completus. Series Latina*, ed. J. P. Migne, 221 vols. (Paris, 1879–1890)
PRO	Public Record Office
WAM	Westminster Abbey Muniments

1

Pilgrimage in Prehistoric Britain?

RICHARD BRADLEY

There must always have been difficulties in discussing pilgrimage in British prehistory, for the entire literature amounts to less than a single article. The only modern discussion is a brief commentary by Colin Renfrew which forms part of a more general account of the archaeology of Orkney.[1] In a discipline where so much else has been written, it is worth reflecting on the sources of such reticence.

1994 saw the publication of a volume of the journal *World Archaeology* concerned with the 'Archaeology of Pilgrimage'.[2] The subject was devised during a meeting of the editorial board and that particular issue was entrusted to a medievalist. Each number of the journal is structured around a single theme, which is advertised well in advance. There is a general call for contributions, and at the editor's discretion this can be supplemented by a number of solicited articles. The progress of this volume was most revealing. Although two writers with direct experience of prehistoric archaeology did submit papers to the journal, in each case these were concerned with relatively recent periods. Norman Hammond considered the re-use of Maya monuments in Belize after the Spanish conquest of the region, whilst Peter Harbison discussed Christian pilgrimage in the Dingle peninsula of south-west Ireland. There were no articles concerned with the prehistoric period, and those authorities who were approached to write papers on this subject all declined the invitation. Why was this?

A superficial reading of the contents page of that issue of *World Archaeology* might suggest that pilgrimage is only worth discussing in historically documented societies. Alternatively, it may be that the very concept of pilgrimage is so nebulous that it cannot be used in studies of the more distant past. Neither argument is convincing. Pilgrimage is widely attested in the ethnographic record and there seems no reason for prehistorians to reject this subject out of hand. In fact many of the concepts used in their research are drawn directly from disciplines like social anthropology, where they have been formulated on

---

1 C. Renfrew, 'Epilogue', in *The Prehistory of Orkney*, ed. C. Renfrew (Edinburgh, 1985), pp. 255–6.
2 J. Graham-Campbell (ed.), 'Archaeology of Pilgrimage', *World Archaeology* 26/1 (1994).

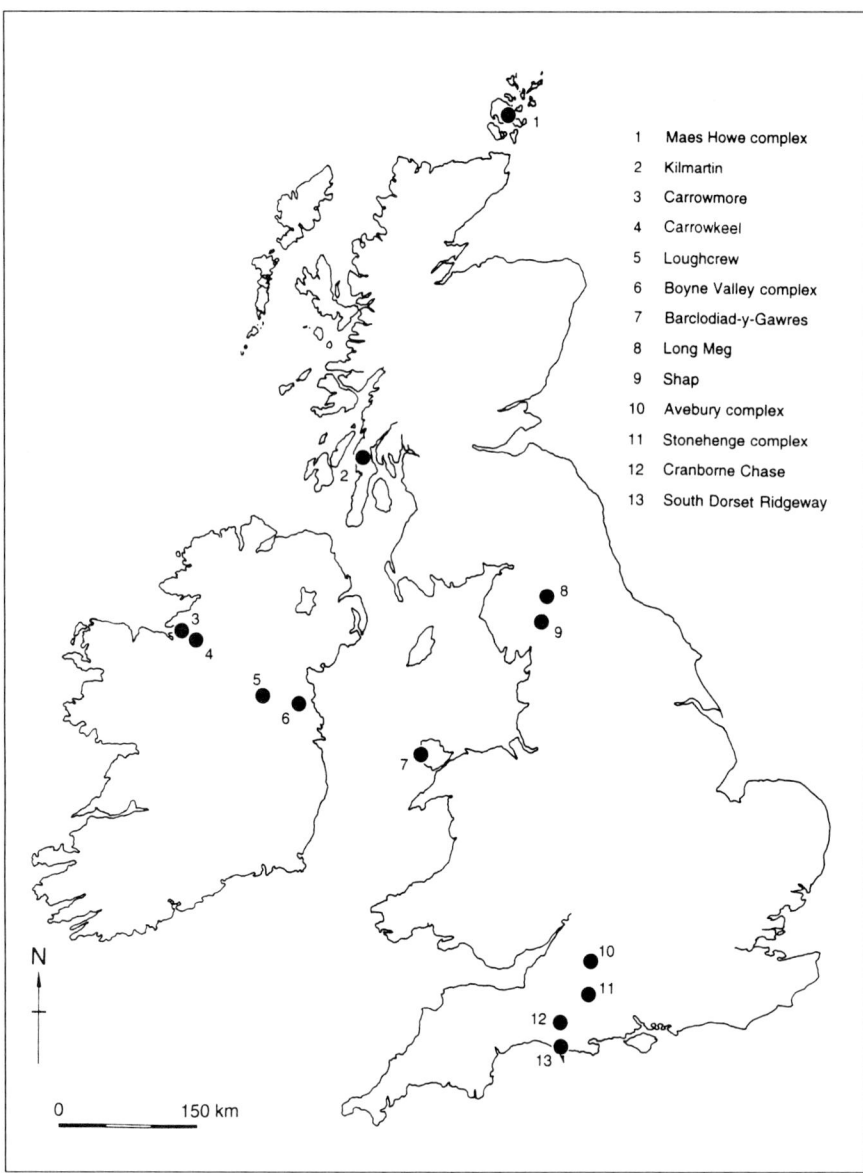

Figure 1 The sites and regions considered in the text. The Maes Howe complex in Orkney includes Barnhouse, the Ring of Brodgar, the Stones of Stenness and the Ring of Bookan. The Boyne Valley complex in Ireland includes Newgrange and Knowth. Temple Wood is at Kilmartin. In southern England, the Avebury complex includes West Kennet and Silbury Hill, and the Stonehenge complex includes Woodhenge and Durrington Walls.

the basis of cross-cultural generalisation. The basic conception of the pilgrimage ought to be no exception.

A *caveat* must be entered at this point. Anthropological generalisations are only useful in archaeology so long as they are treated as a source of ideas. Those ideas must be accepted or rejected according to their utility in investigating specific problems. In no sense can they override the details of the archaeological record: they are an aid to theorising, but that is all. Nor is this to suggest that the sole object of archaeological research is to arrive at general statements similar to those borrowed from social scientists, for by doing so there is a danger of overlooking the distinctive character of particular societies in the past. Unless archaeologists take enough account of their own raw material, the discipline will be impoverished. There is a paradox here. Prehistorians cannot discuss the past without employing concepts that have a wider application, for otherwise they will be unable to communicate with anyone else. But unless they can offer case studies that respect the distinctive character of their own subject matter, their analyses will be of little interest.

For this reason pilgrimage is considered here as a model which may or may not assist in archaeological interpretation. It is not a monolithic institution which must be present or absent in prehistory. Rather, this paper examines some of the aspects of pilgrimage found in historical and anthropological accounts – ritual centres, their operation and the journeys to them – and asks whether any of these may shed light on behaviour in the past. Pilgrimage as a coherent concept is returned to only at the end.

The brevity of the existing literature has already been noted. It consists of a single section in Renfrew's discussion of Neolithic Orkney, and significantly its title takes the form of a question: 'Prehistoric pilgrimages?' Although Renfrew has referred to this topic in his more recent writing, he has still to elaborate on his original suggestions.[3]

He makes several important points. In Orkney, as in many other regions, there are what seem to have been major ceremonial centres. In his words these were probably used for 'periodic meetings and gatherings'.[4] The constructions at these centres are of types that are shared between widely separated regions of Britain and Ireland. Contacts between these different areas are also evidenced by the movement of portable artefacts which can often be traced back to their original sources. As Renfrew says, it is 'against such a background of movement' ... [that] 'the parallel development of rituals, of monuments and of symbolic systems in different parts of Britain becomes much easier to comprehend'.[5] One possibility is that these contacts were effected through the institution of pilgrimage. In Renfrew's carefully chosen words 'one is tempted

---

[3] C. Renfrew, 'Trade beyond the material', in *Trade and Exchange in Prehistoric Europe*, ed. C. Scarre and F. Healy (Oxford, 1993), pp. 5–16.
[4] Renfrew 1985, *op. cit.* note 1, p. 256.
[5] Renfrew 1985, *op. cit.* note 1, p. 255.

to wonder whether there may not have been some agency of greater mobility at work in the spread of ritual ideas. Were there perhaps seasonal festivals at many of the great ritual centres and holy places of Britain, which attracted worshippers and adherents not simply from the outlying parts of their own territories, but from much further afield?'[6] This is the question addressed here.

In order to keep the discussion within bounds, and to draw on the same material as Colin Renfrew, this account is limited to the Late Neolithic period in Britain and Ireland (Figure 1). Four kinds of evidence are considered. The first to be discussed is the distinctive nature of the ceremonial centres referred to in Renfrew's paper. It is particularly important to establish whether these places played a major role in relations with the supernatural and whether they were visited by people who were not usually resident in the area. Secondly, the ways in which some of these places were used is considered. Then some evidence is offered for the distinctive character of movement to and from such monuments in relation to our wider understanding of prehistoric society in the British Isles. And, finally, there is consideration of the more general questions with which this paper began. How useful is the idea of pilgrimage in the interpretation of early prehistory?

The Geography of Observance

The period considered by Renfrew is called the Late Neolithic and this discussion will be concerned with developments that happened between approximately 3300 and 2300 BC, although some developments that occurred during the following phase, the Early Bronze Age will also be described.[7] This period saw the creation of no fewer than four major types of monument. The first of these were the megalithic tombs usually referred to as passage graves. These consisted of circular mounds or cairns with a corbelled chamber at their centre. They take their name from the low passages which communicated between the chamber and the outside world. Passage graves were often succeeded by a series of open enclosures or arenas. Those confined by a circular earthwork, often with an internal ditch, are described as henge monuments, whilst the name of the other type is the stone circle, whose most famous example is Stonehenge in Wiltshire. During the Early Bronze Age both forms of enclosure could be found in close proximity to unchambered burial mounds or 'round barrows'. The history of this last group of monuments began in the Neolithic period but most examples are of later date.

As Renfrew recognised, few of these constructions exist in isolation. On the Mainland of Orkney, for example, the great passage grave of Maes Howe is

---

[6] Renfrew 1985, *op. cit.* note 1.
[7] The background is summarised in J. V. S. Megaw and D. D. A. Simpson, *Introduction to British Prehistory* (Leicester, 1979) and T. Darvill, *Prehistoric Britain* (London, 1987).

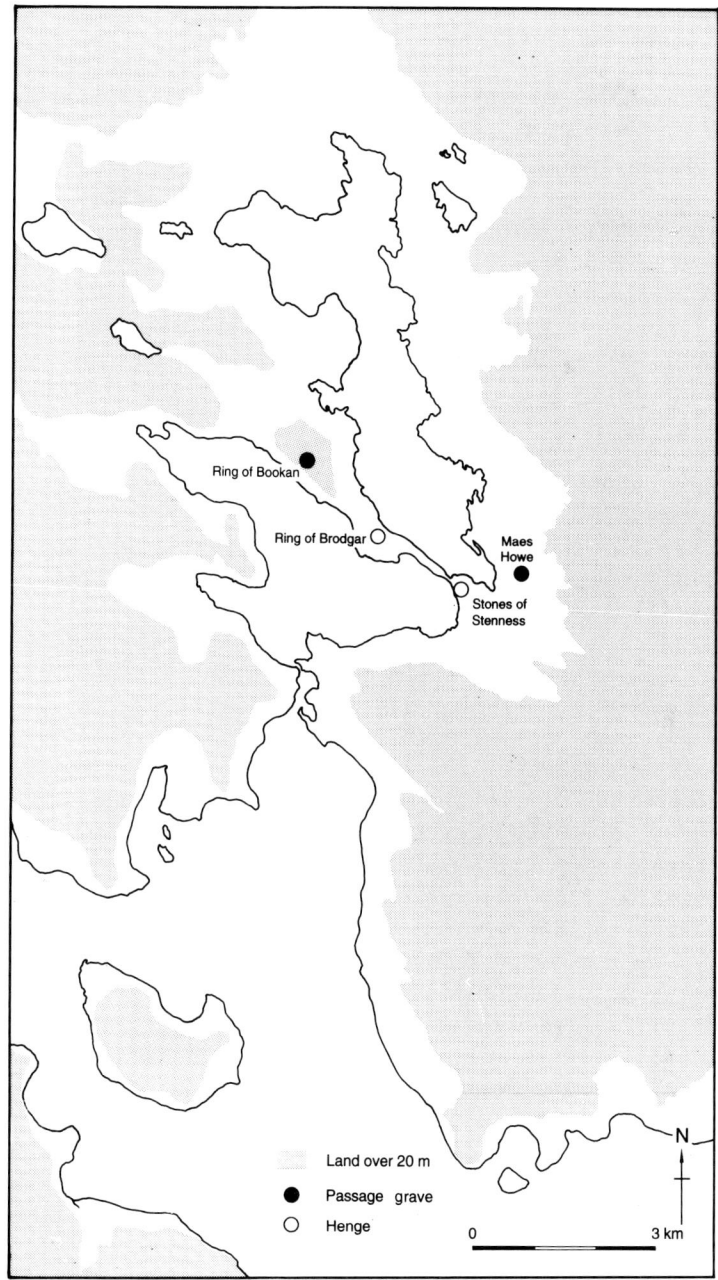

Figure 2 The concentration of major monuments in the Maes Howe complex, Orkney. The sites are located in a natural basin with a continuous horizon of higher ground.

located close to two circular earthworks each of them containing a stone circle. In archaeological parlance all these monuments belong to the Neolithic period (Figure 2). There is also a dense distribution of round barrows in the vicinity which probably date from the Early Bronze Age.[8] Exactly the same can be said of monuments in southern England. The area immediately around Stonehenge includes at least three circular enclosures, all of them containing the remains of timber circles, and several hundred round barrows.[9]

The first question to ask is whether such monument complexes necessarily served a non-local audience. Much of the evidence is equivocal. For some years it was supposed that large concentrations of sites of this kind existed in virtual isolation, so that such areas could be described, rather vaguely, as 'ritual landscapes'. Now it is known that they are by no means lacking in evidence of settlement. The ploughed fields around Stonehenge, for example, contain many thousands of worked flints which form the residue of everyday activities taking place in the landscape surrounding the monument,[10] whilst recent work on the Orkney Mainland has located an entire village amongst the group of major monuments located near to Maes Howe.[11] How is such evidence to be interpreted? At first sight we might suppose that these monuments were directed towards an entirely local audience, but there are serious objections to this view. The Orkney settlement of Barnhouse may be located amidst the most impressive monuments anywhere in the Northern Isles, but other very similar settlements with no major monuments in the vicinity are known elsewhere in the region. In the same way, it seems most unlikely that a massive structure like Stonehenge could have been built entirely by the people living in the area. Its construction demanded a considerable labour force and yet the archaeological and environmental evidence from the surrounding region does not suggest that the local population was greater than anywhere else. The inhabitants do not seem to have worked unaided.

Part of the problem is that field research has concentrated on major monuments and their surroundings, and so it is far from clear whether other parts of the landscape were occupied on the same scale. One exception is fieldwork in south Dorset where the systematic collection of surface artefacts in a number of sample areas suggests that the density of human occupation actually increased with distance away from one of these monument complexes.[12] In that case the ceremonial centre – if that is what it is – may have been towards the edge of the settled landscape and people could have visited it

---

[8] C. Richards, 'Monuments as landscape: creating the centre of the world in Neolithic Orkney', *World Archaeology* 28/2 (1996), pp. 190–208.
[9] J. Richards, *The Stonehenge Environs Project* (London, 1990).
[10] J. Richards 1990, *op. cit.* note 9.
[11] C. Richards 1996, *op. cit.* note 8.
[12] P. Woodward, *The South Dorset Ridgeway: Survey and Excavations, 1977–1984* (Dorchester, 1991), pp. 73–95.

from the surrounding area. Taken together, such arguments might well support Renfrew's suggestion that such places were the ritual *foci* of Neolithic societies.

A second characteristic of these monument complexes is their siting in the landscape. Two observations are often made in the literature. Monuments or monument complexes may be spaced at approximately equal distances from one another, as if each of them was at the centre of a different territory.[13] At the same time, the regions that saw the growth of major ceremonial centres usually include areas of particularly productive farmland.[14] It is easy to conclude that the growth of these complexes depended on an agricultural surplus and that henges and similar sites dominated the surrounding area.

Neither of these arguments is particularly satisfactory. It may be true that major building projects could only be supported where there were the means to sustain a labour force, but there are many equally productive areas of Britain where similar evidence is rare or even absent. In East Anglia, for instance, henge monuments are uncommon and those that were constructed were built on a smaller scale than many of the sites in other regions. In the same way, the spacing of these monuments is by no means self-explanatory; their immediate setting in the landscape also needs to be considered. This can be very revealing. Many of the most important sites are actually located along major rivers, or, in northern England, at the mouths of important valleys providing access through the high ground. Other sites may be found towards the heads of those valleys and some stone circles are located in mountain passes. Many of the most imposing monuments are near modern main roads. These relationships may be more than coincidental. Such sites may not have been located in order to dominate political territories, as Renfrew's work suggests: at a detailed local level these monuments may have been sited on long-established route ways so that they were accessible from the surrounding area.

Even if we accept that such locations served a wider region, we still have to ask whether there is sufficient evidence to identify them as sacred places. This is the conventional interpretation of such monument complexes but it is actually very difficult to answer this question convincingly; even the excavator of such a massive henge monument as Durrington Walls in Wiltshire later reinterpreted it as a settlement site.[15] The main reason for this confusion is that it is not appropriate to distinguish so sharply between the sacred and secular domains in Neolithic Britain. None the less Renfrew has drawn attention to certain features which seem to characterise religious activity in a number of

---

[13] C. Renfrew, 'Monuments, mobilisation and social organisation in Neolithic Wessex', in *The Explanation of Culture Change*, ed. C. Renfrew (London, 1973), pp. 539–58; J. Barnatt, *Stone Circles of Britain* (Oxford, 1987), pp. 166–226.
[14] R. Bradley, *The Social Foundations of Prehistoric Britain* (Harlow, 1984), p. 63.
[15] G. Wainwright, 'Religion and settlement in Wessex, 3000–1700 BC', in *Recent Work in Rural Archaeology*, ed. P. Fowler (Bradford-on-Avon, 1975), pp. 57–71.

different societies.[16] Although such arguments can never be decisive, they do incorporate the most distinctive features associated with this particular group of monuments. Among them are the positioning of such earthworks in relation to particular kinds of natural landform; the presence of placed deposits that clearly refer to the dead; and the provision of what are usually interpreted as intentional offerings. These sites conform to his scheme in other ways too, for their boundaries were often the focus for considerable symbolic elaboration, whilst at a more general level their architecture is designed to enhance the impact of certain activities and to conceal others from view.

A few examples of these patterns may be helpful here. Many of the locations of the monuments may have been selected because they possessed a similar topography. Recently a number of writers have commented on the way in which circular enclosures – both stone settings and henges – echo the natural features of the areas in which they were built (Figure 2). They might be located within low-lying valleys or basins in positions that commanded a continuous horizon of hills.[17] The form of the monument itself reflected that circular configuration and sometimes the close relationship between the natural arena and the form of the enclosure could be emphasised by other features. For example, the far horizon might be breached by astronomical alignments, like the orientation of Stonehenge on the midsummer sunrise, or the natural backdrop of hills might be highlighted by an array of burial mounds visible from the edges of the monument. The argument is obviously very tentative, but the choice of such locations for the construction of circular enclosures suggests that their placing in the landscape was often influenced by a more basic cosmology.

The boundaries of some of these monuments were enhanced by specialised symbols, which in their turn may have referred to the dead or the supernatural. Thus the edges of some of the greatest passage graves in Ireland were marked by deposits of quartz, whilst the kerbstones retaining the monuments carried elaborate carved decoration. Both these features are also found at monuments with open arenas. Many stone circles contain deposits of quartz and the edges of other monuments are decorated in the same style as the chambered tombs. Pottery bearing similar motifs might occasionally be deposited in the equivalent position at henges.[18]

The provision of intentional offerings is indicated by significant differences between objects deposited along the outer boundaries of these sites and those found within the interior. Thus there are sites where wild animal bones were deposited on the boundary whilst the bones of their domesticated equivalents

---

[16] C. Renfrew, 'The archaeology of religion', in *The Ancient Mind*, ed. C. Renfrew and E. Zubrow (Cambridge, 1994), pp. 47–54.

[17] C. Richards 1996, *op. cit.* note 8; R. Bradley, *The Significance of Monuments* (London, 1998), pp. 101–15.

[18] R. Bradley, *Altering the Earth* (Edinburgh, 1993), pp. 45–68.

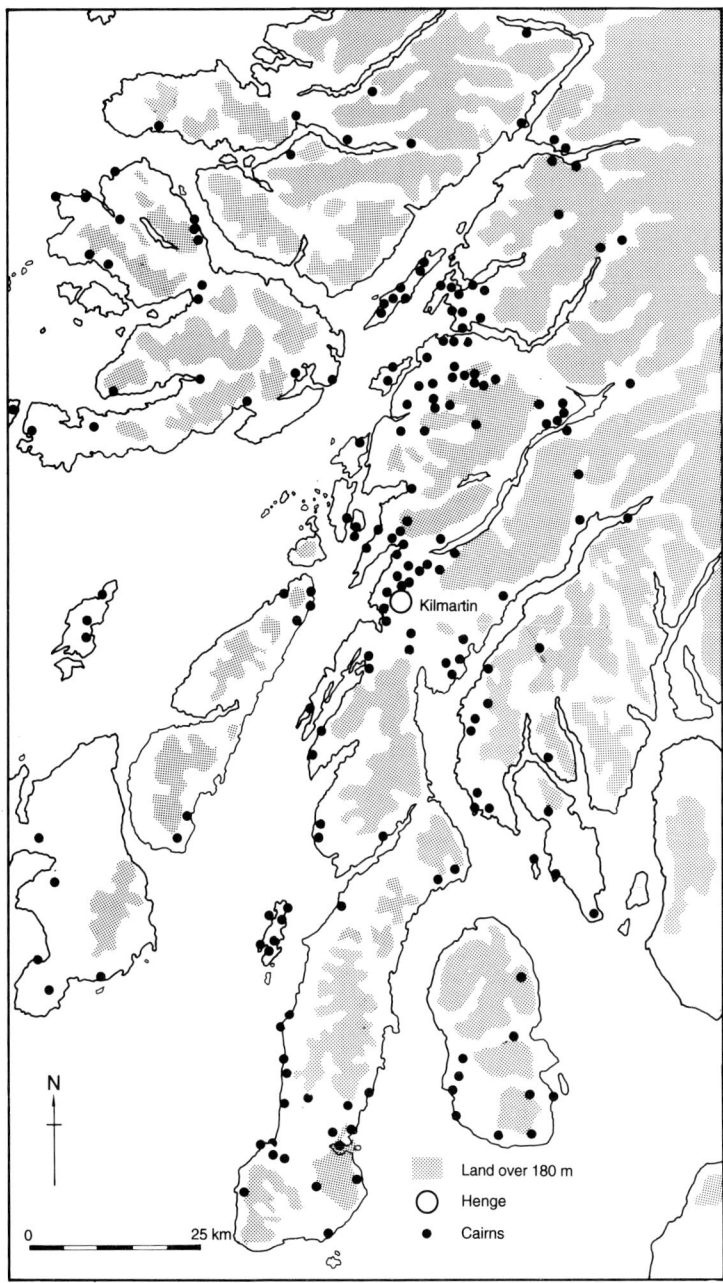

Figure 3 The location of the Kilmartin monument complex in relation to the wider distribution of prehistoric cairns (information from Ritchie 1997, op cit. note 20). The henge monument at Kilmartin is towards the centre of a concentration of ceremonial monuments and is accessible from a wide area in which similar structures are absent. It also dominates the land route across the head of the Mull of Kintyre, the promontory running down the centre of the map.

were placed inside the enclosure. Similarly, there are non-local objects like stone axes that are only found at or beyond the limits of these sites. Sometimes these distinctive groups of artefacts and animal bones were accompanied by relics of the dead. On certain sites, for example, human cremations may have been placed at the base of standing posts, or even in the positions where such features had stood in the past.[19]

A typical site, or collection of sites, which illustrates many of these features, is the monument complex at Kilmartin in Argyll on the west coast of Scotland. It is located on the land route across the head of the promontory known as the Mull of Kintyre; a journey of just seven kilometres as opposed to the 150 km of coastline between the same points.[20] The overland route is marked by a series of important prehistoric monuments which are located mainly in Kilmartin Glen (Figure 3). Here there were at least two stone circles, a henge monument and a barrow cemetery, as well as several stone alignments and a wide variety of rock carvings. Although the area is accessible from all directions, and the soils could have supported year-round settlement, it seems most unlikely that all these monuments served the needs of a resident population. Several of the sites share characteristics with places mentioned earlier. The stone circles at Temple Wood, for instance, are surrounded by a ring of higher ground and echo the natural topography of this area. There are two carvings on the perimeter of the larger circle, which depict motifs shared with passage graves in Orkney, and one of these sites was reused as a cemetery during the Early Bronze Age. Whilst the stone rows that are found nearby are decorated in the same style as natural surfaces in the surrounding landscape, they seem to be directed towards the position of the moon. Although the evidence is limited, there are also finds of non-local artefacts from this area. These features are characteristic of other prehistoric ceremonial centres in Britain and Ireland.

So far the argument is that monument complexes like those discussed by Renfrew most probably played a specialised role in relations with the supernatural and that they need not have been permanently occupied. Moreover it seems more than likely that they were visited by people from a wide surrounding area. Is there any evidence of how these monuments were used?

Stage and Screen

The key elements in these monument complexes can be characterised as stages and screens. Each helped to focus the attention of the audience on certain individuals or activities and at the same time they protected others from view.

---

[19] J. Thomas, *Rethinking the Neolithic* (Cambridge, 1991), pp. 29–78.
[20] G. Ritchie, 'Monuments associated with burial and ritual in Argyll', in *The Archaeology of Argyll*, ed. G. Ritchie (Edinburgh, 1997), pp. 67–94.

Pilgrimage in Prehistoric Britain?

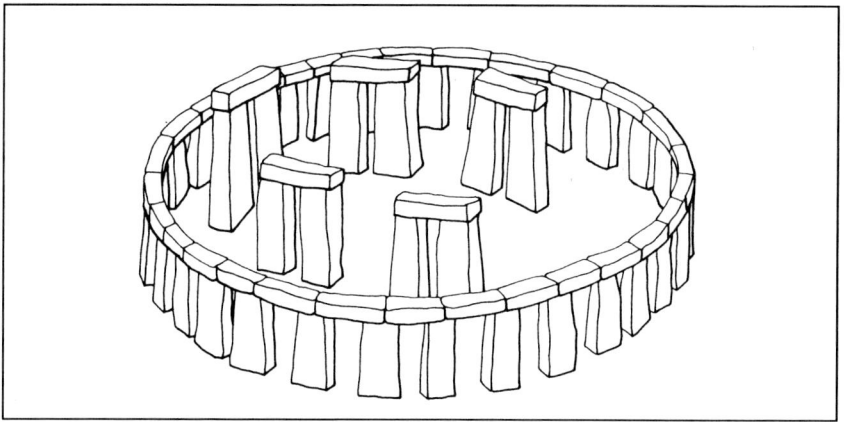

Figure 4 Simplified reconstruction of the principal stone structure at Stonehenge, showing how the horseshoe- shaped structure, in the centre of the monument, is enclosed by a continuous ring of uprights. It faces towards the entrance to the structure which is to the right of the drawing.

Such activities may have included the use of the symbolically charged material which was deposited within these structures.

The 'stages' take many forms, and their character changed during the currency of Late Neolithic and Early Bronze Age monuments. The earliest were probably the monumental facades that flanked the entrances of some of the chambered tombs which, perhaps, gained added definition from a backdrop of massive kerbstones. There are individual sites where these elements were further emphasised by carved designs or by the unusual size or colour of the stones. At a small number of megalithic tombs the cairn was raised above the surrounding area by a platform built against the kerb. This is where certain of the participants in funeral ceremonies may have stood, allowing them to be distinguished from the other people who were present.[21] The same effect could be achieved by building free-standing mounds. John Barrett has suggested that Silbury Hill, the largest prehistoric monument of its kind in Europe, may not have covered a burial at all.[22] Rather, it may have acted like a stage to raise certain individuals high above the surrounding area and to separate them from the rest of the community. Bronze Age round barrows sometimes had the same effect, for not all of them were associated with human burials. One recently published site in Hampshire covered a small

---

[21] Bradley 1998, *op. cit.* note 17.
[22] J. Barrett, *Fragments from Antiquity* (Oxford, 1994), pp. 29–32.

platform bounded by a fence and was littered with animal bones resulting from an episode of feasting.[23]

In other cases free-standing stone structures may have played a similar role. Inside several of the stone circles, most notably Avebury, there are horseshoe-shaped settings of upright stones, which form a kind of megalithic apse. These may have been rather like the forecourts of older tombs, highlighting the position of some of the participants and the importance of their activities within the monument. This principle finds its most complex expression in the Early Bronze Age at Stonehenge where the rings of upright stones enclose a semicircular setting of this kind (Figure 4). It is from this position that the midsummer sunrise can be observed.[24]

Access to such places might have been carefully controlled, and again the architecture of these monuments helped to make such distinctions explicit. The characteristic structure of the passage graves has already been mentioned. With these monuments the distinctions were rather basic ones, for they could accommodate a very limited number of people, who might need to approach the central chamber bent double or on their hands and knees.[25] Once in that chamber they would be cut off from any source of natural light apart from the entrance passage. The walls of the chamber and passage might be decorated with abstract motifs, possibly evoking the sensations experienced during trance. In the great tombs of the Boyne Valley in Ireland the decoration seen by those permitted to enter the monument was very different from the more public motifs on display around the edges of that structure.[26] Like Stonehenge, a number of these structures are aligned on the movements of the sun, but once again such striking features could be observed from only one position inside the building.

This practice of restricting access to certain events or observations did not end with the megalithic tombs. It extended to the open arenas which seem to have taken their place. Some of these, like Stonehenge and Avebury in Wiltshire or the great Shap Circle in Cumbria, had to be approached along a prescribed path or 'avenue'. At Stonehenge this comprised two banks and ditches, but elsewhere it was formed by rows of massive stones. This directed movement to and from the monuments, and the sheer scale of these constructions suggests that large numbers of people were involved. Again such avenues may have directed the viewer's attention towards certain points, but it may also have helped to separate some of the participants from others. Such alignments would also control the visitor's experience of the place. At Stone-

---

[23] M. Allen, M. Morris and R. Clark, 'Food for the living: a reassessment of a Bronze Age barrow at Buckskin, Basingstoke', *Proceedings of the Prehistoric Society* 61 (1995), 159–89.
[24] Barrett 1994, *op. cit.* note 22, pp. 40–7.
[25] Bradley 1998, *op. cit.* note 17.
[26] Bradley 1993, *op. cit.* note 18, pp. 63–6.

henge the avenue links the monument to the River Avon, but for most of its length the stone circle is invisible, although the route does pass across an important barrow cemetery. It is only as the visitor comes very close to Stonehenge that the monument can be observed in any detail and at this point it looks all the more impressive because anyone approaching the entrance must do so by walking uphill.[27] A similar effect is contrived by the West Kennet avenue at Avebury. Not only is it difficult to make out the earthwork of the henge monument until the visitor has travelled a considerable distance, the avenue itself bends so that it does not run straight through the entrance of the enclosure. Two huge monoliths help to screen the interior from those who are not permitted to enter. No doubt some of them would have been able to observe what was going on from the enclosure bank, but they would have been prevented from participating in that activity by a massive rock-cut ditch. At the same time, those spectators would have been the only people who could observe the relationship between such monuments and the wider world. They could look down into these enclosures and the specialised buildings inside them, but they could also refer back at the wider horizon of hills with conspicuous burial mounds distributed along the skyline. Those inside the enclosure could have seen no further than the earthwork barrier itself, which cut them off entirely from the area outside. Even when the participants left those specialised arenas they may have had to follow a prescribed path. Avebury originally had two avenue, each of which led to another stone-built monument, raising the interesting possibility that movement between such places may have been just as important as movement in and out of them.[28]

Some of the specialised structures found within great earthwork arenas have been mentioned already. These often took the form of concentric rings of massive posts. They were once interpreted as the positions of large roofed buildings, but this now seems unlikely. It is much more probable that they were open to the elements, although the individual uprights might well have been linked by screens. The unusual construction of Stonehenge with its upright monoliths and lintels is probably a copy of such constructions in a more durable material; a suggestion reinforced by recent radiocarbon dates which would indicate that this building was erected not long after the timber circles in the surrounding area.[29]

These timber circles are deceptively complex. Certain examples are approached by miniature avenues of upright posts, which would have obliged the visitors to move in single file. Once within the structure their path was by

---

[27] Bradley 1993, *op. cit.* note 18, pp. 45–68.
[28] J. Thomas, 'The politics of vision and the archaeological landscape', in *Landscape: Politics and Perspectives*, ed. B. Bender (Oxford, 1993), pp. 29–44.
[29] A. Gibson, 'Excavations at the Sarn-y-bryn-caled cursus complex, Welshpool, Powys, and the timber circles of Great Britain', *Proceedings of the Prehistoric Society* 60 (1994), 143–223.

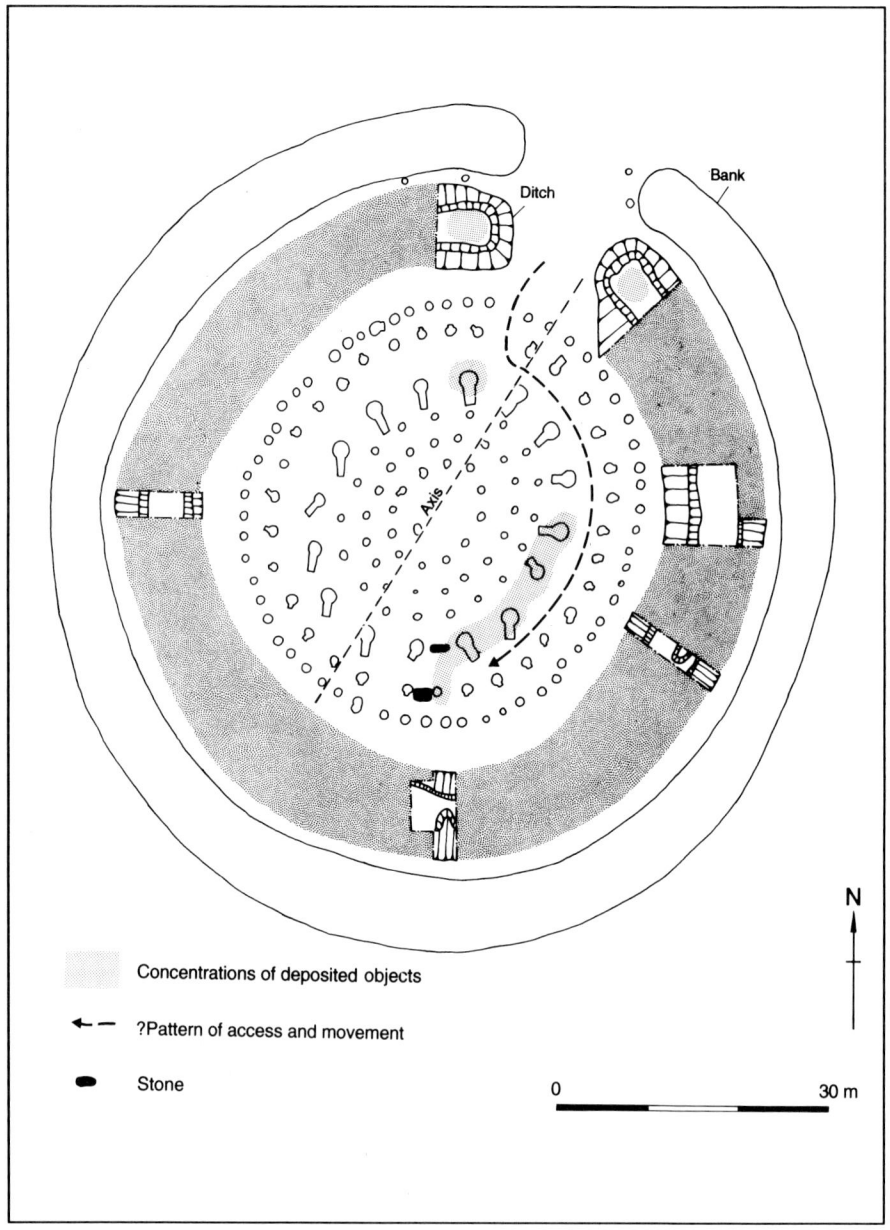

Figure 5 Outline plan of the timber circles at Woodhenge, showing the sockets for the upright posts, the locations of offerings within the site and the path from the entrance to the back of the monument (information from Pollard 1995, *op. cit.* note 30).

no means straightforward. Although the ground plan often suggests that people would have proceeded straight to the centre, there is considerable evidence that in fact this did not happen. Offerings seem to have been placed against the upright posts, but there are significant differences in the character of those at the outer and innermost rings. In the same way, most of those offerings might be found within only one sector of the monument. At Woodhenge in Wiltshire, a massive building whose distinctive ground plan may have influenced the organisation of Stonehenge, most of the deposits were found in the left half of the monument (Figure 5). At the same time, people entering that structure do not seem to have been allowed to proceed directly to its centre. Instead they followed a circuitous path that led them around the concentric rings making up the monument.[30]

The evidence that the timber monuments were sacred is, again, largely circumstantial, perhaps because the distinction between the sacred and the profane had no significance in Neolithic society. But even in our own, modern European, terms there are certain important clues. The restriction on the use of space seems to concern three main elements, each of which may be directly connected to relations with the supernatural. First, there are a surprising number of cases, Woodhenge among them, in which access was restricted to specific points from which astronomical events could be observed. The most important of these seem to have concerned the longest and shortest days of the year. There are certainly a number of passage graves where that alignment may have forged a direct connection between the movements of the heavenly bodies and the position of the dead.[31] Secondly, such restrictions in the use of space within these monuments must have been closely linked to specialised kinds of knowledge. To build these monuments at all must have required a detailed understanding of the cycles of the sun and moon, and to observe the interplay of such cycles with the architecture of the buildings would require information which may not have been generally available. Moreover access to particular locations within the structure of these monuments may have entailed an obligation to make appropriate offerings. This would explain why different places within these sites contain specialised deposits. Inside the henge monument at Durrington Walls, for instance, there is a direct relationship between the nature of the flint artefacts in such deposits, the decoration on the pottery placed in the same positions and even the quality of the meat joints that seem to have been consumed there.[32] Lastly, the use of symbolically charged material at appropriate points in the layout of these monuments

[30] J. Pollard, 'Inscribing space: formal deposition in the Later Neolithic of Woodhenge, Wiltshire', *Proceedings of the Prehistoric Society* 61 (1995), 137–56.
[31] A. Burl, 'Science or symbolism? problems of archaeo-astronomy', *Antiquity* 54 (1980), 191–200.
[32] C. Richards and J. Thomas, 'Ritual activity and structured deposition in later Neolithic Wessex', in *Neolithic Studies*, ed. R. Bradley and J. Gardiner (Oxford, 1984), pp. 189–218.

seems to have extended to the deposition of human remains. It is perhaps no accident that, on either side of the entrance to Woodhenge, there were deposits of human bone. Three more had been placed against posts inside the monument, while at its central point there was the burial of a child.

Distance as Enchantment

The importance of specialised kinds of knowledge has been mentioned. These seem to have been shared over great distances, so that monuments of quite different kinds, located in different parts of Britain and Ireland, might have been aligned on exactly the same events. Thus passage graves in the Boyne Valley were typologically linked with a similar monument in Orkney but also observed the same astronomical events as sites of a quite different type in the south of England. Even inside the monuments there seems to have been a common code dictating where and how certain forms of material culture should be used. So pottery decorated with circular motifs might be deposited around the entrance, whilst axes were excluded from the interior.

Such connections extend to the architecture of monumental sites, and can also be interpreted as incorporating cross references between different locations within the British Isles. Although there is certainly some regional patterning in the organisation of megalithic tombs, henges and stone circles, there also appears to be long distance links between these local traditions. Thus the newly discovered timber circles in Ireland are very like those in northern Britain, and there is an equally strong resemblance between stone circles in Cumbria and Ulster. Such links are found very widely, as Colin Renfrew recognised in his discussion of Neolithic Orkney, but their identification raises certain problems. How are they to be understood? And assuming that such resemblances were a conscious feature of the way in which these monuments were designed, what are the implications of these relationships for the wider pattern of communication?

These questions go to the heart of the problem. Even if the Neolithic and Early Bronze Age monument complexes of Britain and Ireland served a non-local audience, can we say that people travelled great distances to visit them? At this point the evidence of portable artefacts becomes vitally important. This is of several kinds. First, there is the distinctive decoration on a number of portable artefacts which seems to stem from a common source in the decorated tombs of Neolithic Ireland.[33] These motifs were translated into several different media, both in Ireland and across the British Isles, at about the time that henge monuments first developed. The commonest of these media is a style of decorated pottery known as Grooved Ware, although there are also links with decorated stone and antler objects including mace heads, plaques

[33] R. Bradley, *Rock Art and the Prehistory of Atlantic Europe* (London, 1997), pp. 49–66.

Pilgrimage in Prehistoric Britain?

Figure 6 The occurrence of 'horned spirals' in different parts of Britain and Ireland (after Bradley 1997, *op. cit.* note 33). A: Decorated stone from a passage grave at Pierowall, Orkney; B: incised decoration on a flint macehead from Knowth, Boyne Valley; C: pecked decoration on a stone circle at Kilmartin, Argyll; D: pecked decoration on a rock outcrop near Kilmartin; E: the same motif on decorated pottery from Radley, Oxfordshire.

and a curious group of carved stone balls found almost exclusively in north-east Scotland. The link between these decorative motifs also extends to abstract carvings on natural surfaces in the landscape.

There are two important points to consider here. First, virtually all these objects not only share a common source in megalithic art, they are also associated with ceremonial sites and places in the natural landscape. Thus Grooved Ware is found in henge monuments on both sides of the Irish Sea, although this particular style of pottery may have originated in Orkney. The most elaborately decorated mace head comes from the passage grave at Knowth in the Boyne Valley and the carved stone balls share their characteristic distribution with one particular class of stone circle. In the same way, there are a number of stone-built monuments in north-west England which are embellished with the same motifs as Irish megaliths, and there are other monument complexes which are found together with panels of rock art.

The second feature recalls the evidence of some of the monuments themselves, for certain of the individual artefacts show very close similarities over an enormous distance. An excellent example is the 'horned spiral' motif which has been identified in a series of different contexts, including a flint mace head from the Boyne Valley, a decorated passage grave in Orkney, a carved monolith in a west Scottish stone circle and a Grooved Ware vessel found in the Thames Valley (Figure 6). Not only could certain motifs be echoed at great distances; as we have already seen, the objects that carried them may have been used and deposited according to rather similar conventions. Once again the links go beyond a purely visual resemblance and presuppose a common body of knowledge uniting all these areas.

That was very much the point made by Colin Renfrew in his discussion of Neolithic Orkney, but do connections of this kind imply the sort of formalised movement that is so characteristic of pilgrimage? Let us consider some more of the evidence mentioned in Renfrew's account. He refers quite explicitly to the long distance movement of stone axes during this period. These came from a number of sources, but in the Late Neolithic period three kinds of location were especially important.[34] There were a small number of sites where suitable flint was obtained by mining, although this was a technology which had been employed much more widely towards the beginning of the Neolithic period. There is also some evidence that the production of flint axes and other elaborate artefacts took place in settlements located on or near surface exposures of suitable raw material. The bulk of the evidence, though, suggests that the main sources were in the north and west, and that most of the quarries in these areas were located in remote mountainous regions. These quarries were not selected simply for the quality of the stone and some of the working sites seem to have located in areas that were especially dangerous or inaccessible. For example, one group of axe production sites is found within a few hundred metres of the summit of the highest mountain in England. As Renfrew recognised, axes from such locations seem to have gravitated towards the ceremonial centres of the Late Neolithic period, so that the area immediately around these monuments can contain a particular concentration of these artefacts. The same applies to some of the finer flintwork, which may also have been produced in a small number of locations. We know all too little about the contexts of many of these finds. Although axes were normally excluded from

---

[34] R. Bradley and M. Edmonds, *Interpreting the Axe Trade* (Cambridge, 1993), pp. 43–58.

the interior of henge monuments, occasional examples have been found on their periphery or associated with their entrances. Many others are found in the vicinity, and where suitable evidence exists it seems that a significant proportion of them had been buried in pits, together with fine flintwork, decorated pottery and a quantity of animal bones.[35] Some of these objects were still serviceable, although others may have been damaged deliberately before they were committed to the ground.

It is by no means clear whether the stone axes were brought to such sites directly from their source areas, although this does not seem likely. More probably they had been moved across country through a whole series of exchanges. By the time they were deposited in these specialised locations they had, perhaps, attracted a complex history to themselves. This is important for it would be quite wrong to suppose that such artefacts were *either* votive offerings *or* work tools. In fact they could have served both purposes depending on the nature of the transactions in which they were employed. One indication that their movement across country was often a lengthy process is that many of them had been resharpened at least once before they reached their final destination.

There is a further complication, for the overall distribution of stone axes in relation to their parent sources often suggests the main routes by which they were distributed. This is most important as these routes so frequently include the locations of stone circles and henges that some writers have supposed that their movement was organised through those sites. According to one interpretation, it may have been during the large gatherings that took place at these monuments that many of the artefacts changed hands.[36] An older view, which emphasised the purely economic character of this process, saw these as embryonic markets where the movement of axes was controlled by 'middlemen'.[37] That interpretation has little to commend it, for it imposes a modern economic concept onto the past, when it is more appropriate to view such processes as part of prehistoric social life. Rather than supposing that such monuments were positioned to control the movement of valuables across country, it may be more plausible to see them as important locations where some objects changed hands and others were deposited.

The case for the long distance movement of people has still to be demonstrated. A very striking variant of this practice of visiting major monuments is found in the passage graves of the Boyne Valley, where pebbles of imported stone were deposited against the flanks of the monument; indeed, large fragments of quartz may even have been employed to embellish the surface of the cairn. At first sight this seemed to be a simple way of enhancing the

---

35 Thomas 1991, *op. cit.* note 19, pp. 56–78.
36 Bradley and Edmonds 1993, *op. cit.* note 34, pp. 179–99.
37 W. Cummins, 'Neolithic stone axes: distribution and trade in England and Wales', in *Stone Axe Studies*, ed. T. Clough and W. Cummins (London, 1979), pp. 5–12.

appearance of the monument but, once the different stones had been identified, it became clear that the situation was more complicated.[38] Although some of the largest pieces could have been employed in building the structure, this would hardly apply to the smaller pebbles, some of which were used to create miniature circular settings in the lee of the cairn. Nor do any practical considerations explain why the small stones used for these purposes came from a very wide area of the east coast of Ireland; material of similar dimensions could be gathered near at hand. It seems probable that these stones, unlike the axes, were imported directly to the tombs. If so, this kind of evidence may indicate the size of the region from which people came to visit this monument. Such finds may also illustrate the ways in which they recorded those journeys by providing an offering. A similar process might be illustrated by the more mundane deposits of sea shells found at megalithic tombs located far from the coast in Scotland and Ireland.

There is another side to this question. Although it seems unlikely that relics of already completed structures were taken away, there is a little evidence to suggest that certain types of artefact were made in the vicinity of the major ceremonial monuments and removed to other locations. This idea has received very little discussion but, again, some clues exist. There are cases in which henge monuments or similar structures are located very close to sources of raw material. A good example is found in Cranborne Chase on the border of Wiltshire and Dorset. Here Andrew Brown has commented on the careful deposition of the flint waste from artefact production within a series of Late Neolithic pits located close to two henge monuments of this period.[39] He points out how the debris from working poor quality gravel flint was kept separate from the by-products of flaking more suitable flint obtained from the chalk, but he does not consider what was being made. Although he comments on the care taken in flint working within the monument complex, there is nothing to indicate where the finished artefacts were deposited. In such cases it seems possible that they were removed from the area entirely. If so, it might be suggested that two related processes were taking place. One was the formal deposition of artefacts that had originated in distant areas of the British Isles. Its counterpart was the creation of other artefacts from raw material obtained within the monument complex. The unusual qualities of such places may have imbued these objects with special properties and this could be one reason why they were taken away.

None of these arguments is convincing in isolation, but, taken together, they

---

[38] F. Mitchell, 'Notes on some non-local cobbles at the entrances to the passage graves of Newgrange and Knowth, County Meath', *Journal of the Royal Society of Antiquaries of Ireland* 122 (1992), 128–45.

[39] A. Brown, 'Structured deposition and technological change among the flaked stone artefacts from Cranborne Chase', in *Papers on the Prehistoric Archaeology of Cranborne Chase*, ed. J. Barrett, R. Bradley and M. Hall (Oxford, 1991), pp. 101–33.

do seem to indicate a network of close relationships between different areas which was articulated through visits to specialised and apparently sacred monuments. The evidence has all been of a traditional kind – the stylistic affinities that can be identified between different artefacts and different monuments; the movement of certain types of object whose course can be traced by geological characterisation – but there is one other kind of relationship to consider, and this could hardly take a less substantial form. For some years it has seemed likely that the major groups of passage graves in the centre and the east of Ireland might be aligned on one another.[40] The main focus for such attention was the greatest megalithic cemetery of all, in the Boyne Valley. More recently, the same kind of analysis has been extended to the west coast and Bergh has shown that the two major concentrations of tombs there – Carrowmore and Carrowkeel – were aligned on one another.[41] At first sight this is not so surprising in view of the Irish preference for siting such monuments on high ground, but in practice the distances between them are so great that few of these locations are intervisible with one another. In particular, the tombs of the Boyne Valley, which are sited on a relatively inconspicuous ridge, cannot be seen from the important cemetery at Loughcrew. In other words this arrangement expresses an ideal set of relationships rather than one which can actually be traced on the ground.

There are also a few monuments in Scotland and Wales which have especially strong stylistic links with megaliths in Ireland. It would be misleading to suppose that every one of these conforms to the same basic pattern but the two most striking instances of monuments with Irish affinities – Maes Howe in Orkney and Barclodiad Y Gawres in Anglesey – stand out from the general pattern in the vicinity by adopting westerly alignments; almost all the other tombs found in the same regions are aligned towards the east. In the case of Maes Howe it is the largest tomb in Orkney and the only one with strong affinities in the Boyne Valley. It faces south-west towards Ireland and shares the same alignment on the midwinter sun as Newgrange. The stone circle known as Long Meg and her Daughters in Cumbria is decorated in the same style as Irish passage graves and again it faces west. Like Maes Howe, it is aligned on the midwinter sunset, but on another level it may also be orientated on Ireland. Here we may have evidence for a symbolic connection between widely separated groups of monuments. This emphasises more clearly than anything else how such links were a fundamental feature of the Neolithic world view.

---

[40] J. Patrick, 'Megalithic exegesis', *Irish Archaeological Research Forum* 2/2 (1975), 9–14.
[41] S. Bergh, *Landscape of the Monuments* (Stockholm, 1995), pp. 111–40.

Beginnings and Ends

The main elements that might make up a prehistory of pilgrimage – the existence of sacred places serving a wider constituency, the practice of travelling there on special occasions – may perhaps be recognised in Late Neolithic Britain, but it would be idle to pretend that the case is especially strong. What is far more striking is how many strands of evidence come together in this period and at no other time in the prehistoric sequence. Before the Late Neolithic there were widespread traditions of monumental architecture in the British Isles. Particular styles of artefact were distributed across large areas and certain objects, notably axes, were moved over considerable distances. The important difference is that these patterns do not seem to have been systematically related to one another. There were certain resemblances between artefacts and monuments in different parts of Britain and Ireland, but the links were generalised ones, with nothing to suggest close connections between particular locations or the practices that took place there. Similarly, whilst there is some evidence for mobility in relation to specialised earthwork enclosures, such movement was on a rather local scale.[42] There was none of the interplay between different categories of material culture that characterises the Late Neolithic.

It was with the Late Neolithic that the situation began to change, and it is a change that is aptly symbolised by the provision of platforms or enclosed areas outside the megalithic tombs known as passage graves.[43] These were places where large numbers of people could gather who might never be permitted to enter the buildings. The carved motifs that they were allowed to view on the exterior of the tombs find echoes in other media, including decorated pottery, carved stonework and the abstract motifs pecked into natural surfaces in the landscape. These connections represent something new. The same features are found at other monuments which provide significant evidence for the long distance movement of artefacts, shells and unworked stones. Connections may also be indicated by the way in which different groups of monuments were aligned on one another across considerable areas of country or even across the Irish Sea.

The tombs were gradually replaced by open arenas, the form of which reflected the natural setting in which they were built. This represents an important departure, for the new constructions were capable of accommodating much larger numbers of people than the passage graves. They were also associated with a wider variety of structures and a richer material culture. These arenas were not always located in the most densely settled areas. Instead they seem to have been built where they would be accessible from many

---

[42] Bradley 1998, *op. cit.* note 17, pp. 68–83.
[43] Bradley 1998, *op. cit.* note 17, pp. 101–15.

different directions and could, therefore, be visited by a large number of people. Some indication of the importance of this process comes from the growing number of exotic items deposited in and around these monuments. There is also some evidence that artefacts were made at these sites and taken away.

The closest links between the monuments, and the artefacts associated with them, were often between places that were a considerable distance apart. There were similar links in the ways in which some of the items were deposited in different parts of the country. In each case we can trace a network of associations that links individual sites across Britain and Ireland. The sequence begins with the use of passage graves, and in many cases it ended with the replacement of timber circles by more massive settings of monoliths.

These various elements had a quite specific context in prehistoric Britain. They first appeared in the same cultural contexts, and they also disappeared together. The translation of some of the timber circles, into stone, marks the end of a lengthy history; during the Early Bronze Age many of these distinctive patterns vanish from the record. Some of the ceremonial centres were no longer maintained, and new ones were rarely, if ever, built on the same scale. The wide spacing of the major monument complexes gave way to a much denser cluster of small stone settings and barrow cemeteries, although the most imposing structures built during the Neolithic period still formed the focus for large numbers of burial mounds.

If one development symbolises the breakdown of the old order it is this treatment of some of the open spaces or arenas at Neolithic monuments. It seems as if a growing proportion of the stone circles were taken over as burial sites, so that the open spaces that originally existed there were filled by a series of graves.[44] There are even cases in which an entire monument might be buried beneath an enormous cairn. The emphasis was no longer on the large numbers of people who might have congregated inside the enclosures. These places had become the cemeteries of an elite. Material culture also changed during this period, so that a stereotyped funerary assemblage was shared between many different areas of Europe. Of the specialised links between particular monuments in Britain and Ireland not a trace remained. The ritual tradition which has formed the subject of this paper had finally run its course.

So has this study of pilgrimage in British prehistory. Is the concept a useful one? It is possible that in those two pages devoted to Neolithic Orkney Renfrew set the agenda for a whole field of research. The prehistorian's journey in search of enlightenment has only just begun.

Acknowledgements   The figure drawings were prepared by Steve Allen.

---

[44] Bradley 1998, *op. cit.* note 17, 132–46.

2

Were there Christian Pilgrims before Constantine?

E. D. HUNT

At some point in the later second century AD a leader of the Christian community at Sardis in Asia Minor (possibly the local bishop) travelled eastwards to Palestine. In a letter to a fellow-Christian, preserved in Eusebius' *Church History*, Melito of Sardis describes the purpose of this journey.[1] His correspondent Onesimus had wished to have 'extracts from the Law and the Prophets concerning our Saviour and all our faith, and to know the accurate facts about the ancient writings, how many they are and in what order'. In answer to this zeal for the faith and the Scriptures, Melito made his way to the East and to 'the place where [these things] were preached and done', with the intention of discovering the authoritative Old Testament canon. The approved books are then listed, from which Melito went on to compile the significant extracts (like most of Melito's literary output, this work does not survive).

This expedition to Palestine, as pre-eminently the land of biblical authority, finds echoes a century or so later in an oration delivered in the agora in Smyrna – again in Asia Minor – by the local Christian presbyter Pionius, who was imminently to meet a martyr's death at the hands of the Roman government. Pionius told his hearers how he had seen with his own eyes the wrath of God when he had travelled all over the land of Judaea.[2] Crossing the Jordan, he beheld parched and infertile ground, the burnt-up evidence of God's punishment for the sins of the inhabitants; and the waters of the Dead Sea which, in fear of a repetition of divine anger, would support no living creature, and rejected human bodies to the surface (rather than allow them to sink). For Pionius the biblical fate of Sodom and Gomorrah was revealed as present reality in the landscape of contemporary Palestine, and with it a foretaste of the biblical wrath of God still to come.

Were Melito and Pionius in any sense 'pilgrims'? Elsewhere I have argued

---

[1] Eusebius, *Historia Ecclesiastica* IV.xxvi.13–14, ed. E. Schwartz (Leipzig, 1903). In this chapter Eusebius had referred to Melito as 'bishop' of Sardis, yet an earlier source, Polycrates of Ephesus, cited by Eusebius at *Historia Ecclesiastica* V.xxiv.2–7, lists Melito among the 'great luminaries' of Asia separately from the bishops.
[2] *Martyrium Pionii* 4.18–20, *The Acts of the Christian Martyrs*, ed. H. Musurillo (Oxford, 1972). On Pionius see further R. Lane Fox, *Pagans and Christians* (Harmondsworth, 1986), pp. 460–92.

that they were, and as such pioneers of a long tradition; but it has more recently become fashionable to deny them the label, and with them the other few known pre-Constantinian Christian travellers to the Holy Land.[3] Scholars have neutralised their journeys and diluted them into mere inquisitive tourism, a display of specialised and erudite curiosity devoid of any religious feeling: 'those who found travel helpful for making Scripture vivid' is one such summary of these first Holy Land ventures.[4] In a recent book Joan Taylor has concluded that there is no such phenomenon as Christian pilgrimage – or holy places – prior to the development of the Holy Land initiated by Constantine, and has insisted on dissociating the learned study-tour of the occasional biblical scholar from the devotional objective of the pilgrim. In her view, Melito and Pionius belong with the former, not the latter.[5]

While the real frame of mind in which they and others approached the places of the Bible can never be known, there is at least a powerful sense of reverence conveyed by their words: in the one case, reverence for the biblical authority of the Holy Land 'where these things were preached and done', and in the other, reverence for the continuing signs of God's power and anger. It may be granted that there is no indication that these early travellers 'took to the road as a form of asceticism or penitence, or to secure therapy for body and spirit';[6] nor did they go in search of holy relics, nor in large numbers in some collective demonstration of pious enterprise. But this means no more than that they were unlike later, medieval pilgrims, not necessarily that they were not pilgrims at all. Such defining characteristics of more fully-fledged pilgrimage are equally inapplicable to their more immediate fourth-century successors – the Bordeaux pilgrim, Egeria, or Jerome's ascetic soul-mate Paula – to whose travels around the holy places it would be impossible to deny the inspiration of religious fervour.

The purpose of this paper is to reassert that there is something which may legitimately be termed 'pilgrimage' already at work in these second- and third-century forays to the Holy Land, and to restate some of the essential features of such pilgrimage, viewed on its own terms and in its historical

---

[3] For these first 'pilgrims', see still H. Windisch, 'Die ältesten christlichen Palästinapilger', *Zeitschrift des deutschen Palästina-Vereins* 48 (1925), 145–58; E. D. Hunt, *Holy Land Pilgrimage in the Later Roman Empire AD 312–460* (Oxford, 1982), pp. 2–4. For reluctance to regard them as pilgrims, see P. Maraval, *Lieux saints et pèlerinages d'Orient* (Paris, 1985), pp. 25–7.

[4] K. G. Holum, 'Hadrian and St. Helena: Imperial Travel and the Origins of Christian Holy Land Pilgrimage', in *The Blessings of Pilgrimage*, ed. R. Ousterhout (Urbana, 1990), pp. 66–81 (p. 69); for similar dissatisfaction at equating biblical tourism with pilgrimage, see further Holum's review of Hunt 1982, *op. cit.* note 3, in *Classical Philology* 80 (1985), 377–80.

[5] J. E. Taylor, *Christians and the Holy Places: the myth of Jewish-Christian origins* (Oxford, 1993), especially summary at pp. 295–332.

[6] Holum 1990, *op. cit.* note 4, p. 70.

context. The analysis of those modern anthropologists who impose structural patterns differentiating pilgrimage (for example, as a movement towards the 'Center') from, say, tourism (as a movement towards the 'Other') is misleading when applied to the journeyings of Melito, Pionius and the rest.[7] Their approach fails to make room for the unique place of the Bible in the formation of Christian pilgrimage, and its role in turning expeditions of scholarly investigation into *at the same time* a devotional quest for the basis of the faith.

There should by rights, of course, be no such thing as Christian pilgrimage. Christ had enjoined on his followers the worship of God 'in spirit and in truth' (John 4. 24). As St Paul reminded his pagan audience on the Areopagus in Athens (Acts 17. 24–5), the God of the Christians did not live in shrines built by men; he was not isolated in specific and preferentially 'holy' places, but dwelt everywhere in the hearts of all the faithful. It was this universal revelation which separated the New Covenant from the Old, with its highly 'place-specific' focus on the cult of the Temple in Jerusalem. As the power of Rome encompassed the physical destruction of the Temple building, so the coming of Christ signalled the breaking of boundaries in space (and time). Such themes resonate through the arguments of Christian purists down the centuries who have objected to the veneration of holy places and the practice of pilgrimage associated with them.[8] None the less, they have been swimming against the tide: whatever the Gospel injunctions, Christians from the start have gone on pilgrimage. The Temple in Jerusalem may have been destined for oblivion, yet the Palestine into which Christianity was born was already dotted with places rendered sacred to the Jews by their Old Testament past: memorials of patriarchs and prophets which could serve as the focus of veneration and annual festivals. In some cases sites commemorating the same person or event were duplicated, an indication of competing traditions in the 'market' for attracting gatherings of devotees.[9]

The New Testament record of the initial interest in the tomb of Christ itself bears witness to this background of Jewish recognition of holy places. Two disciples on the road to Emmaus discussing the recent fate of Jesus of Nazareth are recounted in Luke's gospel (24. 19–24) speaking of him as a powerful

---

[7] For one such analysis see E. Cohen, 'Pilgrimage and Tourism: convergence and divergence', in *Sacred Journeys: the anthropology of pilgrimage*, ed. A. Morinis (Westport, 1992), pp. 47–61.

[8] As, for example, Jerome's famous 'non Hierosolymis fuisse, sed Hierosolymis bene vixisse laudandum est' (*Epistle* 58.3.4: 'it is not having been present in Jerusalem, but having led a good life in Jerusalem which is praiseworthy'); cf. Hunt 1982, *op. cit.* note 3, pp. 88–92.

[9] See J. Wilkinson, 'Jewish Holy Places and the Origins of Christian Pilgrimage', in *The Blessings of Pilgrimage*, ed. R. Ousterhout (Urbana, 1990), pp. 41–53; cf. J. Jeremias, *Heiligengräber in Jesu Umwelt* (Göttingen, 1958). R. L. Wilken, *The Land Called Holy: Palestine in Christian History and Thought* (Yale, 1992), pp. 105–8, is less convinced of Jewish pilgrimage other than to Jerusalem.

prophet, whose tomb has already been visited by his followers and said to be the scene of miraculous visions of angels. St John (19. 41–2) displays what advocates of Pauline universality might take to be an inappropriate interest in the actual location of the tomb, 'at the place where he was crucified there was a garden, and in the garden a new tomb, not yet used for burial. There because the tomb was near at hand . . . they laid Jesus.' Was John aware of a specific tomb in Jerusalem sacred to the first Christians, and already a focus of devotion for them? Another New Testament tomb may have generated similar reactions. After Stephen was stoned to death, he was buried by 'certain devout men, who made a great lamentation for him' (Acts 8. 2). No location is mentioned, and it would not be until the early fifth century (415) that a tomb claimed to be that of Stephen was discovered, and his influential cult rapidly disseminated across the Mediterranean world:[10] yet it is tempting to speculate that the author of Acts knew of a spot already honoured in apostolic times as the burial place of the first Christian martyr.

In the annual commemorations which came to surround the cults of Stephen's martyr-successors one species of Christian pilgrimage can be seen coming into being. Probably by the time that Melito set off from Sardis on his Holy Land journey, the Christian community at nearby Smyrna had begun the yearly remembrance of their martyred bishop Polycarp, gathering around his tomb on the anniversary of his 'birthday' (the day of entry into eternal life effected by his martyrdom).[11] Polycarp was the example for Pionius to emulate. In succeeding generations, the growth of martyr cults in areas beyond Asia Minor can be traced in the rudiments of the Roman celebration of Peter and Paul, for example, and the martyr tradition in the north African church, which was strongly evident by Cyprian's day.[12] Such (primarily local) festivals brought together congregations of the faithful who may not have journeyed far in terms of distance, but who certainly forged a great gap in other ways between themselves and the world which they had, albeit temporarily, left behind them. If pilgrimage is indeed some sort of 'movement towards the Center', then their 'Center' was transported to the margins of the society in which they lived, amid the burial-grounds which lay at the perimeter, beyond the boundaries of city-based civilisation.[13] In attending martyr commemorations, the faithful moved themselves outside their secular world, on a

---

[10] See Hunt 1982, *op. cit.* note 3, pp. 212–20. The narrative of the discovery is provided by the so-called *Epistula Luciani*, *Patrologia Latina* 41, 807–18.

[11] *Martyrium Polycarpi*, *op. cit.* note 2. On Polycarp as the prototype of Christian martyr-cult, see G. W. Bowersock, *Martyrdom and Rome* (Cambridge, 1995), pp. 13–17.

[12] For Cyprian's encouragement of martyr commemorations, see his *Epistles* 12.2 and 39.3; on Peter and Paul, Ch. Pietri, *Roma Christiana* (Rome, 1976), pp. 366–89.

[13] On the extra-mural location of the first martyr celebrations, see R. Markus, *The End of Ancient Christianity* (Cambridge, 1990), pp. 142–52; and on the importance of martyr-cult in the formation of Christian holy places, R. Markus, 'How on earth

pilgrimage to encounter the glorious forebears who were the formative and identifying influences on their Christian community. Nor was it just some nostalgic trip into the past. It is the common parlance of martyr cult that the saint whose remains had been so assiduously preserved was perceived as a continuing presence in the tomb, the moment of his or her glory recalled vividly to life each year in the recitation of the *acta* – the record of the martyr's glorious moment of death and triumph. In time, as in space, these pilgrims travelled to confront the reality of the martyr's experience, and its 'witness' to the founding faith of their church.[14]

Melito's Holy Land expedition can surely be seen as something analogous to these pilgrimages to the shrines of martyrs. The physical displacement entailed was more extensive than a procession out to a local cemetery, but was, none the less, a journey to a destination perceived to be a source of historical authority and religious definition. In Melito's case this involved the whole unfolding of Christian history foreshadowed in the Law and the Prophets of the Old Testament. In travelling to the land 'where these things were preached and done' in his quest for authoritative biblical sources, Melito was moving through space and time to come face to face with the 'witness' to the faith represented by the Scriptures, in those very places which had seen the events enacted. Just as local Christians relived their past and sought out the roots of faith around the tombs of their martyrs, so Melito was engaged on a similar pilgrimage – writ larger on the map of the eastern Mediterranean – in search of the defining Christian identity. Comparison with contemporary martyr-festivals is rendered explicit in the language attributed to Pionius in the agora in Smyrna: in traversing Judaea and crossing the Jordan, he affirms that he beheld 'the land which to this day *bears witness to* ('μαρτυροῦσαν') the anger of God which has afflicted it'.[15] Pionius' vision of the landscape around the Dead Sea was present evidence of the ancient biblical narrative at the roots of Christian faith.

What *was* there for these first Christian visitors, equipped with 'eyes of faith', to behold in the pre-Constantinian Holy Land? For Pionius, his gaze sharply concentrated by the imminent prospect of martyrdom, the physical characteristics of the land itself (and the Dead Sea) were enough to evoke a vivid realisation of the angry God of the Old Testament. Others would go in search of more specific locations and memorials, to sites already handed down in Jewish tradition. These formed the physical record of the people and events of the Old Testament, which Christian travellers to Palestine would incorpo-

---

could places become holy? Origins of the Christian idea of holy places', *Journal of Early Christian Studies* 2 (1994), 257–71.

[14] On the early martyr-acts, see Bowersock 1995, *op. cit.* note 11, pp. 23–39; for the 'praesentia' of the saint, P. Brown, *The Cult of the Saints* (London, 1981), pp. 86–105.

[15] *Martyrium Pionii* 4.18, *op. cit.* note 2. On the Christianisation of the Greek word for 'witness', see Bowersock 1995, *op. cit.* note 11, pp. 5–21.

rate into their own vision of biblical history. When we reach the first full pilgrim narratives of the fourth century, it is noticeable how large a proportion of the places visited derived their sacred significance from Old Testament associations.[16] To this extent Christian visitors inherited, not to say appropriated, a pre-existing biblical panorama.

Much of the physical record had already been demolished. Biblical Jerusalem had fallen to the ravages of Roman destruction, replaced by the *colonia* of Aelia Capitolina, and presided over by Jupiter and other deities of the Roman pantheon (not least the deified Hadrian, founder of the new city).[17] It would be claimed by Eusebius in the fourth century that Hadrian's builders, in an act of pagan desecration, had deliberately obliterated the tomb from which Christ was raised from the dead, only for it to be miraculously rediscovered in God's good time under the new Christian rule of Constantine. It is much more likely that the site was an incidental casualty of the extensive construction work on the monumental area of forum and temples at the heart of Roman Aelia.[18] The layout of Jerusalem had in any case been transformed since biblical times by the building of a more northerly wall-circuit within a decade or so of Christ's crucifixion, and it is a matter of speculation with what degree of success local Christians were able to retain a memory of the sacred topography hinted at in the Gospels.[19]

Melito's Holy Land travels may afford some help. In his own account of his journey 'where these things were preached and done', he is silent about any specific destination, even Jerusalem (or Aelia Capitolina, as it was in his day). Yet in his surviving *Paschal Sermon* he repeatedly declares that the Lord was crucified 'in the middle of Jerusalem', or (at one point) 'in the middle of the street and in the middle of the city'.[20] Hence the attractive and influential suggestion that Melito had actually seen the new monumental centre of Aelia, and had had pointed out to him the Golgotha of the Gospels, the spot where the local Christian community believed the place of the crucifixion to be, with the tomb of Christ nearby. The unanimous message of the Gospels, and standard Roman practice, is that Christ was led *out* of Jerusalem to be crucified, to an extra-mural place of execution which also served as a burial-ground.[21] Melito could not, so the argument runs, have employed this language in the

---

[16] See above, p. 27.
[17] For Hadrian and Jerusalem, see E. Schürer (revised, G. Vermes and F. Millar), *The History of the Jewish People in the Age of Jesus Christ* (Edinburgh, 1973), I, 534–57; F. Millar, *The Roman Near East 31 BC – AD 337* (Cambridge, Mass., 1993), pp. 106–7.
[18] See most recently S. Gibson and J. E. Taylor, *Beneath the Church of the Holy Sepulchre* (London, 1994), pp. 65–71; with Eusebius, *Vita Constantini* iii.26, ed. F. Winkelmann (Berlin, 1975).
[19] Taylor 1993, *op. cit.* note 5, pp. 113–42.
[20] Melito, *On Pascha*, ed. S. G. Hall (Oxford, 1979), pp. 72 and 93–4.
[21] The topographical significance of Melito's text was first spotted by A. E. Harvey, 'Melito and Jerusalem', *Journal of Theological Studies* New Series 17 (1966), 401–4.

sermon, especially the reference to the 'middle of the street', without knowledge of the actual layout of the city in the later second century.

On the other hand, it is well to acknowledge that Melito's wording may be meant not literally, but figuratively. It was symbolically and theologically significant to locate the murder of Christ at the very heart of Judaism, just as Eusebius would affirm when talking of Constantine's Christian reclamation of the site.[22] Nowhere else in the sermon does Melito display the slightest interest in the topography of earthly Jerusalem – on the contrary, he evinces precisely that pure and boundless universalism which is characteristic of New Testament Christianity: 'the Jerusalem below is worthless now because of the Jerusalem above ... for it is not in one place nor in a little plot that the glory of God is established, but on all the ends of the inhabited earth his bounty overflows, and there the almighty God has made his dwelling through Christ Jesus'.[23] If it was the case that Melito was led to the perceived site of the Crucifixion in Aelia Capitolina, surrounded by the monuments of pagan Rome, then he drew from the experience rather different biblical conclusions than from his more straightforwardly literal encounters with the prophetic world of the Old Testament. Pagan Aelia served as 'witness' to the worthlessness and insignificance of 'the Jerusalem below', which could no longer confine the glory of God. The 'eyes of faith' characteristic of the pilgrim might well thus penetrate the actual invisibility of the tomb beneath pagan temples to behold the deeper realities enshrined in the scene.

If Melito's evidence leaves us uncertain about Christian recognition of the place of the Crucifixion in second-century Jerusalem, we are on surer ground when it comes to Bethlehem and the site of Christ's Nativity. A tradition evident in apocryphal works, and in the pages of Melito's contemporary, Justin Martyr, spoke of a 'cave' in the vicinity of Bethlehem to which Joseph led Mary before the birth of Jesus.[24] The manger of Luke's gospel might, indeed, be literally understood to have been a cave on the outskirts of the village. It is uncertain, though, whether the apocryphal tradition reflects the existence of an actual cave around Bethlehem identified as the place of Christ's birth, or is reproducing more symbolic imagery (for example, that of the light of the world emerging from the depths of darkness). Justin's allusion, for instance, is bound up with his interpretation of the Septuagint reading of a passage of Isaiah (33. 16) about what he terms the 'symbol of the cave'.[25] These unpromising hints yield to more substance by the middle of the third century, when an often-quoted passage of Origen's *Contra Celsum* confirms that, by then at least,

---

[22] *Tricennial Oration* ix.16: 'in the heart of the Hebrew kingdom'.
[23] *On Pascha, op. cit.* note 20, p. 45. In his edition of the text (Paris, 1966), O. Perler explained away the references to the centre of the city as 'une exagération rhétorique' (p. 177); while Taylor 1993, *op. cit.* note 5, invokes 'poetic licence' (p. 122).
[24] Justin Martyr, *Dialogue with Trypho* 78, Patrologia Graeca 6, 657–60; cf. *Protevangelium Jacobi* 18, ed. H. R. Smid (Assen, 1965), pp. 125–7.
[25] So Taylor 1993, *op. cit.* note 5, pp. 99–101.

a specific cave which had seen the birth of Christ was located *in* Bethlehem (Justin's cave had merely been 'nearby'), and that this cave was 'famous even among people alien to the faith'.[26] Origen was resident in Caesarea, the principal city of Roman Palestine, and, displaying the biblical scholar's interest in the topography of the contemporary Holy Land (which we can document elsewhere in his scriptural works), he had every reason to know of the celebrated cave at Bethlehem.[27]

In singling out this cave, Christians may have been laying claim to what was in fact a pagan cult site, if we are to believe the testimony of Jerome who, many years later at the end of the fourth century, would affirm that prior to Constantine the cave of the Nativity had been the heart of a sacred grove of Adonis, the doomed lover of Venus/Aphrodite.[28] On the basis of this evidence Joan Taylor has sought to nullify any Christian significance for pre-Constantinian Bethlehem, arguing that the shrine's pagan guardians may have willingly shown their cave to the occasional visiting Christian traveller or biblical scholar, as inquisitive outsiders with some alternative understanding of the site's religious import.[29] Yet even if Jerome's account of the cave's pagan background were to be accepted (despite the absence of other evidence, and suspicions that he was inventing for Bethlehem a history of pagan desecration to parallel the same Venus cult which had disfigured the place of the Crucifixion and the Tomb in Jerusalem),[30] we are not obliged to deny the Bethlehem site a tradition of Christian pilgrimage going back before the advent of Constantine. Origen's language is admittedly prone to the exaggeration of Christian apologetic, but still implies something of greater significance for the Bethlehem cave than mere intellectual curiosity. It suggests, rather, a destination arousing devotional response from Christians who *saw* there the fulfilment of biblical prophecy (Micah 5. 2, 'and thou Bethlehem are not the least . . .') and its realisation in the Gospel narrative of the Nativity – in Melito's words, 'where these things were preached and done'. The site's pagan-ness need not preclude its being regarded by Christians as sanctifed by its biblical history: indeed its very desecration, when seen through the lens of the 'eyes of faith', may even serve to reinforce the image's conviction, just in the way that the pagan monuments of earthly Jerusalem may have summoned up for Melito the truths of the Bible.

Our best guide to the pre-Constantinian Christian 'map' of the Holy Land is Eusebius, bishop of Caesarea in the early fourth century and metropolitan of the Roman province of Palestine. In using the term 'pre-Constantinian' of these

---

26 *Contra Celsum* i.51, ed. M. Borret (Paris, 1967).
27 Cf. Hunt 1982, *op. cit.* note 3, pp. 92–3. See below, p. 35.
28 Jerome, *Epistle* 58.3.5.
29 Taylor 1993, *op. cit.* note 5, pp. 96–112: for example, 'the pagans may well have taken some delight in convincing the occasional Christian visitor of the third century that Christ was born in the sacred cave of Tammuz-Adonis' (p. 104).
30 As argued by P. Welten, 'Bethlehem und die Klage um Adonis', *Zeitschrift des deutschen Palästina-Vereins* 99 (1983), 189–203.

eastern regions of the Roman empire, it should be recalled that the crucial date is 324, when in September Constantine defeated his rival Licinius and established Christian rule unchallenged in the East. It was only then, for Eusebius and the populations of the eastern Mediterranean, that the Christian Roman empire began. Thus Eusebius' huge literary output in defence of Christianity compiled in the decade prior to 324 (principally the pair of works known as the *Preparation of the Gospel* and *Proof of the Gospel*) is, in effect, pre-Constantinian material, and reflects the world of the eastern Mediterranean *before* it came to feel the impact of undiluted Christian rule.[31] The Bethlehem mentioned in several places in the *Proof* is still as it had been known to Origen some seventy years earlier. Christian visitors are shown the cave in which Jesus was born (in fulfilment of the ancient prophecy of Micah), and the fame of the place is such that they arrive 'from the ends of the earth' to *see* it.[32] We may allow for the enthusiasm of the apologist bent on proving prophecy correct, but the implication of Eusebius' words is still that Bethlehem was answering to more than scholarly enquiry. Visitors came in faith to see where Christ was born, as the Old Testament had predicted and the New had fulfilled.

Another passage in the *Proof* focuses attention around the summit of the Mount of Olives. Here Eusebius describes the congregation of 'those who believe in Christ from all over the world', as people assembled there to see scriptural prophecy accomplished in the destruction and desolation of the Temple site, across the valley in Jerusalem. They were also shown on the Mount another cave, this one 'where the Lord prayed and handed on to his disciples the mysteries of the End, and from where he made his ascent into heaven'.[33] Much difficulty of interpretation surrounds this mysterious and significant cave on the Mount of Olives, associated in the written tradition with Christ's last moments on earth. It has no Gospel authority and appears to originate in some kind of Gnostic setting early in the third century.[34] What is beyond dispute is that Eusebius, writing before 324, knew of the summit of the Mount of Olives as a place frequented by the Christian faithful, for the purpose, as he saw it, of visualising and reliving the biblical fate of Jerusalem. It was a place which had been rendered sacred by no less than the presence of Christ himself at the moment of his Ascension – itself a realisation of Zechariah's prophecy of the last day, when 'the Lord's feet will stand on the Mount of Olives to the east of Jerusalem' (14. 4).

---

[31] On the nature of Eusebius' apologetic writings in this period, see T. D. Barnes, *Constantine and Eusebius* (Cambridge, Mass., 1981), pp. 178–86.
[32] *Demonstratio Evangelica* I.i.2; cf. III.ii.47 and VII.ii.15, ed. I. A. Heikel (Leipzig, 1913).
[33] *Demonstratio Evangelica* VI.xviii.23, *op. cit.* note 32. For this congregation of the faithful at the summit of the Mount of Olives, cf. Eusebius, *Onomastikon*, ed. E. Klostermann (Leipzig, 1904), p. 74.
[34] Argued principally by Taylor 1993, *op. cit.* note 5, pp. 143–56. P. W. L. Walker, *Holy City, Holy Places?* (Oxford, 1990), pp. 199–210, sets the Mount of Olives cave in a more mainstream Christian tradition.

This passage poses a challenge for those who would deny the existence of Christian holy places prior to Constantine. It is difficult to avoid the conclusion from Eusebius' observation that there was something powerfully devotional present in these overlapping biblical perceptions of the Mount of Olives, and that the faithful who congregated there under the impulse of Scripture did so in the guise of pilgrims. Three components of Eusebius' teminology will repay examination: (1) the cave on the Mount is 'shown' (δεικνμένῳ) to those who visit the spot; (2) the believers come with the intention of 'enquiring into' (ἕνεκεν ἱστορίας) the capture and desolation of Jerusalem as foretold by the prophets; and (3) they assemble to 'worship' (προσκυνήσεως) on the Mount.

The 'showing' of the cave to the faithful is language of the sort already encountered in connection with Bethlehem, inherited by Eusebius from Origen's description of visits to the place of the Nativity. Moreover, the verb δείκνυται forms a persistent refrain through the list of biblical place-names assembled in Eusebius' own Palestinian gazetteer known as the *Onomastikon* (*On the Place-Names in Holy Scripture*), another text which, although it cannot be precisely dated, certainly bears witness to the pre-Constantinian state of the Holy Land.[35] The preface of this work makes clear that it was meant primarily as an aid to biblical scholarship and topography ('... setting out the meaning, the location, and the contemporary name, whether similar to the ancient or different, of the cities and villages which occur in the Holy Scripture'), and not as some kind of practical handbook for the use of pilgrims.[36] None the less, the contemporary world of the Holy Land it reflects was one in which the places of the Bible exerted a more potent authority than would sites of only occasional learned curiosity. From its very first entry under 'Ararat', where 'they say that to this day remains of the Ark *are shown* in the mountains of Armenia',[37] through the numerous Old Testament monuments and memorials which make up most of its scriptural topography, to the Gospel locations marking episodes of Jesus' earthly life, the *Onomastikon* is a testament to the embodiment of the Scriptures in the landscape, beheld as living and visible reality by those with eyes to see. So in and around Jerusalem, for example, the 'field of blood' purchased with the money paid to the traitor Judas 'is still now shown in Aelia to the north of Mount Sion'. A similar phrase is used to place Golgotha 'where the Lord was crucified' (Eusebius thus knows, as had perhaps Melito of Sardis earlier, of a location for the Crucifixion in the central area of Aelia

---

[35] For the character of this work, and its early (possibly pre-fourth century) date, see Barnes 1981, *op. cit.* note 31, pp. 106–11 (although this perhaps relies too heavily on the assumption that Eusebius precisely reflected current Roman administrative boundaries); D. Groh, 'The *Onomasticon* of Eusebius and the rise of Christian Palestine', *Studia Patristica* 18 (1985), 23–31. The standard edition is that of Klostermann 1904, *op. cit.* note 33.

[36] Pace Hunt 1982, *op. cit.* note 3, pp. 97–9.

[37] *Onomastikon*, *op. cit.* note 33, pp. 2–4.

Capitolina).³⁸ In the village of Bethany, on the slopes of the Mount of Olives, the place is 'still shown to this day' where Christ revived Lazarus from the dead. In Jerusalem the pool of Bethesda, scene of Christ's healing miracles, 'is still shown' as one of the city's water cisterns.³⁹ Many of these locations, listed by Eusebius as 'shown' to visitors, will hardly have been holy places or pilgrim destinations – certainly not places of worship – in the fullest sense of such terms. When lost amid the secular and pagan surroundings of Aelia Capitolina this biblical topography must in any case have been somewhat notional, evident only in the eye of the beholder. Yet there is nothing notional, casual, or even just touristic, about Eusebius' repeated emphasis on the places 'being shown' – they are shown to those who *see* them, and what is seen is nothing less than the plain truth of the biblical past. Here seeing *is* believing. Just as for Eusebius' predecessor, Origen, the display of the famous cave at Bethlehem had been proof of the realisation of Old Testament prophecy in the birth of Jesus. Just as Origen's martyr-contemporary, Pionius, had seen the landscape of Judaea as 'witnessing' to the angry deeds of God. Eusebius' witnesses in the *Onomastikon* are the biblical locations 'shown', produced in evidence, in confirmation of the sacred history represented in them.⁴⁰ In characterising this kind of response to the places of the Bible, we may opt for a genuine spirit of piety and devotion, or dismiss it as mere unthinking credulity. However understood, it is neither neutral nor detached, nor indifferent to the religious potential of retracing Scripture in the contemporary Holy Land.

Returning to Eusebius' throng of the faithful assembled on the Mount of Olives, the second key term, ἱστορία, implies that they had come to explore and search out *in situ* the roots of their Christian 'history', as set out in the pages of the Old Testament prophets, and duly accomplished in the gospel narratives. Again Eusebius takes up the theme from Origen, who in the course of commenting on St John's gospel had spoken of his own travels around Palestine 'in search of (ἐπὶ ἱστορίαν) the traces of Jesus and his disciples and the prophets'.⁴¹ At first reading this sounds like the voice of the biblical scholar that Origen was, in this passage investigating the accuracy of the received text concerning the location of the ministry of John the Baptist. Recent discussion has been eager to disclaim any idea of pilgrimage lurking in Origen's depiction of his peripatetic researches into biblical topography.⁴² The context is indeed that of the erudite scriptural commentary, and nothing in it reveals any devotional inspiration attaching to his Holy Land movements; yet further

---

38 *Onomastikon, op. cit.* note 33, p. 74; and for Aceldama, the 'field of blood', see p. 38.
39 *Onomastikon, op. cit.* note 33, p. 58.
40 For the *Onomastikon* understood in this fashion, cf. Hunt 1982, *op. cit.* note 3, pp. 96–101.
41 Origen, *Commentary on John* VI.xl.40, ed. C. Blanc (Paris, 1970).
42 For example, Taylor 1993, *op. cit.* note 5, p. 311: '... an *historia* was not a pilgrimage'.

consideration of the notion of ἱστορία will suggest that it is capable of embracing elements more suited to the travels of a pilgrim.⁴³

The term has a long history in classical antiquity, denoting the kind of erudite, investigative tourism favoured by leading men of learning and leisure, and reaching its heyday in the freedom of mobility afforded by the *pax Romana*. Apologists of the high Roman empire placed universal travel and ease of communication high on the list of the blessings of imperial rule, and it is against such a background that Melito and Pionius were able to make the journey from western Asia Minor to the land of the Bible. An example of this vogue for ἱστορία is the story of the teacher, Demetrius, from Tarsus in Cilicia. Demetrius is one of the *dramatis personae* of Plutarch's dialogue *On the Decline of Oracles*, set in Delphi, most likely in AD 83. During an expedition undertaken on imperial orders as far afield as Britain, Demetrius had visited islands off the coast 'for the purposes of investigation (ἱστορίας) and sightseeing (θέας)'. Reaching Delphi, on his way home, he reported on the inhabitants' primitive religious explanations for the severe storms which beset them.⁴⁴

In bringing the results of his learned expedition to the setting of Delphi, Demetrius was 'carrying coals to Newcastle', in that Delphi was itself a central destination on the itinerary of those many educated travellers of antiquity (and not only of antiquity) who made Greece the object of voyages of ἱστορία. From emperors, such as Hadrian, downwards, the élite of the Greco-Roman world went in search of their cultural origins amid the landscape of the classical past. In another dialogue of Plutarch's (*The Oracles at Delphi*), a group of such travellers can be observed being escorted on a tour around the monuments of Delphi, by guides who were not always able to satisfy the intellectual curiosity of their visitors, despite being pre-programmed with a litany of stories.⁴⁵

A more substantial dossier of the spirit of ἱστορία actively abroad in the second-century Greek world is afforded by Pausanias' *Description of Greece*. This is a complex work, part guidebook, part literary and historical treatise, which reflected the needs of the erudite and cultured traveller on the look-out

---

43 For what follows, cf. E. D. Hunt, 'Travel, Tourism and Piety in the Roman Empire: a context for the beginnings of Christian pilgrimage', *Echos du Monde Classique/Classical Views* 28 (1984), 391–417.

44 Plutarch, *De Defectu Oraculorum* 419–20, *Plutarch's Moralia*, trans. F. C. Babbitt, 15 vols., Loeb Classical Library (London, 1936), V, 402–4. The official nature of Demetrius' travels brought him, it appears, to the northern provincial headquarters at York, where he made religious dedications recorded in Greek on two bronze tablets which were unearthed during the building of the railway station (and are now in the Yorkshire Museum): see *Roman Inscriptions of Britain*, ed. R. G. Collingwood and R. P. Wright (Oxford, 1965), I, 662–3, with H. Dessau, 'Ein Freund Plutarchs in England', *Hermes* 46 (1911), 156–60.

45 For various allusions to guides and their shortcomings, see Plutarch, *De Pythiae Oraculis* 395a, 397e, 400d–e, *Plutarch's Moralia*, *op. cit.* note 44, pp. 260, 276 and 292. On Roman travellers to Greece, see S. E. Alcock, *Graecia Capta; the landscapes of Roman Greece* (Cambridge, 1993), pp. 224–30.

for the classical heritage in its native land. The very title of Pausanias' text, Περιήγησις (= 'conducted tour'), makes it the literary equivalent, for Greece as a whole, of those περιηγηταί (= guides) who escorted visitors around Plutarch's Delphi.[46] The *Description* is the result of years of travel on Pausanias' part around his Greek homeland, and a preoccupation with its mythical and historical past almost to the exclusion of the realities of the present. Its panorama is dominated by the vestiges of Greek antiquity, rather than the contemporary condition of Greece as a province of the high Roman empire.[47] Far from being just a casually inquisitive or touristic enterprise, ἱστορία for him was a committed search for what he perceived to be the roots of Greek culture and identity.

Enlarging on this point, John Elsner has recently introduced the vocabulary of pilgrimage into modern discussion of Pausanias.[48] Noting the predominance of religious sites and ceremonies among Pausanias' interests, Elsner has convincingly cast him in the role of religious devotee, even the initiate, seeking out the sacred places which defined for him what was meant by being Greek; and he has made illuminating comparisons between Pausanias' quest for this religious self-identity and the Christian traveller's immersion into the biblical landscape of the Holy Land. In Pausanias, classical ἱστορία and the religious conviction of the pilgrim may thus be seen to converge.

Even if this analysis of Pausanias' own perceptions is discounted, his narrative endures as a panoply of ancient remains which attracted travellers eager to enter and relive the legacy of the Greek past – its mythical heroes and historical figures – and to be *shown* its physical remnants. They could be present at Aulis, for example, and see again Agamemnon and the massing of the Greek fleet setting sail for Troy, or walk among the celebrated tombs of Athens' cemetery quarter and behold the tableau of history there represented.[49] It is, of course, impossible to enter the minds of Pausanias' visitors to these places, but it is hard not to conclude that their enterprises of ἱστορία were marked by at least a *quasi*-devotional attachment to the objective – as much pilgrimages as 'special interest' tourism.

Another favoured destination for enterprises of ἱστορία in antiquity was the land of Egypt, where the ancient tombs and temples of the Nile valley

---

46 On the nature and purpose of Pausanias' work, see C. Habicht, *Pausanias' Guide to Ancient Greece* (Berkeley, 1985), pp. 1–27.
47 For Pausanias' ambivalence towards the Roman present, and preference for the distant past, cf. Habicht 1985, *op. cit.* note 46, pp. 117–40.
48 J. Elsner, 'Pausanias: a Greek pilgrim in the Roman world', *Past and Present* 135 (May 1992), 3–29, and in his *Art and the Roman Viewer* (Cambridge, 1995), pp. 125–55; cf. Alcock 1993, *op. cit.* note 45, p. 174.
49 See Pausanias, *Description of Greece*, trans. W. H. S. Jones, 5 vols., Loeb Classical Library (London, 1918–1935), I.xxix. Habicht 1985, *op. cit.* note 46, p. 23, observes that the latest of the graves mentioned by Pausanias date back to some 450 years before his own time. For Aulis, see Pausanias, *Description of Greece* IX.xix.

regularly attracted both passing visitors and determined travellers. Some of these were individual explorers, others belonged to the retinues of the 'high and mighty', and there was even the occasional emperor. Many surviving inscriptions carved on the monuments remain a vivid testimony to these expeditions in search of the Egyptian past.[50] The language of these texts is again familiarly that of ἱστορία, but often coupled with other forms of reaction to the places visited: words for 'marvel', 'wonder', are common, and so too is the vocabulary of prayer and worship (προσκυνέω, προσκύνησις, etc.). The act of inscribing the names becomes an appeal to the gods on behalf of the travellers themselves, or on behalf of others left behind, and these distant places take on a sanctity inspired by some perceived divine presence. Among the inscriptions are some which exhibit a language of personal devotion and religious commitment extending far beyond conventional formulae of tourist graffiti. Most notable is the famous hymn of praise to the local sun-god Mandulis, inscribed in the portico of his temple at Talmis, in the remote southern reaches of Egypt. Here, in metrical Greek, the worshipper (his name is Maximus) communicated his experience of the god's presence.[51] Journeying with these travellers in Roman Egypt, perhaps even more explicitly than in Pausanias' Greece, we are confronted by an ancient sacred landscape which drew from those who came in search of it a vivid sense of awe and wonder, and a spirit of reverence for the gods who inhabited it.

It is time to return to those Christian believers drawn to congregate at the summit of the Mount of Olives overlooking Eusebius' Jerusalem. This paper has attempted to elucidate something of the religious potential inherent in the terminology favoured by Eusebius, in which biblical sites are described as being 'shown' to those who came to see them. With the aid of comparable evidence from the classical, pagan, world it has also tried to demonstrate that participation in those learned enterprises of ἱστορία, which occupied Origen's and Eusebius' tracing of the Scriptures, need not be devoid of religious significance. The third key term isolated from Eusebius' description of the assembly on the Mount of Olives now speaks for itself – the believers gathered there for the purpose of *worship* (προσκυνήσεως) in the face of the glory of the Lord revealed through the Bible on that spot. In the *Onomastikon* too he had noted the faithful 'hastening to make their prayers' at the site of Gethsemane on the slopes of the Mount, 'where Christ prayed before his suffering'.[52] In the *Church History* he had told of an early third-century bishop, Alexander, 'from the land of the Cappadocians', who journeyed to Jerusalem 'for the purpose of prayer

---

[50] Hunt 1984, *op. cit.* note 43, pp. 404–8; cf. J. Lindsey, *Men and Gods on the Roman Nile* (London, 1968), pp. 315–39.

[51] A. D. Nock, 'A Vision of Mandulis Aion', *Harvard Theological Review* 27 (1934), 53–104, reprinted in his *Essays on Religion and the Ancient World*, ed. Z. Stewart (Oxford, 1972), I, 357–400; cf. Lane Fox 1986, *op. cit.* note 2, pp. 166–7.

[52] *Onomastikon* 74, *op. cit.* note 33.

and investigation (ἱστορία again) of the [holy] places', only to be detained by the congregation there as their new bishop.[53]

The motives for visiting Jerusalem accorded to Alexander perhaps have more affinity with Eusebius' own day and the context of composition of the *Church History*, than with pre-Constantinian reality. Yet it should be remembered that, like the other works of Eusebius on which this paper has been based, the *Church History* was a substantially 'pre-Constantinian' product.[54] The Jerusalem around which Eusebius depicted the Christian faithful on their quest to retrace the Scriptures, to behold before their eyes biblical prophecy brought to life in the events of the New Testament, and to respond as pilgrims in reverence and worship, was still the paganised Roman colony of Aelia Capitolina. The Christian advent of Constantine in the East, with its dramatic consequences for Jerusalem and elsewhere in the Holy Land, was yet to come.

When the Constantinian development of the holy places did materialise, in the years after 324,[55] a new Christian topography of biblical sites did not have to be invented *from scratch* for the attendant pilgrims. There was a pre-existing tradition of the location of key moments in the scriptural record, albeit only occasionally and dimly documented. These places already attracted the attention of devotees, and their quest was at the same time 'intellectual' and 'religious'; they gained the satisfaction of *seeing* the Bible enshrined in its proper and unique place, and of having their faith confirmed. The three principal locations around Jerusalem which saw the building of Constantinian churches (aided by the involvement on the spot of the empress-mother Helena) were the Golgotha area of Calvary and Sepulchre, the sacred cave at the summit of the Mount of Olives, and the cave of the Nativity in Bethlehem. All of these had, as has been seen, a prehistory of some kind of Christian interest, which had drawn the faithful of earlier generations even when (as in the case of Golgotha and, perhaps, Bethlehem) their object was obscured beneath a superstructure of pagan cult.

A fourth Constantinian basilica in the Holy Land arose at the site of Mamre, near Hebron. This was the place of the terebinth tree, which in Genesis 18 had provided shelter for the three strangers visiting Abraham, who arrived to foretell the late pregnancy of his aged wife, Sarah. Christian interpretation identified the spokesman who voiced the promise of the future seed of Abraham, the father of all nations, as nothing less than the preincarnate Christ

---

[53] *Historia Ecclesiastica* VI.xi.1–2, *op. cit.* note 1.

[54] The dating of its various editions is a complex and contentious question, but all are agreed that it was substantially complete in its present form well before 324: for differing views, see T. D. Barnes, 'The editions of Eusebius' *Ecclesiastical History*', *Greek, Roman and Byzantine Studies* 21 (1980), 191–201 and A. Louth, 'The date of Eusebius' *Historia Ecclesiastica*', *Journal of Theological Studies* New Series 41 (1990), 111–23.

[55] See *Vita Constantini* iii.33, *op. cit.* note 18, for the 'new Jerusalem' arising opposite the ruins of the old on the Temple Mount.

('the Lord appeared to Abraham . . .'). Mamre was at least as significant for Christian believers as were the gospel locations of Christ's subsequent earthly existence.[56] What, then, of the pre-Constantinian history of the actual site? In both *Onomastikon* and *Proof of the Gospel* Eusebius noted that the terebinth tree 'where Abraham had his tent' was to be seen and was 'still to this day being shown', and that it was a place of worship (θρησκεύεται) 'for those who live in the neighbourhood' (cf. ὑπὸ τῶν ἐθνῶν in *Onomastikon*: 'by native peoples').[57] The implication would appear to be that, here at least, it was not the Christian faithful who frequented the spot and derived satisfaction from the sight of the venerable tree, but rather that Mamre was a centre of local *pagan* cult.

Confirmation of this emerges from Constantine's surviving letter to the Palestinian bishops in which he instructs them about building the church at Mamre. Acting on the report of his mother-in-law, Eutropia (evidently visiting the Holy Land), the emperor ordered the destruction of the pagan idols, altar and sacrifices which she had seen flourishing at the spot, and the restoration of Abraham's Mamre to its 'ancient holiness'.[58] Despite the new church, Constantine was unsuccessful in obliterating Mamre's paganness. A century later the church historian Sozomen depicted the place as a thriving religious centre for all persuasions, Christian, Jewish *and* pagan.[59] Such was the 'catholic' appeal of the tale of Abraham.

Yet, in the light of the discussion in this paper, it is not necessary to conclude that Mamre had meant nothing to Christians before Constantine, or that its Christian holiness was not in fact 'ancient', but a new Constantinian creation. The place was evidently too minor a focus of Christian interest to serve the apologetic purposes of Origen or Eusebius – hence the silence about Christian visitors in *Onomastikon* and *Proof of the Gospel*. Nevertheless it seems likely that there were other Christian travellers, who preceded Eutropia in the biblical quest for the sacred encounter of Genesis 18, only to lament, and perhaps recoil from, the pagan cult which they discovered monopolising the site, while still recognising the place as that where 'the Lord appeared to Abraham'. Viewed with the pilgrims' eyes of faith, the land of the Bible could not but 'show' forth its holy places, no matter what alien worship might possess them.

---

[56] On Mamre, see Hunt 1982, *op. cit.* note 3, pp. 102–4; Taylor 1993, *op. cit.* note 5, pp. 86–95.
[57] *Demonstratio Evangelica* V.ix.7, *op. cit.* note 32; *Onomastikon, op. cit.* note 33, pp. 6 and 76.
[58] *Vita Constantini* iii.52–3, *op. cit.* note 18.
[59] Sozomen, *Historia Ecclesiastica* II.iv.2–5, ed. J. Bidez and G. C. Hansen (Berlin, 1960).

3

Sacred Journeying: Women's Correspondence and Pilgrimage in the Fourth and Eighth Centuries

JULIE ANN SMITH

Late antique and early medieval pilgrimage sites were places where God was perceived to have made his power manifest. They were places made holy by the events recounted in the Bible and by the lives of the saints. Particularly important were those where miracles had been performed, or where sanctity was endowed by the physical remains of the saints after death.[1] This sacred geography was the fundamental attraction to the women whose letters form the basis of this study and it was to the most important Christian cities, Jerusalem and Rome, and their associated holy places, that they travelled. Many pilgrims journeyed in the hope that they would be able to envision the biblical events mystically (re)happen by simply being at the sites where they had taken place. Other aims were to visit, and take inspiration from, the monasteries and hermitages of renowned holy women and men. The idea of sacred journeying for women of the fourth and eighth centuries was no doubt daunting, but unquestionably achievable and permissible, and 'forgetful of their sex' (in the words of St Jerome[2]) they moved more or less decorously about the holy places.

The chronological limits of this study are dictated by the existence of a small corpus of letters from the late fourth century and the first half of the eighth century. Those from the fourth century relate, first, to the pilgrimage of Egeria and, then, to the travels of Paula and her associates. Those from the eighth century comprise the letters of several Anglo-Saxon women, who took part in the correspondence which has been gathered together under the name of St Boniface. There is little comparable material between these two periods. The absence of correspondence in the fifth and sixth centuries is, no doubt, explained in part by the barbarian migrations. Likewise, the Viking migrations of the ninth and tenth centuries would have reduced the allure of such excursions for even the most devout. The relative stability of the late fourth and

---

[1] The present paper only discusses the notion of pilgrimage as an elective journey to a sacred centre. There will be no discussion of notions of penitential or missionary pilgrimage.
[2] Jerome, *PL* 22, letter 108, c. 14.

early eighth centuries made pilgrimage an achievable goal, even if not a very comfortable one.

The letters refer only to the pilgrimage sites of the Holy Land and Rome; the former as the site of the Old and New Testament stories and the 'miracle' of salvation, the latter as the *limina apostolorum* (threshold of the apostles) where SS Peter and Paul had preached and been martyred for the faith. The fourth-century letters mention a number of holy places within the Holy Land to which pilgrims had access. These letters suggest that there were few obstacles to pilgrimage by women of the Roman aristocracy; they travelled extensively and restlessly about the biblical sites (only Egeria was once deflected from travelling to a site which was not under the direct protection of Rome) and money seems not to have been a problem. The eighth-century letters focus on Rome. No pilgrimage sites in England or on the way to the holy city are mentioned and, consequently, we know little of how the Anglo-Saxon women actually made their way there. It is likely to have been a long, arduous and dangerous journey. Many pilgrims were either physically unable to survive the outward or return journeys, or fell by the wayside in a spiritual sense.

It is clear that there were many pilgrims, both female and male, during the periods under discussion. Their volume, and governmental support for such journeys, is shown by the provision of hostels in areas under the control of the Roman administration, and of cohorts of soldiers to protect pilgrims and other travellers in unsafe areas. The hostels established by Jerome and Paula in Bethlehem, and that of Rufinus and Melania in Jerusalem, are known examples of the accommodation available to all types of pilgrims in the Holy Land. Hospitality was also provided by the semi-eremitic groups of religious which clustered about many of the holy sites, such as Marcana's monastery near the martyrium of St Thecla, at Seleucia, in the Taurus mountains.

In the first half of the eighth century writers commented on the large numbers of people travelling to Rome. Bede noted the numbers of English people, both male and female, and of all classes, who made the journey.[3] The *Life of Boniface* records that the devout bishop was surrounded by Franks, Bavarians, Anglo-Saxons and other peoples who were living in the holy city when he made his third pilgrimage to Rome in 738.[4] Eangyth, an Anglo-Saxon nun, lamented to Boniface that so many friends and relations had left England either to make the pilgrimage to Rome or to become missionaries.[5] The *Anglo-Saxon Chronicle* made several references to pilgrimages by kings, queens and

---

[3] Bede, *Historia Ecclesiastica Gentis Anglorum*, ed. C. Plummer (Oxford, 1896; reprinted 1985), V, c. 7.

[4] C. H. Talbot, *The Anglo-Saxon Missionaries in Germany* (London, 1954), c. 7, 49.

[5] *Monumenta Germania Historica: Epistolae Selectae, Volume I. S Bonifatii et Lulli Epistolae*, ed. M. Tangl (Berlin, 1955), letter 14. All letters from the Boniface correspondence are numbered according to Tangl's edition. The dating established by Tangl, and the editors of the other letters used, is followed here.

bishops.[6] In this later period it is less clear whether official hostels or protection might be expected along the way. Such provision is unlikely to have been available to any but the most wealthy or noble. Concern over these matters is shown by a letter from Cardinal-Deacon Gemmulus, who assured Boniface from Rome that the women pilgrims commended to his care had been well protected and accommodated.[7] The issue of financial provision for pilgrims is mentioned in a letter by Pope Gregory II and again in a confessional handbook ascribed to Archbishop Theodore.[8]

In recent years scholarly attention has focused on the gendered nature and discourses of travel as intrinsically a male endeavour or pastime denied to women, with a language which is used in its description, which reinforces this notion of exclusion. This is particularly the case in relation to travel undertaken for what is perceived to be beneficial purposes, that is educational, heroic, scientific or ennobling.[9] In travel narratives the place of women is usually marginalised and degraded.[10] This creates difficulties for women who undertake any form of journeying and also creates problems of self-definition which usually involves a negation or denial of sexuality.[11] The freedom of movement accessible to women during the late antique and early medieval periods has been examined by Joyce Salisbury, who concludes that their independence was enabled by their embracing a life of chastity.[12] The denial of their sexuality placed them outside the normal gender requirements of their culture and allowed them the freedom to travel; something which was not open to women who did fulfil their gendered roles. In his letter to Eustochium, Jerome describes Paula as 'forgetful of her sex' when she desired to live among the Egyptian monks, which he says she could have done if her desire to return to Bethlehem had not been so strong.[13] This personal freedom was seized upon by the women whose letters form the basis of this study, and was used by them to undertake formidable sacred journeys.

6 *Anglo-Saxon Chronicle, sub anni* 688, 709, 721, 726/8, 737, ed. C. Plummer, *Two of the Saxon Chronicles Parallel* (Oxford, 1892).
7 Tangl 1955, *op. cit.* note 6, letter 62.
8 Tangl 1955, *op. cit.* note 6, letter 18: 'He is to divide the revenues of the church and the offerings of the faithful in four parts ... the third for the poor and pilgrims'; Penitential of Theodore, Book II, XIV, 10, *Councils and Ecclesiastical Documents relating to Great Britain and Ireland. Volume III: The English Church, 595–1066*, ed. A. W. Haddan and W. Stubbs (Oxford, 1964), p. 203: 'It is not lawful to give tithes except for the poor and for pilgrims.'
9 J. Clifford, 'Travelling Cultures', in *Cultural Studies*, ed. L. Grossberg, C. Nelson and P. Treichler (New York, 1992), pp. 105–6.
10 J. Wolff, 'On the Road Again: Metaphors of Travel in Cultural Criticism', *Cultural Studies* 7/2 (1993), 229.
11 Wolff 1993, *op. cit.* note 10, p. 234.
12 J. E. Salisbury, *Church Fathers, Independent Virgins* (London, 1992). See also J. A. McNamara, *Sisters in Arms: Catholic Nuns through Two Millenia* (Cambridge, Mass., 1996).
13 Jerome, *PL* 22, letter 108, c. 14.

The letters discussed here have never been used as a corpus or compared with one another, nor have they been used to assess the nature of women's pilgrimage. They are extraordinary, not only because they have survived but also because there is no comparable male correspondence. On the other hand, they are a meagre legacy of the experiences of what were probably large numbers of women travelling long, difficult and dangerous journeys across the ancient world. The letters contain all the written evidence we have for the pilgrimages of these women in the late antique and early medieval periods.

The letters of Egeria, Paula, and the Anglo-Saxon nuns reveal something of how these women conceived of the notion of pilgrimage. There are no stories of miracles in any of the preserved letters. The visitors to Jerusalem saw the most important of all Christian relics, the True Cross, but none of the stories recounted of visiting or touching it suggest anything miraculous in the event, nor do they witness or receive any evidence of miracles which may have been associated with the Cross. None of the letters indicate that the writers were ill or in need of physical healing though some of them sought healing for maladies of the spirit. Among the Anglo-Saxons there was a tradition of self-imposed exile or alienation from home and community. Nuns and monks travelled to the Continent to visit the holy places, or to become missionaries, in isolation from family and customary social contacts. This notion of exile and homelessness, which is part of the Anglo-Saxon social and literary culture, was alien to the experience of the Roman women. When women like Melania, Paula, and their many unnamed followers set out on their journeying they were denying more than family ties.

The aim of this paper is to understand something of the nature of the sacred journeys made by the women who wrote these letters, and to reconstruct how they defined themselves as pilgrims. Victor Turner's theory of liminality, in relation to pilgrimage and monasticism, is used to provide a number of concepts against which the letters can be analysed.

Pilgrimage, Liminality and Tourism

In one of his papers on the concept of pilgrimage, Turner compared the processual nature of sacred journeying with those of rites of passage.[14] He found that pilgrims shared many attributes with ritual passage candidates, and expanded Arnold van Gennep's[15] transitional phases of

separation → margin → reaggregation (serial phases) or
preliminality → liminality → post-liminality (spatial phases)

[14] V. Turner, 'Pilgrimage as a Liminoid Phenomenon', in *Image and Pilgrimage in Christian Culture: Anthropological Perspectives*, ed. V. and E. Turner (Oxford, 1978), pp. 1–39.
[15] Turner 1978, *op. cit.* note 14, p. 2.

to encompass the behaviour and symbolism of pilgrimage. The pilgrim's journey to the 'Sacred Centre' becomes an extended period of separation from the 'Primary Centre';[16] s/he exists in an ongoing marginal state during the period spent at the Sacred Centre; and the return journey to the Primary Centre becomes a period of reaggregation. Turner was not, of course, equating pilgrimage with passage rites, simply observing that the transitional state of a ritual candidate resembles the temporary marginality of a pilgrim. The liminal state is outside the normal structures of society, 'symbolically, all attributes that distinguish categories and groups in the structured social order are here in abeyance'.[17] Passage ritual liminars move from a mundane centre to a sacred periphery which transiently becomes a new centre; they are removed from the influence of power in their societies; they form a *communitas* with other liminars in which they are characteristically anonymous, equal and sexless; and they exist outside the concepts of place and time of their societies. Pilgrimage has similar features: pilgrims move from a mundane (Primary) Centre to a holy site which is always the Sacred Centre of their world; they form a community in which class and gender are *less* significant; they have removed themselves from the influences of power, place and time of their societies. But the liminality of pilgrimage is most clearly distinguished from that of rites of passage by its voluntary nature; it is not required for transition from one status to another. Hence, Turner defined Christian pilgrimage as 'the quintessence of voluntary liminality'.[18] And because the features of pilgrimage resemble, rather than equate to, those of ritual passage liminality Turner concluded that they are best described as liminoid, or quasi-liminal, rather than liminal in van Gennep's full sense.[19]

The liminal phase of ritual has also been compared by Turner to the marginal nature of monasticism. He found that liminality in a highly-structured society can achieve a religious or quasi-religious state with a 'full complement of structural roles and positions'.[20] In monasticism, liminality has been institutionalised and is permanent. The individual chooses to enter a secondary *communitas* that is separate from the Primary Centre, and in which members are anonymous, sexless and equal. Unlike the liminality of pilgrimage, though, the nun or monk remains permanently separated and marginalised from the primary community; there is no element of reaggregation. As with pilgrimage, entry into the monastic life is voluntary and might be defined as liminoid. The liminoid state is, then, one of voluntary alienation

---

[16] 'Primary Centre' is used here to denote the community by which the pilgrim defines her/himself and from which s/he moves away when travelling toward the 'Sacred Centre'.
[17] V. Turner, *The Ritual Process: Structure and Anti-Structure* (London, 1969), p. 103.
[18] Turner 1978, *op. cit.* note 14, p. 9.
[19] Turner 1978, *op. cit.* note 14, p. 35.
[20] Turner 1969, *op. cit.* note 17, p. 167.

from a Primary Centre, undertaken that the individual might become a stranger to the things of the world.

In contrast to pilgrimage, with its concentration on a Sacred Centre, its elements of *communitas* and of religious reaffirmation, is touristic experience. Erik Cohen has defined a typology of touristic experience[21] of which three types may be relevant to this study. Recreational tourism is essentially travel for relaxation, for moving away from the Primary Centre and its associated cares and responsibilities, while retaining central social values. The experiential tourist desires to encounter the authentic lives of other cultures but, again, retains central social values. Existential tourists enter into alien or other cultures and adopt them as their own. The feature which most strongly distinguishes touristic experience from pilgrimage is that the tourist is in search of the 'Other'. In its benign aspect the Other is simply alien but in its malignant aspect it is dangerous, chaotic or heretical.[22] Visiting the Other may recreate or revitalise, but the tourist will remain alienated from the Primary Centre while s/he remains there. Existential tourists redefine Other as an elective centre and more or less permanently alienate themselves from their own culture and community. According to Cohen, although sacred journeying toward a Sacred Centre and touristic journeying towards Other are 'conceptually distinct, they are not completely discrete, as each possesses some qualities of the other'.[23] Both Sacred Centre and Other are liminal; in both cases the normal order of things is suspended. But, unlike the Other, the Sacred Centre is ideologically sited within the pilgrim's society or culture. And the Sacred Centre has a fundamental potential for order, while the Other does not.[24]

According to Turner's thesis, pilgrims leave their Primary Centre to journey to the Sacred Centre where they join a liminoid community. They then journey back to the Primary Centre and are reaggregated. During the period of reaggregation, pilgrims share their experiences, recounting tales of the people they have met, the sights seen, ideas and rituals encountered, which are outside the experience of most people at the Primary Centre. In this way pilgrims change their communities. In monasticism, the candidate separates from the Primary Centre and is permanently aggregated into a liminoid community. The monastery is paradoxically both a new Primary Centre and a state of permanent liminality. Each of these liminoid states (pilgrimage, monasticism

---

[21] E. Cohen, 'Pilgrimage and Tourism: Convergence and Divergence', in *Sacred Journeys: the Anthropology of Pilgrimage*, ed. A. Morinis (Westport, Connecticut, 1992), pp. 53–5.

[22] Cohen 1992, *op. cit.* note 21, p. 151

[23] Cohen 1992, *op. cit.* note 21, p. 50.

[24] Cohen 1992, *op. cit.* note 21, p. 51. Cohen also points out that 'while the experience of the existential tourist at the elective centre is homologous to that of the idealised pilgrim, his structural position is not. The pilgrim's centre is within his own society or culture, whereas that of the existential tourist is not; rather, the latter transforms a point in the periphery of that world into his elective centre', p. 55.

and touristic experience) is used here to try to understand the nature of the pilgrimages undertaken by the women correspondents, and their reasons for undertaking them.

The Correspondents: Egeria[25]

Egeria was a nun or canoness from a religious community in Galicia, northern Spain,[26] travelling in the Holy Land c. 381–384. The material surviving from her correspondence is incomplete and when we meet up with her she has already been journeying among the holy places for over a year. Although she appears to have been the only member of her community on the journey, her constant use of 'we' suggests that she travelled in groups. She was widely read with an extensive knowledge of the scriptures.[27] Her claim to unimportance belies the attention she was constantly afforded by bishops and other holy men and women. Her energy and enthusiasm during her long and often difficult journeys suggest that she was youngish, or at least not elderly. She shared a warm relationship with her sisters at home, often addressing them with such endearments as 'ladies of my heart', 'ladies, my light' or 'ladies, reverent sisters'.[28]

Egeria's correspondence was written over a three-year period though only two sections survive: the journey from Mt Sinai back to Jerusalem and then on to Constantinople, and part of her description of the liturgy of Jerusalem. The surviving material does not make it clear whether the original was one long letter or a series of letters later copied as continuous text. The final instalment was written from Constantinople. She had intended to return home from there but then decided to continue her travels to other holy places in Asia Minor. She told her sisters that she was not sure if her journeying would ever be finished or if she would ever return home. It saddened her that she might never see them again and she asked them to remember her in their prayers. Her letters consist of detailed descriptions of places, events and liturgical practices which

---

25 'Itinerarium Egeriae', in *Itineraria et Alia*, ed. A. Francheschini and R. Weber, *Corpus Christianorum Series Latina* 175 (Turnhout, 1965), 35–103; *Egeria's Travels*, trans. J. Wilkinson (London, 1971).
26 Little is known about Egeria and her religious status has been the subject of some discussion. However, in her description of the Epiphany liturgy in Jerusalem Egeria writes of the great crowds, 'not just monks, but lay men and women' ('non solum monazontes, sed et laici, uiri aut mulieres'), and later describes 'the people' ('populus') keeping the Easter vigil 'at the same time as us' ('qua hora et aput nos'). She would not need to comment on this lay participation if she were a laywoman herself. 'Itinerarium Egeriae', *op. cit.* note 25, 25.12 and 38.1–2.
27 E. D. Hunt, *Holy Land Pilgrimage in the Later Roman Empire AD 312–460* (Oxford, 1989), p. 119.
28 'Itinerarium Egeriae', *op. cit.* note 25, 3:8, 5:8, 17:2, 19:19, 20:5, 23:10, 24:1: 'domnae', lumen meum' or 'dominae animae meae'.

are invaluable and unprecedented. They were inspired by her intense interest in the holy places as physical witnesses of the biblical narratives, and were written to give her sisters some share in what she had seen and to supplement their pious reading. After creating a detailed account of her visit to Mt Sinai she explained that she had described the places and events one by one so that her sisters would be able to picture what happened when they read the Book of Moses.[29] She endeavoured to create for them a vicarious vision or apprehension of the physical settings of biblical events. She also valued the experience of visiting the sites herself, and asked for the appropriate passages to be read from the Bible, but she was not emotional and sought no mystical union with the episodes related.

It would seem that Egeria had set out with the intention of returning to her community of sisters, or had, at least, expressed the intention of doing so. Several times she explains why she had not returned, why she was extending her time in the Holy Land, visiting sites she had not originally planned to visit or had not heard of before her arrival. After three years of prolonged journeying, when all her planned visits to holy sites had been fulfilled, she declared that her spirit was ready to return to her own country. But once again departure for home was delayed, this time as a result of God's bidding her to go to Eddessa in Syrian Mesopotamia. From Edessa she travelled more or less directly to Constantinople which lay on the western land route used by pilgrims of that time. From Constantinople she wrote that she might never return as she had heard of more holy places to visit near Ephesus. She promised to write if her new plans changed.

During a visit to a monk in the valley of Cherith, Wadi Yabis, Egeria questioned him about why he lived there, because, as she explained to her sisters, she was very curious.[30] This aspect of her personality is most striking in her writings. Although her purpose was ostensibly religious, and she only mentioned visiting places of biblical and Christian interest, Egeria's ever-extended travels were largely driven by curiosity. She carried on regardless of discomfort, danger and possible disapproval from her community at home, and her pilgrimage became a permanent state.

Egeria remained purposely and consciously liminoid. Several times she declared that she intended to begin the journey home, which would have marked the beginning of the process of reaggregation with her community, only to postpone it in order to undertake yet another holy detour. Her final comment was that she might die before her sacred journeying was over. She chose the permanence of her liminality. She had obviously enjoyed travelling and was consciously extending, for as long as possible, the liminoid state.

---

[29] 'Itinerarium Egeriae', *op. cit.* note 25, 3:8; 5:8; 17:2; 19:19; 20:5; 23:10; 24:1.
[30] 'Itinerarium Egeriae', *op. cit.* note 25, 5:8.

The Roman Women

Many Roman women journeyed to the Holy Land during the fourth century but few are identifiable and little is known of their personal experiences there. However two letters survive which give some insight into the pilgrimages of such women and how they defined themselves as pilgrims. The letters pertain to two patrician women, Paula and her daughter Eustochium, who had joined the movement of Roman women who left families and fortunes in Rome and chose the ascetic life in the Holy Land, many with the express intention of remaining there. Paula and Eustochium made a pilgrimage through the Holy Land before jointly establishing a religious community with St Jerome in Bethlehem. This journey was described by Jerome in a eulogistic letter to Eustochium written shortly after Paula's death in c. 404.[31] He related that, after leaving their family in Rome, Paula and Eustochium journeyed to Antioch where he joined them and they travelled together about the holy places of Palestine. The letter concentrates upon Paula's fervour and her mystical perception of the holy places[32] but makes scant reference to the fact that Eustochium, an unspecified number of virgins, and Jerome himself accompanied her. After travelling as far as Egypt to meet some of the holy monks there, she returned to Bethlehem where she built monasteries, cells and hostels for different kinds of pilgrims.[33] It is not clear if she travelled again after settling in Bethlehem, although she encouraged another Roman woman, Marcella, to join them there, saying that she would visit the holy places with her if she came. The other letter which relates to this extended pilgrimage of Paula and Eustochium in the Holy Land was written by the two women to their friend, Marcella, in Rome.[34] The letter was written from Bethlehem, c. 386, recounting for Marcella the wonders of the Holy Land, enticing her to join them and to encounter with them the spiritual experience of the holy places of Palestine, especially Jerusalem and Bethlehem.[35]

There has been an assumption among some, though not all, modern translators and commentators that this second letter was written by Jerome. Paula

---

[31] Jerome, *PL* 22, letter 108.
[32] For instance, Jerome describes Paula's response upon entering the cave of the nativity in Bethlehem, *PL* 22, letter 108, c. 10: 'She declared in my hearing, that she saw with the eyes of faith the infant Lord, wrapped in cloths and crying, the Magi adoring, the star shining from above, the Virgin mother, the careful nursing, the shepherds coming by night to see the word which had been made.'
[33] Jerome, *PL* 22, letter 108, c. 14.
[34] Jerome, *PL* 22, letter 46.
[35] Jerome, *PL* 22, letter 46, c. 13. This letter is couched in both emotional and mystical language: 'Will that day never be when we may be permitted to enter the Saviour's cave? To weep in the sepulchre of the Lord with our sister, our mother? Then to touch the wood of the Cross, and to be lifted up in spirit on the Mount of Olives with the ascending Lord.'

and Eustochium often acted as his secretaries but there is no reason for assuming that they could not or did not write letters for themselves. Their learning and language skills were praised by Jerome and it is inappropriate to assume they did not have the expertise to write such a letter. Marcella wrote letters which have survived and perhaps they also wrote other letters which are no longer extant. Indeed the letter is quite different in tone from those of Jerome, especially when compared with a letter he wrote to Desiderius and Serenilla exhorting them to come to Bethlehem, c. 393.[36] His letter does not suggest the places they might visit nor does it describe the mystical, affective nature of the journey they would make as does the letter to Marcella.

Many Roman women, such as one named Fabiola who visited the Bethlehem community in 394, made the journey to the Holy Land and then returned to Rome, thereby completing the pilgrimage process. Paula and her followers did not return to Rome. They separated from their Primary Centres and journeyed to the holy places, but they remained at the Sacred Centre, choosing not to be reaggregated with their Primary Centres. They chose to live in communities which had been established for the purpose of allowing pilgrims to visit or live at the holy sites. They altered their lives, removing themselves from their families in Rome, and from whatever remained of their patrician lifestyle there. They journeyed to the Sacred Centre, only to redefine themselves in relation to that centre, making in it a new *communitas*. Paula and Eustochium made this clear in their letter to Marcella when they pointed out the superiority of the monastic life in Jerusalem and Bethlehem.[37] Admittedly, they said, Rome was holy, but its display and power were contrary to the principles and quietude of the monastic life.[38] They were adamant that 'those who stand first throughout the world are here gathered side by side'[39] and that 'of all the ornaments of the Church, our company of monks and virgins is one of the finest'.[40]

Paula and her companions fell outside Turner's model, having redefined themselves in relation to the Sacred Centre. They no longer existed in the liminoid phase of pilgrimage but they had not reaggregated themselves to their Primary Centre. In relation to that Primary Centre they were still liminoid. They had made for themselves a new, or secondary, centre which was homologous with the liminality of monasticism and in which the new or secondary centre was located at the Sacred Centre.

---

[36] Jerome, *PL* 22, letter 47.
[37] Jerome, *PL* 22, letter 46, c. 10.
[38] Jerome, *PL* 22, letter 46, c. 12.
[39] Jerome, *PL* 22, letter 46, c. 10.
[40] Jerome, *PL* 22, letter 46.

The Anglo-Saxon Women

By the early eighth century the Sacred Centre of western Christianity was Rome, the site where SS Peter and Paul had preached and achieved martyrdom. The shrine of St Peter validated the power of the popes who were his successors. Clerics, monks, nuns, and lay-folk yearned to make sacred journeys to the threshold of the apostles. Many of them were aged and planned to see out their days in Rome. Others were younger but still chose to remain, as many Romans had done in the Holy Land three centuries earlier. Among these intrepid travellers there seems to have been a large company of Anglo-Saxons, both women and men. The eighth-century letters are to be found among the correspondence associated with St Boniface. This small corpus consists of seven letters and concerns a number of Anglo-Saxon nuns and their pilgrimages to Rome. Some of the letters were written by women planning to make the pilgrimage, and others were from Boniface concerning such pilgrimages. The letters also mention women who had already made the journey to the holy city, some of them having stayed there, while others had returned home.

The principal correspondents were Eangyth, Ecgburg, Eadburg (Bugge), Ælffæd and Boniface. Eangyth, an abbess of an unnamed community which, it seems, had fallen upon hard times, wrote to Boniface about her desire to abdicate her abbacy, which had become too great a burden, and to make a pilgrimage to Rome with her daughter, Eadburg.[41] Her community consisted of both monks and nuns for she reported having trouble with the monks. They had also fallen into disfavour with the royal house. She requested that the will of God be revealed to herself and Eadburg through Boniface who was to pray to God on their behalf and relay the divine message back to them. Eangyth was not asking Boniface's permission, but rather his advice, based on divine revelation. It is not known if Eangyth ever made her journey to Rome or if she returned to England afterwards, but her purposes in making or desiring to make her pilgrimage were not solely to visit the holy places. She confessed to Boniface that she needed to be relieved of her burdens of office as she was weary from dealing with the worldly cares of the monastery. It was recreation and spiritual healing that she sought in her sacred journeying.

Ecgburg was not planning to make a pilgrimage herself, though it is not clear in her letter written to Boniface, c. 716–18, if this was her own choice or if she had been prevented from going.[42] She did not seek the good offices of Boniface in this respect, merely lamented the fact that so many of her kin and friends had gone either to Rome or the mission fields leaving her feeling both lonely and inadequate. She considered that Boniface and pilgrims like her sister Wethburg, who had entered an anchorage in Rome, would occupy a

---

[41] Tangl 1955, *op. cit.* note 5, letter 14.
[42] Tangl 1955, *op. cit.* note 5, letter 13.

more distinguished place than herself in the heavenly hierarchy. Evidently she considered pilgrimage as spiritually far superior to her own monastic life.

Around 713, Abbess Ælfflæd of Whitby wrote briefly to Abbess Adela of Pfalz requesting accommodation and protection for an unnamed fellow-abbess who was making the journey to Rome.[43] The tone of this letter suggests that Ælfflæd was accustomed to making such requests, and no doubt there were many such letters of introduction written on behalf of women pilgrims although no others have survived.

The most prolific writer to participate in the Boniface correspondence was Abbess Eadburg[44] though only six letters survive from the enduring friendship between them. Some are in answer to letters which are now lost, while others are apparently part of an ongoing conversation. The two friends provided each other with gifts, advice and spiritual comfort, and it was in the mode of advice, and in answer to a non-extant letter from Eadburg, that Boniface replied, *c*. 738, concerning her desire to journey to Rome.[45] He expressed some surprise that she felt she would find greater peace in Rome than she had found since giving up her abbacy for quiet and the contemplation of God. She was living in retirement in her own monastery and it seems as if she had already marginalised herself from her secondary *communitas*. Nevertheless, Boniface did not criticise her as he believed it to be entirely her own decision. He advised waiting until the holy city was no longer under threat from Saracen attack, suggesting that in the meantime she should begin her preparations so as to be able to depart as soon as it was safe.

Eadburg did make her pilgrimage, meeting up with Boniface himself in Rome where they made their devotions and observances together. She returned to the convent where she had once been abbess, but does not seem to have resumed her office. She did, however, share her experiences with King

---

[43] Tangl 1955, *op. cit.* note 5, letter 8.

[44] Tangl 1955, *op. cit.* note 5. It seems likely that there were two, or even three, women called Eadburg who took part in the Boniface correspondence. In Tangl, letter 10 (dated 716), Boniface writes to a woman named Eadburg whom he describes as 'monastice normulæ conversationis emerite'. This is unlikely to be the same Eadburg whose mother Eangyth wrote in Tangl, letter 14 (dated 719–22), of her desire to give up her abbatial duties and journey with her daughter to Rome. It is also unclear if this younger Eadburg is the same Abbess Eadburg (affectionately known as Bugge) who conducted the long and close correspondence with Boniface. Eadburg/Bugge became abbess of Minster-in-Thanet on the death of St Mildryth. Eangyth was abbess of a monastery which was certainly not Minster-in-Thanet and which was out of favour with the royal house. If Eadburg was daughter of Centwine, king of the West Saxons, as cautiously suggested by W. G. Searle, *Anglo-Saxon Bishops, Kings and Nobles* (Cambridge, 1899), p. 335, then perhaps their monastery was somewhere in the West Saxon kingdom. It would not be impossible for a West Saxon Eadburg to become abbess of a Kentish royal monastery, but Tangl's dating of the letters does make it impossible for Eangyth's daughter to have been abbess of St Mildryth's monastery in 716.

[45] Tangl 1955, *op. cit.* note 5, letter 27.

Æthelbeorht II. The latter mentioned their conversations, and the experiences she related to him, in a later letter to Boniface.[46] Eadburg is one of the few women of this period, for whom letters survive, who completed the pilgrimage process as defined by Turner. She not only returned home, but also shared their experiences with those who had remained there.

In the same letter from Boniface to Eadburg, Boniface mentioned 'our sister, Wiethburg' who was already living in Rome, and commented on letters he had received from her in which she had described the peace she had found 'at the threshold of St Peter'.[47] If Wiethburg was the same as the Wethburg whose absence was lamented by Ecgburg in another letter to Boniface,[48] dated 716–18, then she had been living in an anchorage in Rome for twenty years. Like Paula and her companions, Wiethburg/Wethburg does not fit Turner's model. All these women adopted a mode of monastic life at the Sacred Centre and redefined the nature of their liminoid status.

Comparisons and Conclusions

The surviving correspondence about pilgrims in the late fourth and early eighth centuries is exclusively concerned with women and contains most of what is known about pilgrimage in these periods. The two groups of letters were written in very different circumstances. Egeria and Paula's letters were written during their travels, from pilgrimage sites. Their letters, and other contemporary sources, give details of itineraries, places, events, people and, even, liturgy. There are few such details for the Anglo-Saxon women who travelled, or wished to travel, to Rome in the eighth century. However, all these letters allow us to understand how the women who journeyed to the Sacred Centres of their worlds perceived of themselves as pilgrims.

There are many similarities between the pilgrimages of Egeria, of the Roman women and the Anglo-Saxon women, and there are also differences which affect the nature of their journeys and of their ideas of themselves as pilgrims. The major distinction was the manner in which they lived before and after journeying. The Anglo-Saxon women, and possibly also Egeria, were nuns; they were living in a state of monastic liminality, that is at a secondary centre, prior to journeying to the Sacred Centre. They were no longer in a position to separate from a Primary Centre or to reaggregate with it on completion of pilgrimage. Their ways of life when at the Sacred Centre were also quite different. Egeria chose to regard all the holy places which she visited as constituting the Sacred Centre; her journeying does not seem to have ended or found resolution in access to any particular sacred place. The experience of Paula and

---

[46] Tangl 1955, *op. cit.* note 5, letter 105.
[47] Tangl 1955, *op. cit.* note 5, letter 27.
[48] Tangl 1955, *op. cit.* note 5, letter 13.

Eustochium and their followers contrasts strongly with this as they built hostels and monasteries, demonstrating concretely their intention of permanently inhabiting the Sacred Centre. Their communities at Bethlehem and Jerusalem included accommodation for both the permanent residence of virgins and monks, and for temporary visitors. The building complexes also had communal areas, for group prayer and study, which were the principal funtions of the communities.[49] They had moved from a Primary Centre to the Sacred Centre and established there a secondary *communitas* thus compounding their liminal status as pilgrims, as well as signalling their intention of remaining permanently liminal. There is less information about the daily life of the Anglo-Saxon women in Rome. Ecgburg's sister, Wethburg, entered an anchorage, and this would have to have been attached to a monastery of some sort. The letter from Gemmulus to Boniface mentions the reverend sisters and handmaids of God who had arrived in the holy city with letters of introduction from Boniface. Gemmulus assured Boniface that they had been cared for as he had requested, and as God would deem proper, but supplies no details of the sort of hospitality provided.[50] What the women pilgrims would actually do once they arrived in Rome is never made clear. It seems either to have been understood, needing no discussion, or else they simply did not concern themselves with such mundane matters.

The women who wrote the letters incorporated in this study had different notions of the nature of pilgrimage. Paula and Eustochium and their followers visited the holy places as pilgrims but remained at the Sacred Centre redefining the relationship between that centre and their *communitas*; they had achieved permanent alienation. They did not return home to relate their experiences to, and thereby enlarge the experience of, those who had never made the journey. Egeria remained permanently and intentionally liminal. Elements of her experience were touristic, for example, travel for pleasure, and her desire to encounter authentic experience, but she was not a tourist because she was not moving towards Other. No matter how far or how long she journeyed, while ever she continued to visit holy sites associated with the biblical or early Christian stories she was still within the extended Sacred Centre of the Holy Land. In this she was distinctly a pilgrim, though she did not align with the Turnerian archetype because of her permanent liminality. Indeed, she was unlike any of the other women pilgrims encountered in these letters.[51]

The Anglo-Saxon women did not request Boniface's permission to make their journeys. They asked his advice, perhaps his blessing upon their abdication of duty, but they assumed their prerogative to make the journey. Eangyth

---

[49] Jerome, *PL* 22, letter 108, c. 19.
[50] Tangl 1955, *op. cit.* note 5, letter 62.
[51] There do, however, seem to have been other shadowy women pilgrims who wandered about the holy sites without any fixed monastic relationship or spiritual guidance, such as Silvia of Aquitaine and Poemenia. Jerome did not always approve of their behaviour; see letter 54, c. 13.

imposed a recreational element upon her notion of pilgrimage which was not expressed in letters written by her contemporaries (though this is not to say it did not otherwise exist). It is not possible to compare her with Turner's model as it is not known if she either made the journey or returned afterwards. Wethburg's journey is comparable with that of Paula and her followers as she remained at the Sacred Centre, redefining that centre as a new secondary *communitas*. Of the correspondents, only Eadburg is documented as completing the pilgrimage process, returning to the community in which she lived before setting out and relating or sharing her experiences with other members of that community.

These women either returned to a Primary Centre (Fabiola) or to a secondary *communitas* (Eadburg), or remained at the Sacred Centre and were absorbed into monastic communities there (Wethburg), redefining a place within the Sacred Centre as another secondary *communitas*. That is, they integrated pilgrim liminoid status with monastic liminality. The potential for prolongation in the pilgrimages of Paula and Egeria was influenced by the nature of the Holy Land sites. These were many, scattered from Asia Minor to Egypt, and continuous, active liminoid status, at least for a long time, was not impossible. The Roman sites, on the other hand, were limited in number and geographical extent making continuous journeying comparable to that of Egeria more difficult. By not returning to their primary or monastic communities to share their observations of sights, ideas, rituals and people vastly outside the experience of those at home they were, in a sense, failing in their responsibility as pilgrims for the benefits remained purely personal, though this is not to say that their experiences were thereby invalidated or their pilgrimages not authentic. However, viewed in this light Egeria's voluminous correspondence may have been an endeavour to make up for her failure to return. She attempted to recompense her sisters for her absence by writing in such detail of her pilgrim experience.

Like Jerome in the fourth century, twentieth-century anthropologists have attempted to define the process of pilgrimage, but the letters of these holy women show that they participated in the process as they saw fit. Both Turner and Cohen provide useful analytical tools for the study of pilgrimage but their models do not incorporate women's pilgrimage in the fourth and eighth centuries. The women found their own ways of defining pilgrimage. They constructed themselves through chastity which allowed them to separate from their primary communities. They then felt free to choose the location of their secondary *communitates* either through pilgrimage and relocation at the liminal site of the Sacred Centre, or through entering the nunnery. And, of course, some chose both. The women saw themselves as part of a culture of pilgrimage, or lamented not being part of it. They longed to experience sacred journeying. Their pilgrimages were undertaken for personal reasons at one level, but also were part of the process of alienation from community and visitation of sacred sites which was a widely practised social phenomenon.

Pilgrims had come to occupy a special position within Christian society; they had almost become a class with its own ecclesiastical and secular legislation, and hostels and networks. When the women reached the holy places they found fellowships of others who had chosen to remain in the liminoid state, and perhaps the permanent presence of these pilgrim communities reduced the sense of liminality.

There is one sense in which the pilgrims who remained permanently at the Sacred Centre were *liminal*, that is, more closely resembling the liminal phase of processual ritual than ordinary pilgrims who did return home and complete the pilgrimage process. They had left their primary or secondary communities abdicating all responsibilities and ties to journey to the Sacred Centre where, according to Turner's thesis, they entered a liminoid state. They remained in this liminoid state until they commenced the process of reaggregation, not by returning home to be reaggregated with their earthly communities but to make the return journey home to Heaven. They elected an ongoing liminal status that was not simply the liminoid phase of pilgrimage but effectively also the liminal phase between life and death. It is this enhanced liminality which Ecburg yearned for and which she felt gave pilgrims the advantage over non-pilgrims, like herself, in the heavenly hierarchy. The Anglo-Saxon nuns already lived at one remove from their primary communities; they had already made one step along the journey of which the pilgrimage to Rome was in some ways a natural continuation – a journey which was meant to bring the soul ever closer to Heaven. The liminoid phase of pilgrimage actually became the transitional stage between this life and the next, the final liminal state in the soul's sacred journey to God.

Acknowledgements   I am very grateful for discussion and contributions made by Dr Keith Beattie and Mr Basil Poff.

4

Patrons, Pilgrims and the Cult of Saints in the Medieval Kingdom of León

SIMON BARTON

Relics and the Cult of Saints

The cult of the relics of saints enjoyed a particular vogue in all parts of the Latin West between the eighth and the twelfth centuries.[1] The widespread belief that physical proximity to the tombs of saints was beneficial encouraged men and women of all ranks in society to travel as pilgrims to shrines in search of divine favour, a cure from illness or some other miraculous act. Relics were regarded not merely as sacred objects in their own right, but as sources of power which, God willing, might help those who invoked the assistance of a saint. As Patrick Geary has observed, relics

> provided the point of contact between mundane existence and the divine world. They were part of the sacred, the numinous; but incarnated in this world, as had been Christ, without losing their place in the other. Moreover, they provided the only recourse against the myriad ills, physical, material, and psychic, of a population defenseless before an incomprehensible and terrifying universe. The miraculous power of the saint was the basis upon which his other power rested, and from this ability and willingness to perform miracles developed his following, his *famuli*, his devoted slaves. This following was the basis of his propagandistic value, his economic strength, and his political leverage.[2]

At a time when political instability and territorial fragmentation meant that central authorities were frequently unable to offer any real protection to religious bodies, churchmen looked to the supernatural support of saints to protect their institutions and their properties from attack. Saints had an important role to play as fund-raisers for religious communities, by inspiring

---

[1] See, for example, H. Fichtenau, 'Zum Reliquienwesen im früheren Mittelalter', *Mitteilungen des Instituts für österreichische Geschichtsforschung* 9 (1952), 60–89; P.-A. Sigal, *L'homme et le miracle dans la France médiévale (XIe–XIIe siècles)* (Paris, 1985), pp. 35–45; P. J. Geary, *Furta Sacra: Theft of Relics in the Central Middle Ages* (Princeton, 1978), pp. 16–37.
[2] Geary 1978, *op. cit.* note 1, p. 25.

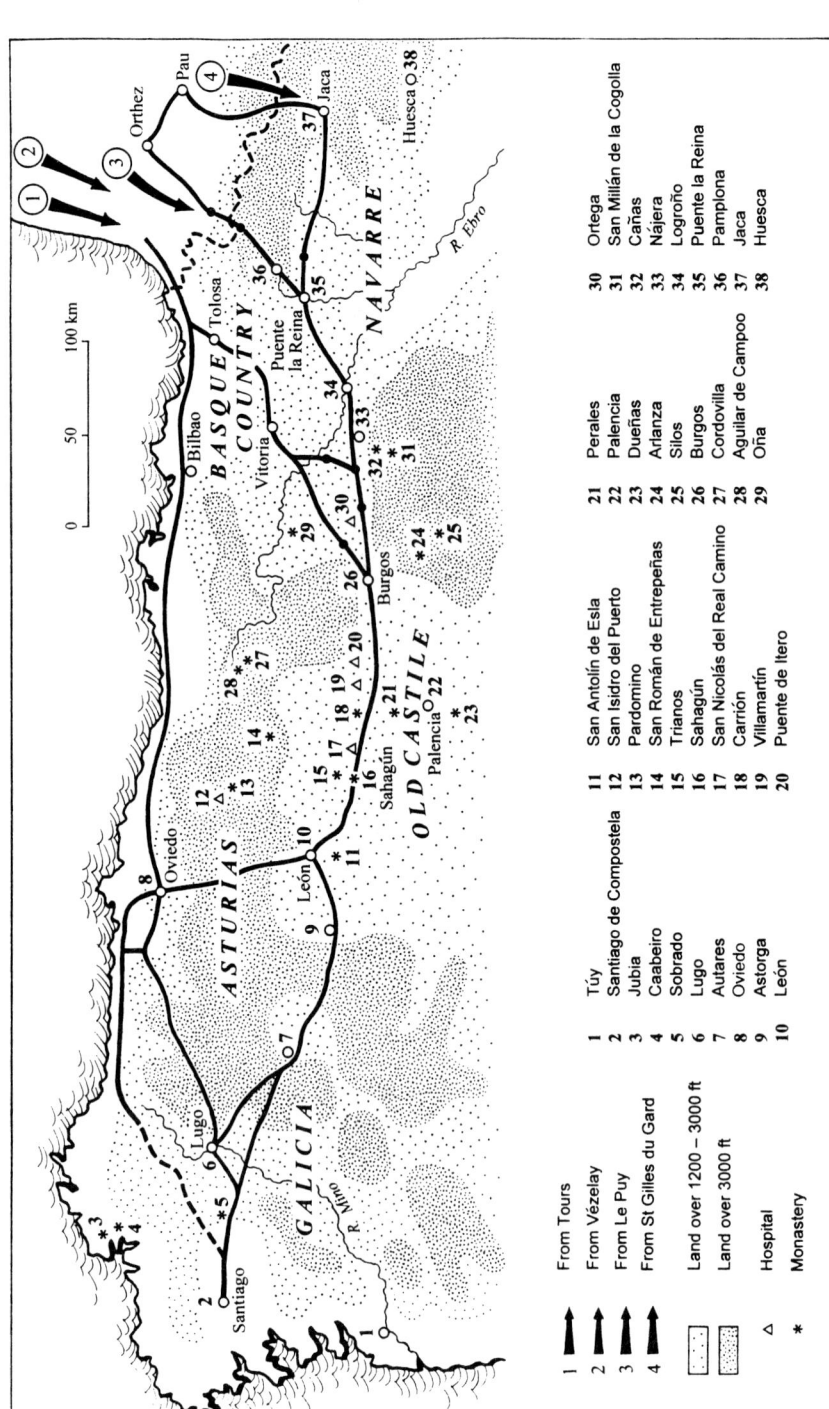

Northern Spain, showing sites mentioned in the text.

the laity to give alms in their honour. For their part, secular rulers firmly believed that the power of saints could help them to be victorious in war and to rule their kingdoms justly and well.[3]

In the late summer of 1038, a Leonese nobleman named Rodrigo Galíndez and his wife Sancha Muñoz founded a Benedictine monastery in the village of San Lorenzo, near León.[4] In the charter that was drawn up to record this act of pious munificence, Rodrigo Galíndez declared that, having heard of the many miracles worked at the tomb of St Antoninus, he had resolved to travel to France in person in order to visit the shrine.[5] He had subsequently brought back relics of the martyr and miracle worker, and had them installed in the monastery erected for the purpose on the banks of the River Esla. The new monastery, where Rodrigo wished to be buried, came to be known as San Antolín de Esla, and was lavishly endowed by its noble patrons. Their largess included a valuable collection of silver altar goods, eleven liturgical and other religious books, tableware and bedding of the highest quality, seven Moorish slaves and four Moorish slave girls, together with a large body of livestock. Rodrigo Galíndez also donated the village of Matallana, while Sancha Muñoz made over to the monastery no fewer than seventeen separate properties in the territory of León, including the village of San Lorenzo itself. Finally, Sancha granted the estates which had belonged to her daughter Elvira Pérez, thereby fulfilling a promise made on Elvira's death-bed, that her lands would also be delivered to the monastery of San Antolín de Esla.

The cult of St Antoninus, a fourth-century martyr of Apamea in Syria, is first known to have been propagated in Europe in the early ninth century, initially at the French abbey of Saint-Antonin-du-Rouergue in the Tarn valley, which claimed to possess the head and other relics of the saint, and subsequently at the monastery of Frédelas (later known as Pamiers), south of Toulouse.[6] The

---

[3] See, for example, the illuminating comments of R. A. Fletcher, *St. James's Catapult: the Life and Times of Diego Gelmírez of Santiago de Compostela* (Oxford, 1984), pp. 68–77. Cf. G. M. Spiegel, 'The Cult of Saint Denis and Capetian Kingship', *Journal of Medieval History* 1 (1975), 43–69.

[4] *Colección documental del archivo de la catedral de León (775–1230): IV (1032–1109)*, ed. J. M. Fernández Catón (León, 1990), nos. 970 (dated 31 August 1038), 971 (dated 2 September 1038). The latter charter records only the endowments promised by Sancha Muñoz to the monastery; the former was dismissed as a forgery by G. del Ser Quijano, 'Un monasterio benedictino leonés olvidado: San Antolín', in *Semana de historia del monacato cántabro-astur-leonés* (Oviedo, 1982), pp. 175–94 (p. 176, n. 8), but its authenticity is defended by Fernández Catón, pp. 106–7. On Sancha Muñoz, and her murder at the hands of her nephew Nuño Pérez, see M. Torre Sevilla and F. Galván Freile, 'La condesa doña Sancha: una nueva aproximación a su figura', *Medievalismo* 5 (1995), 9–29. The village of San Lorenzo has been identified as the modern settlement of Granja de San Antolín by Ser Quijano 1982, see above, p. 178. See the map above for the location of sites mentioned in the text.

[5] *Colección documental de León IV, op. cit.* note 1, no. 970.

[6] On the cult of St Antoninus, see *Bibliotheca Sanctorum*, 12 vols. (Rome, 1961–70), II, cols. 79–81. In a Spanish context, see C. J. Bishko, 'Fernando I and the origins of the

cult grew rapidly. By the second decade of the tenth century, the fame of the saint was such that, according to Adémar of Chabannes, large numbers of pilgrims were visiting the shrine at Frédelas annually.[7] While the appeal of the Syrian martyr appears to have been limited among the Christian realms of eastern Spain, devotion to St Antoninus soon became widespread in the west of the peninsula, in the kingdom of León. 'From at least 1035, a wave of enthusiasm for the Antoninian devotion swept through the upper classes of the Leonese Empire', Charles Bishko has commented.[8] For it was on 17 February of that year that King Vermudo III and Queen Jimena of León dedicated the newly-restored cathedral church of Palencia to the Virgin Mary and to St Antoninus.[9] Later tradition would claim that the restoration of the see of Palencia was, in fact, the work of King Sancho III 'the Great' of Navarre (1004–35).[10] According to the account recorded in the early thirteenth century, King Sancho had chanced upon a crypt and altar which had been erected in honour of St Antoninus whilst out hunting in the vicinity of the ruins of Palencia.[11] Sancho, in hot pursuit of a wild boar for his dinner table, followed his quarry into the crypt, but when he raised his spear-arm to dispatch the animal the king was miraculously immobilized and the boar escaped unharmed. The astonished king promptly prayed to St Antoninus and ordered that the ruined city be rebuilt, that a church be erected on the site of the shrine and that a bishop be appointed to the place.

Although it might be rash to accord too much credence to Archbishop Rodrigo's colourful account of the restoration of the church of Palencia, eleventh-century benefactors of the see were also firmly of the opinion that the holy relics reverently held within the cathedral walls were those of St Antoninus.[12] What is more, after 1035, doubtless encouraged by royal example, a significant number of other churches and monasteries in the Asturias, Galicia and Portugal were dedicated to the martyr. Judging from the evidence of various liturgical manuscripts the feast day of the saint also began to be widely celebrated.[13] In short, the foundation of the monastery of San Antolín de Esla by Rodrigo Galíndez and Sancha Muñoz in 1038 appears to have been not so much a ground-breaking exercise in lay piety, than merely

Leonese-Castilian alliance with Cluny', in *Studies in Medieval Spanish Frontier History* (London, 1980), no. II, 1–136 (pp. 10–14).

7   Bishko 1980, *op. cit.* note 3, p. 95, n. 56.
8   Bishko 1980, *op. cit.* note 3, p. 13.
9   *Documentación de la catedral de Palencia (1035–1247)*, ed. T. Abajo Martín (Burgos, 1986), no. 1.
10 *Documentación de Palencia, op. cit.* note 9, nos. 2, 4 and 9.
11 Rodrigo Jiménez de Rada, 'Historia de rebvs Hispanie sive Historica Gothica', *Corpus Christianorum Continuatio Mediaevalis* 72, ed. J. Fernández Valverde (Turnhout, 1987), 184.
12 *Documentación de Palencia, op. cit.* note 9, nos. 10 and 12.
13 Bishko 1980, *op. cit.* note 6, pp. 11–13.

the latest, albeit one of the most spectacular, manifestations of a burgeoning popular cult.

Popular though the cult of St Antoninus was, the Syrian martyr was merely one among hundreds of other saintly men and women who were the object of veneration in the eleventh-century Latin West. None the less, some saints' shrines managed to stand out from among the throng of competing cult centres and to attract devout suppliants to them from much further afield. More often than not this was because they managed to secure the backing of a particularly influential patron. So, for example, the cult of St Léonard de Noblat in the Limousin came to flourish, thanks to the enthusiastic support of Jordan, bishop of Limoges between 1022 and 1051, and that of Bohemond, prince of Antioch. Bohemond visited Noblat in 1106 claiming that it was the intercession of St Leonard that had secured his release from captivity in Turkey.[14] Alternatively, a cult might achieve prominence thanks to the energetic efforts of its publicists, in the way that the monks Benedict and William of Canterbury broadcast to the wider world the miracles of their recently-martyred archbishop, Thomas Becket, between 1171 and c. 1184.[15]

Likewise, when Rodrigo Galíndez and Sancha Muñoz invested their own considerable financial – as well as spiritual – resources in their monastic foundation by the River Esla in the late summer of 1038, they evidently harboured high hopes that in time their shrine to St Antoninus would itself become a major centre of veneration and pilgrimage for the sick, needy and pious.[16] But if that were the case, they were to be sorely disappointed. On 1 August 1040, barely two years after its foundation, the monastery of San Antolín de Esla lost its independent status when, for reasons unknown, Sancha Muñoz granted the house and its endowment to Bishop Servando of León.[17] To compound matters, in the years that followed the abbey-shrine does not appear to have attracted either pilgrims or further benefactors in sufficient numbers to enable it to flourish.[18] This might have been because St Antoninus did not prove the miracle-worker he was advertised to be, but the simple truth of the matter was that the timing of the initiative was far from propitious. St Antoninus was by all accounts a mightily powerful as well as popular saint, but in western Spain he was to come up against some formidable competition.

King Fernando I of León-Castile (1037–65) was a particularly enthusiastic

---

14 M. Bull, *Knightly Piety and the Lay Response to the First Crusade: the Limousin and Gascony, c.970–c.1130* (Oxford, 1993a), pp. 235–49.
15 B. Ward, *Miracles and the Medieval Mind: Theory, Record and Event 1000–1215* (London, 1982), pp. 89–109.
16 *Colección documental de León IV, op. cit.* note 4, no. 970 (p. 110); cf. no. 971 (p. 115).
17 *Colección documental de León IV, op. cit.* note 4, no. 992 (pp. 144–6).
18 The grant of properties to San Antolín by Sancha Muñoz's nephew, Nuño Pérez, on 2 November 1040, is the only benefaction known to us: *Colección documental de León IV, op. cit.* note 4, no. 993 (pp. 146–8). Cf. the comments of Ser Quijano 1982, *op. cit.* note 4, pp. 183–4; Torre Sevilla and Galván Freile 1995, *op. cit.* note 4, pp. 20–2.

collector of holy relics. Some time before 1062 he translated the mortal remains of SS Vincent, Sabina and Christeta from Avila and donated them to the cathedral church of Palencia. Then, having had second thoughts about the matter, he shared them out between the monastery of San Juan Bautista in the city of León and the Castilian abbey of San Pedro de Arlanza near Burgos.[19] In 1063, moreover, towards the end of his long and highly successful reign, King Fernando dispatched a task-force to the court of al-Mu'taḍid, the Muslim ruler of Seville.[20] The party comprised Bishop Alvito of León, Bishop Ordoño of Astorga and Count Muño Muñoz, together with an escort of knights.[21] Their mission was to locate and bring back to the city of León the earthly remains of St Justa, who had been martyred in Seville in the third century. However, when the party reached Seville the relics of St Justa were nowhere to be found. When Bishop Alvito prayed for divine assistance with his quest, St Isidore, bishop of Seville and foremost scholar of the Visigothic age, is said to have appeared to him in a dream to declare that God had decided that the city of Seville was not to be deprived of one of its favourite daughters. However, so that the party did not return home empty-handed, the relics of St Isidore himself were vouchsafed to the good bishop and his companions, although Alvito himself immediately fell gravely ill, dying the week after St Isidore's coffin was opened.

The recovery of the mortal remains of St Isidore of Seville was a considerable coup for Fernando I. Despite the absence of the hapless bishop, the returning party were greeted with jubilation by the king. On 21 December 1063, in the presence of all the notables of his realm, including Bishop Ordoño of Astorga (who was soon to be rewarded by the king for his leading role in the translation of the relics), Fernando formally dedicated to St Isidore the newly-revamped monastery of San Juan Bautista in León, where, two years later, the king was to find his own final resting-place.[22]

---

[19] *Documentación de Palencia, op. cit.* note 9, no. 12; *Cartulario de San Pedro de Arlanza*, ed. L. Serrano (Madrid, 1925), no. 62. Cf. *Crónica del obispo don Pelayo*, ed. B. Sánchez Alonso (Madrid, 1924), p. 74.

[20] For what follows, see *Historia Silense*, ed. J. Pérez de Urbel and A. González Ruiz-Zorrilla (Madrid, 1959), pp. 198–204; and the so-called 'Actas de la Traslación' published in *Historia Silense*, ed. F. Santos Coco (Madrid, 1921), pp. 93–9. See, in this context, A. Viñayo González, 'Cuestiones histórico-críticas en torno a la traslación del cuerpo de San Isidoro', in *Isidoriana: Estudios sobre San Isidoro de Sevilla en el XIV centenario de su nacimiento*, ed. M. Díaz y Díaz (León, 1961), pp. 285–97; cf. R. McCluskey, 'The early history of San Isidoro de León (X–XII c.)', *Nottingham Medieval Studies* 38 (1994), 35–59 (pp. 36–41).

[21] The Count Muño to whom both accounts of the translation of the relics of St Isidore refer can be identified as the Asturian magnate Count Muño Muñoz, who was later rewarded by Fernando I for his part in the operation: see *El Libro Registro de Corias*, ed. A. C. Floriano Cumbreño, 2 vols. (Oviedo, 1950), I, no. 198. There are some brief notes on the magnate's career in vol. II, p. 208.

[22] *Colección diplomática de Fernando I*, ed. P. Blanco Lozano (León, 1987), nos. 66–7.

In some respects, Fernando I's decision to deposit the holy remains of St Isidore at the monastery of San Juan Bautista may be construed as an act of political astuteness as much as one of deep-felt piety.[23] In the late tenth century, San Juan Bautista and its sister house, San Pelayo, had been destroyed during the course of one of the many raids launched against the Christian north by the ḥājib (chief minister) and de facto ruler of Muslim Spain, al-Manṣūr. To add insult to injury, the holy relics which the dual monastery had housed had been taken to Oviedo for permanent safe-keeping, along with the remains of the kings of the Leonese.[24] However, a programme of rebuilding had been undertaken in or around 1027 by Fernando I's father-in-law, Alfonso V of León (999–1028), culminating in the latter's decision to establish a mausoleum for his dynasty, the so-called Pantheon of the Kings, in the narthex of San Juan Bautista, where the bodies of the monarchs of the Asturian-Leonese line from Ordoño III to Vermudo II were interred and where, ultimately, Alfonso V himself chose burial. However, Fernando I, the son of Sancho III 'the Great' of Navarre, ruled León by virtue of military conquest, not by birthright; he had killed the previous incumbent, Vermudo III, in battle at Tamarón in September 1037. But his wife Sancha, the daughter of Alfonso V, *was* of the Asturian-Leonese royal line, and it was reportedly at her urging that Fernando decided to designate San Juan Bautista as his ultimate burial place.[25] By choosing to associate himself with the Leonese royal monastery *par excellence*, as well as with the saintly Isidore, Fernando I may have been seeking in part to reinforce his own claims and those of his own dynasty to rule over the kingdom of León.

Be that as it may, the monastery of San Pelayo and San Juan Bautista, or, as it was re-christened after 1063, San Isidoro de León, was to go from strength to strength. It was helped in this respect by two things that the abbey-shrine of San Antolín de Esla appears to have so sorely lacked. First, it was able to attract a stream of benefactions from numerous influential and wealthy patrons. These included Fernando I's daughters, the royal infantas Urraca and Elvira, and a succession of Leonese-Castilian monarchs, from Fernando I himself, to his great-great-great-grandson Alfonso IX of León (1188–1230).[26] Secondly, the shrine of St Isidore soon established itself as an obligatory port of call for pilgrims who visited the city of León. By the time the author of the so-called *Historia Silen*se, which was probably composed in León in or around the year

---

[23] See McCluskey 1994, *op. cit.* note 20, pp. 40–1.
[24] *Crónica del obispo Don Pelayo, op. cit.* note 19, pp. 65–6.
[25] *Historia Silense*, ed. Pérez de Urbel and González Ruiz-Zorrilla, *op. cit.* note 20, pp. 197–8.
[26] See *Patrimonio cultural de San Isidoro de León, I/1: documentos de los siglos X–XIII. Colección diplomática*, ed. M. E. Martín López (León, 1995), nos. 6–13, 15–16, 20, 24, 52–4, 57–9, 61, 65, 67, 72, 85, 88–90, 93–5, 97, 99, 105–6, 114, 117, 125, 127–8, 130–1, 133, 135, 137–9, 149–50, 153, 156, 167–8, 174–5, 183, 186, 191 and 193. On the origins and expansion of the house of San Isidoro, see McCluskey, *op. cit.* note 20, pp. 35–59.

1120, came to write up his account of the translation of the relics of St Isidore, the shrine of the saint had already witnessed numerous miracles and was attracting pilgrims from far and wide.[27] In response to the growing popularity of the cult, on 14 November 1168, Fernando II (1157–88) modified the route of the pilgrim-road to Santiago de Compostela so that the faithful who passed through León on their way to Compostela might have an opportunity to visit the shrine of St Isidore.[28] And early in the following century the cult of St Isidore was to enjoy a new peak of popularity thanks to the efforts of Lucas, a canon of San Isidoro and future bishop of Túy (died 1249), who compiled the *Book of the miracles of Saint Isidore* between the early 1220s and 1235.[29]

The holy Isidore was but one among a plethora of saints who were the object of veneration in the kingdom of León during the Middle Ages.[30] Nevertheless, thanks in large part to the sustained support it received from the Leonese royal family, the house of San Isidoro de León, as well as its patron, came to enjoy a reputation that only a very few other shrine-churches – such as the nearby Benedictine abbey of Sahagún, home to the remains of SS Primitivus and Facundus, and the cathedral church of Oviedo, which housed an extraordinary collection of relics – were able to match.[31] But even the saintly Isidore found it hard to compete with the flourishing cult of St James at Compostela.

The origins and development of the cult of St James at the place that is

---

[27] *Historia Silense*, ed. Pérez de Urbel and González Ruiz-Zorrilla, *op. cit.* note 20, pp. 204–5.

[28] *Patrimonio cultural de San Isidoro*, *op. cit.* note 26, no. 89.

[29] The original Latin text of the *Liber de miraculis sancti Isidori*, which is to be found in MSS 61 and 63 of the Archive of San Isidoro in León, remains unpublished. MS 62 from the same archive, a Castilian translation of the *Liber*, was published by J. Pérez Llamazares, *Don Lucas de Túy: milagros de San Isidoro* (León, 1947). On the career of Lucas of Túy, see B. Sánchez Alonso, *Historia de la Historiografía Española*, 2nd edition (Madrid, 1947), pp. 125–30; F. J. Fernández Conde, 'El biógrafo contemporáneo de Santo Martino: Lucas de Túy', in *Isidoriana 1: Ponencias del Primer Congreso Internacional sobre Santo Martino en el VIII centenario de su obra literaria (1185–1985)*, ed. A. Viñayo González (León, 1987), pp. 305–34; P. A. Linehan, *History and the Historians of Medieval Spain* (Oxford, 1993), pp. 350–412.

[30] On the monastic houses of eleventh-century León, see A. Linage Conde, *Los orígenes del monacato benedictino en la península ibérica*, 3 vols. (León, 1973), II, 559–600.

[31] The shrine of the martyrs Facundus and Primitivus at Sahagún was among those singled out by the author of the twelfth-century guide for pilgrims to Compostela as being particularly worth visiting: see 'Le Livre IV du codex de Saint-Jacques de Compostelle', *Revue de Linguistique et de Philologie Comparée* 15, ed. F. Fita y Colomé (1882), 1–20 and 225–68 (at p. 249). See also J. M. Fernández Catón, 'Datos para la historia del martirio y del culto de las reliquias de los mártires leoneses Facundo y Primitivo', *Bivium* (León, 1983), 67–80. On the cult of relics at Oviedo, see *Colección de documentos de la catedral de Oviedo*, ed. S. García Larragueta (Oviedo, 1962), no. 72; and S. Suárez Beltran, 'Los origenes y la expansión del culto a las reliquias de San Salvador de Oviedo', in *Las peregrinaciones a Santiago de Compostela en la Edad Media*, ed. J. I. Ruiz de la Peña Solar (Oviedo, 1993), pp. 37–55.

known today as Santiago de Compostela may be briefly told. According to Compostelan tradition, it was during the reign of the Asturian king Alfonso II 'the Chaste' (791–842) that Theodemir, bishop of Iria Flavia, in deepest, greenest Galicia, was guided by a star to a nearby cave within which he discovered the remains of St James in a marble sarcophagus.[32] Although archaeological excavations carried out within the walls of the cathedral of Santiago de Compostela have revealed the existence of a Christian cult centre, which appears to have flourished on the site between the fifth and seventh centuries, there is no reliable evidence to substantiate the claim that James the Great, the son of Zebedee and brother of St John the Evangelist, ever actually visited Spain, let alone that he was later buried there.[33] Nevertheless, the belief that the apostle had preached the gospel in the peninsula had begun to gain wide currency among western churchmen by at least the seventh century.[34] Towards the end of the eighth century, during the reign of the Asturian king Mauregato (783–8), a hymn was composed in honour of St James, who was already being portrayed as the guardian and patron of Christian Spain.[35] The precise date when the putative remains of the apostle were located by Bishop Theodemir has not been recorded, although the discovery must have occurred some time between the years 818 and 842.[36] News of the discovery travelled fast. When Usuard of St-Germain-des-Prés, who had visited Spain, came to compile his *Martyrologium* in or around 865, he roundly declared that after St James's martyrdom the remains of the apostle had been translated from Jerusalem to the furthermost region of Spain, where they were revered with the most devout veneration by the locals.[37]

Although a good deal of scholarly ink has been used in trying to establish whether or not the human remains discovered by Bishop Theodemir could possibly have been those of St James, the important point to bear in mind is that, with one or two notable exceptions, Bishop Theodemir's contemporaries were willing to share his belief.[38] That said, the cult of St James does not

---

[32] A. López Ferreiro, *Historia de la Santa A. M. Iglesia de Santiago de Compostela*, 11 vols. (Santiago de Compostela, 1898–1909), III, appendix, no. i; cf. *Historia Compostellana*, ed. E. Falque Rey, *Corpus Christianorum Continuatio Medieualis* 70 (Turnhout, 1988), 9.

[33] On the early history of the cult of St James in Spain, see J. van Herwaarden, 'The origins of the cult of St. James of Compostela', *Journal of Medieval History* 6 (1980), 1–35; Fletcher 1984, *op. cit.* note 3, pp. 53–77; and K. Herbers, *Der Jakobuskult des 12. Jahrhunderts und der 'Liber sancti Iacobi': Studien über das Verhältnis zwischen Religion und Gesellschaft im hohen Mittelalter* (Wiesbaden, 1984).

[34] Van Herwaarden 1980, *op. cit.* note 33, pp. 3–7; Fletcher 1984, *op. cit.* note 3, pp. 54–5.

[35] Van Herwaarden 1980, *op. cit.* note 33, 7–18.

[36] Compostelan tradition records that the discovery of the apostle's tomb occurred in the time of King Alfonso II (791–842) and Bishop Theodemir of Iria (died 847). The latter's predecessor, Bishop Quendulfus, was still alive in 818: Fletcher 1984, *op. cit.* note 3, p. 57.

[37] Van Herwaarden 1980, *op. cit.* note 33, pp. 18–23.

[38] Fletcher 1984, *op. cit.* note 3, p. 81.

immediately appear to have enjoyed the lavish, unconditional patronage of the Asturian royal house. Although King Alfonso II is reported to have had a church built on the site where Bishop Theodemir had found the holy relics, it appears to have been only a modest construction built of rubble and clay.[39] And there is no reliable evidence that Alfonso II's immediate successors on the throne of the Asturias made any further attempt to promote the cult of the apostle, although a number of later, forged charters would have us believe otherwise.[40] Instead, it was not until the reign of Alfonso III (866–910) that an energetic attempt was made to advertise and diffuse the cult of St James on a large scale. Alfonso III held the apostle in particular esteem. It was thanks to the intercession of St James, the king declared in his charters, that he had defeated his enemies and successfully enlarged his kingdom.[41] In repayment of this debt, Alfonso worked energetically to promote the cause of his patron and protector St James: it was Alfonso who rebuilt the church dedicated to St James at Compostela in 899, who made numerous munificent donations of land to the church, and who told the wider world of the discovery of the mortal remains of the apostle James and of the many miracles that had been worked at the shrine of the saint.[42]

Thanks in large part to the efforts of Alfonso III and Bishop Sisnando of Iria-Compostela, the cult of St James soon spread throughout Spain and further afield. Following royal example, prominent laymen and women began to endow the church of Compostela with generous grants of land. Church dedications to St James proliferated and pilgrims began to visit the shrine-church at Compostela.[43] Bishop Godescalc of Le Puy, who is known to have travelled to Compostela with a great following in 951, was but the first recorded pilgrim in a long and distinguished line of the great and the good to visit the shrine of the apostle.[44] Duke William X of Aquitaine won particular fame by dropping dead in front of the altar of St James in Compostela cathedral on Good Friday, 1137.[45] The earliest recorded pilgrim from England was a

---

[39] López Ferreiro, *op. cit.* note 32, II, appendix, no. xxv (p. 51).
[40] Fletcher 1984, *op. cit.* note 3, pp. 66–7.
[41] Fletcher 1984, *op. cit.* note 3, p. 70.
[42] Fletcher 1984, *op. cit.* note 3, pp. 70–3 and 317–23.
[43] Fletcher 1984, *op. cit.* note 3, pp. 78–9.
[44] On Godescalc of Le Puy and his pilgrimage to Compostela, see M. C. Díaz y Díaz, *Libros y librerías en la Rioja altomedieval*, 2nd edition (Logroño, 1991), pp. 55–60 and 279–80. Many other celebrated pilgrims to Compostela are identified by L. Vázquez de Parga, J. M. Lacarra and J. Uría Riu, *Las peregrinaciones a Santiago de Compostela*, 3 vols. (Madrid, 1948–9), I, 39–110. On the international popularity of the pilgrimage, see the studies in *Santiago: la Europa del peregrinaje*, ed. P. Caucci von Staucken (Barcelona, 1993).
[45] *The Ecclesiastical History of Orderic Vitalis*, ed. and trans. M. Chibnall, 6 vols. (Oxford, 1969–80), VI, 480–2.

Yorkshireman, Richard Mauleverer, who travelled to Compostela shortly before 1105.[46]

A miracle story recorded in the pages of the *Historia Compostellana*, the history of the see of Compostela during the pontificate of Diego Gelmírez (1100–40), speaks volumes for the perceived power of St James the apostle during the early decades of the twelfth century.[47] The *Historia* relates that in the summer of 1121 the Almoravid emir, 'Alī ibn Yūsuf, sent a group of ambassadors to visit Queen Urraca of León (1109–26), apparently with a view to establishing a peace treaty between the two rulers. As they made their way westwards into Galicia, where the queen and her court were residing at that time, the ambassadors were reportedly astonished by the vast numbers of pilgrims they encountered who were travelling along the same route. When the Muslims enquired of their Christian guide the reason for this great throng of the faithful, they were told that the apostle James was venerated as a patron and a protector by the inhabitants of France, England, Italy, Germany, and of all the other regions of Christendom, but above all by those of Spain. Later, once they had reached the holy city of Santiago de Compostela and had seen for themselves the cathedral church of St James, the Muslim ambassadors were moved to ask what exactly it was that the apostle did for those who came to honour and venerate him. Their guide responded:

> Such is the grace that through his merits and intercessions he receives from our Lord Jesus Christ, that through God's mercy he permits the blind to see and the lame to walk, and he gives health to lepers and to those suffering from numerous other illnesses. He succours and helps all those who with devotion ask him to do so and he works innumerable miracles on both sides of the Pyrenees. He has freed some who were languishing in prison in chains, he has cured others who were laid low by long illnesses, and he has assisted yet others with difficult enterprises. In all regions God Almighty has displayed his miracles through the merits and intercessions of the Blessed James. That is why such great crowds of people visit his body; that is why so many people do not doubt to ask for his help.[48]

---

[46] *Early Yorkshire Charters*, ed. W. Farrer (Edinburgh, 1915), II, no. 729. See, in this context, D. W. Lomax, 'The first English pilgrims to Santiago de Compostela', in *Studies in Medieval History presented to R. H. C. Davis*, ed. H. Mayr-Harting and R. I. Moore (London, 1985), pp. 165–75.

[47] For what follows, see *Historia Compostellana, op. cit.* note 32, pp. 307–12.

[48] 'Tantam . . . a Domino nostro Iesu Christo meritis et intercessionibus suis consequitur gratiam, quod per Dei misericordiam cecis uisum, claudis gressum, leprosis aliisque diuersorum morborum generibus compeditis salutem largitur. Subuenit atque opitulatur omnibus se deuote deposcentibus et transpirenem et citra innumeris miraculis pollet. Hos enim compeditos et carceri mancipatos liberauit, alios diuturno langore detentos sanauit, illis in difficillimis opem prestitit: ubique terrarum omnipotens Deus meritis et intercessionibus beati Iacobi miracula sua ostendit. Ob hoc corpus eius tanta frequentat multitudo, ob hoc innumeri opem eius indubitanter exposcunt': *Historia Compostellana, op. cit.* note 32, p. 308.

When, later still, the power of the saint reportedly cured one of the ambassadors of a malign tumour that had appeared on his neck, the Muslims were suitably impressed and are said to have promised that on their return home to al-Andalus they would proclaim to their people the power and glory of the mighty apostle.

Donations to Religious Institutions

The collection of relics and the foundation of cult centres were two of the ways in which laymen sought to harness the miraculous power of saints for their own spiritual welfare and that of their families. Yet these were, by their very nature, exceptional acts of piety, often made only once in a lifetime; they were strictly the preserve of only the very wealthiest and most influential members of the secular élite. For the most part, members of the laity – both in western Spain and further afield – appear to have been firmly of the opinion that regular benefaction of religious institutions, and the saints whom they represented, could reap equally important spiritual rewards for the donor and his kin. This much is clear from the many thousands of charters that were drawn up on behalf of patrons to record their acts of pious benefaction to religious communities, which more often than not took the form of a donation of landed property. Given their terse and rigidly formularistic nature, it is hardly surprising that these documents rarely make reference to the specific personal circumstances that had prompted a lay benefactor to favour a particular church. There are nevertheless a number of notable exceptions. Count Martín Flaínez, for example, gave a meadow, money and candles to the Castilian monastery of Santa Eugenia de Cordovilla, some time before 1108, because the monks of the place had apparently exorcised an evil demon from the body of his young son Rodrigo. More prosaically, Vermudo Pérez de Traba made a grant of some serfs to the Cluniac abbey of Jubia in Galicia in 1145 because the monks had given the magnate a mule on the occasion of his impending journey to Portugal.[49] On other occasions, grants were made to religious houses as the donors lay stricken with illness, before they themselves entered religious life, or even before they embarked on a perilous enterprise such as a military expedition or a pilgrimage. Witness, for example, the benefactions that were made to various Galician religious communities by Countess María Fernández as she lay on her death-bed in Santiago de Compostela in January 1169; the generous endowments which Countess Aldonza Rodríguez made to the nuns of Cañas in the Rioja when she entered the nunnery in June 1171; the grant given by Count Gonzalo Salvadórez to the monks of the Castilian abbey

---

[49] *Colección diplomática de San Salvador de Oña (822–1284)*, ed. J. del Alamo, 2 vols. (Madrid, 1950), I, no. 146; *La colección diplomática de San Martín de Jubia*, ed. S. Montero Díaz (Santiago de Compostela, 1935), no. xlvi.

of Oña shortly before he went off to campaign against the Moors in September 1082; or the gift of land that the noble lady Teresa made to the monastery of San Millán de la Cogolla in the Rioja prior to setting out on pilgrimage to Rome in 1096.[50]

In general terms, however, pious benefactions by the laity were motivated and conditioned by two fundamental religious ideas. One, oft-repeated in the preambles to the charters, was the widespread belief that it was the responsibility of the rich and powerful to support and protect the church and that the permanent alienation of material wealth was one of the best ways for them to achieve this.[51] The second was the deep-rooted conviction on the part of lay patrons that their acts of pious generosity would secure divine favour not only in this life, but also effectively pay off part of the penitential debt which they and their kinsmen had amassed in the past. In this way, benefactors might limit the pains that they would have to endure on their passing, as well as reduce the suffering that the souls of their deceased relatives were already experiencing in the afterlife. As one widely broadcast dictum pithily put it, 'Just as water extinguishes fire, so alms extinguish sin.'[52] Accordingly, the overriding concern of lay benefactors was to ensure that after their death the intercessionary prayer of the monks and canons who served in the Army of God would help to secure the salvation of their souls and those of their relatives. Thus, when the Galician knight Suero Menéndez made a grant of various properties to the Cistercian monks of the abbey of Sobrado in 1165, he did so not only for the good of his own soul and those of his kinsmen, but so that he might 'attain the Kingdom of God through the present and future prayers of those who dwell or shall dwell in the aforesaid monastery of Sobrado'.[53]

Sometimes charters set out for all to see the sinful behaviour that had motivated a lay donor to favour a particular religious body. We learn, for example, that between 1120 and 1131 the Galician lady Oñega Fernández

---

[50] *Galicia histórica: colección diplomática* (Santiago de Compostela, 1901), no. ii; Madrid, Archivo Histórico Nacional (hereafter AHN), Clero, 1023/19; *Colección diplomática de Oña, op. cit.* note 49, I, no. 77; *Cartulario de San Millán de la Cogolla (1076–1200)*, ed. M. L. Ledesma Rubio (Zaragoza, 1989), no. 263.

[51] See, for example, the preamble to Countess Elvira Pérez de Lara's donation to the monks of Sahagún on 14 January 1168: *Colección diplomática del monasterio de Sahagún (857–1300): IV (1110–1300)*, ed. J. A. Fernández Flórez (León, 1991), no. 1360.

[52] 'Sicut aqua extinguit ignem, ita elemosina extinguit peccatum'. The phrase, inspired by *Ecclesiasticus (Sirach)* 3.33, occurs in countless charters of this period: see, for example, *Colección diplomática de Sahagún, op. cit.* note 51, IV, no. 1320; *Colección diplomática de Oña, op. cit.* note 49, I, no. 253.

[53] 'Hoc autem facio pro remedio anime mee et parentum meorum et ut merear peruenire ad regnum Dei per orationes presentium et futurorum qui habitant uel habitauerint in predicto monasterio Superaddi': *Tumbos del monasterio de Sobrado de los Monjes*, ed. P. Loscertales de García de Valdeavellano, 2 vols. (Madrid, 1976), I, no. 601 (p. 521).

made a benefaction to the canons of the cathedral church of Túy to expiate the crime of her son Pelayo Díaz, who had murdered a man in the church of Penso.[54] In 1171 another Galician aristocrat, Count Rodrigo Alvarez, made a grant to the canons of Lugo because 'seized by diabolical fury' he had burnt the church of Santa María de Mal to the ground.[55] More often than not, however, charters evoked in only the most general terms the overwhelming sense of sinfulness which had prompted a donor's act of pious generosity. As Marcus Bull has observed, 'Fear was the essential ingredient: fear of the appalling agonies which were befalling dead relatives in the afterlife and which awaited the living. Sinfulness was not a matter of indulging in occasional and especially unusual or enjoyable vices. It was a consequence of everyday existence in the lay environment, touching the lives of arms-bearing kindreds where it hurt most.'[56]

These deep-rooted fears are reflected in numerous charters of the period: in 1038 Rodrigo Galíndez referred to his terror of the fires of Hell when he founded the monastery of San Antolín de Esla; in 1077 Countess Teresa Ovéquiz expressed her fear of damnation when she granted her monastery of San Zoilo de Carrión to the monks of Cluny; and when Munina Froilaz endowed the Galician abbey of Caabeiro in 1114, she freely admitted that she did so fearing the punishments of Hell and the Day of Judgement.[57] Although not all laymen may actually have been able to understand the Latin in which their donation charters were drafted, it does not necessarily follow that they were correspondingly ignorant of the religious ideas which underpinned their acts of pious benefaction. The fact that year after year secular patrons were willing to alienate significant portions of their land holdings to religious communities suggests that laymen knew only too well what was actually at stake. To quote Marcus Bull once more, 'when lords and knights gave their property to a religious community, they were not, on the level of consciousness, simply obeying social imperatives. They knew what they wanted; and what they wanted was that the grant would do them good.'[58]

How did patrons put these ideas into practice? The first point to be made, is that in western Spain, as in most other areas of the Latin West in the Middle Ages, the cult of relics helped to channel the pious impulses of the laity towards specific churches and their patron saints and, as a consequence,

---

54 P. Galindo Romeo, *Tuy en la baja Edad Media*, 2nd edition (Madrid, 1950), appendix, no. viii.
55 E. Flórez, M. Risco, et al., *España Sagrada*, 51 vols. (Madrid, 1747–1879), XLI, 322.
56 M. Bull, 'The roots of lay enthusiasm for the First Crusade', *History* 78 (1993b), 353–72 (p. 369).
57 *Colección documental de León IV*, op. cit. note 4, no. 970; *Documentación del monasterio de San Zoilo de Carrión (1047–1300)*, ed. J. A. Pérez Celada (Burgos, 1986), no. 8; AHN, Códices, 1439B, fols. 37v–38r.
58 Bull 1993a, op. cit. note 14, p. 158.

enabled them to enter into a relationship with the church as a whole.⁵⁹ More often than not, patrons preferred to endow those religious institutions with which their kin had already forged particularly strong ties and which as a rule lay close to their family's seat of power. For example, the Benedictine abbey of San Salvador de Oña, north west of Burgos, was the favoured institution of the local lord Salvador González, who was buried within the precincts of the abbey some time after 1059. A number of donations followed and in 1205 the same institution was granted property by his great-great-great-granddaughter Elvira González.⁶⁰ In like fashion, the Galician abbeys of Jubia and Sobrado were the object of numerous generous endowments by members of the powerful Traba family during the course of the eleventh and twelfth centuries.⁶¹

Other patrons, however, chose to spread their favours more widely, as if in an attempt to maximise the spiritual benefit that their souls would derive from their numerous acts of pious generosity. One of the most notable of all in this respect was Count Pedro Ansúrez who, during the course of his long and highly successful career, is known to have made grants to at least thirteen separate religious bodies, including five cathedral churches, half a dozen Benedictine monasteries, and the abbey church at Valladolid, which was founded and lavishly endowed by the count and his wife in 1095.⁶²

The pious works of Count Nuño Pérez de Lara were equally breathtaking: there was the Cistercian monastery at Perales which he and his wife Teresa founded in 1160; the Premonstratensian abbey of Aguilar de Campoo in the foothills of the Cantabrian mountains, which Nuño and his kinsmen helped to establish in 1169; the cathedral churches of Burgos, León and Toledo to which Nuño made a number of munificent endowments in the 1170s (at Toledo in 1177 he even founded a chapel dedicated to St Thomas of Canterbury where masses and prayers were to be said for his soul and those of his family); the Military Order of Calatrava to which he made a grant of property in January 1172; and the hospital for pilgrims which Count Nuño established at Puente de Itero some time before 1174.⁶³

Tello Pérez de Meneses was a prominent figure at the court of Alfonso VIII

---

59 Bull 1993b, *op. cit.* note 56, pp. 365–7.
60 *Colección diplomática de Oña, op. cit.* note 49, nos. 77 and 359.
61 See, for example, *La colección diplomática de Jubia, op. cit.* note 49, nos. vi, vii, xi, xviii, xix, xxi–xxiii, xxx, xxxii–xxxv, xxxviii–xxxix, xlvi, l–li, liv–lv and lxxv; *Tumbos de Sobrado, op. cit.* note 53, I, nos. 145 and 476; II, nos. 11, 13–14, 19, 513 and 537; AHN, Clero, 526/11, 527/11.
62 For full references, see S. Barton, *The Aristocracy in Twelfth-Century León and Castile* (Cambridge, 1997), pp. 275–7. For further details of the career of Count Pedro Ansúrez, see J. Rodríguez Fernández, *Pedro Ansúrez* (León, 1966).
63 References in Barton 1997, *op. cit.* note 62, 269–70 and 328. On the hospital at Puente de Itero, see *Documentación de la catedral de Burgos (804–1183)*, ed. J. M. Garrido Garrido (Burgos, 1983), pp. 302–3.

of Castile.[64] Among his numerous pious acts, he is chiefly remembered as the founder of the Cistercian monastery of Matallana in the Tierra de Campos in 1173, the hospital for former prisoners-of-war, which he established at Cuenca in 1182 to care for those who had been captured in battle by the Muslims, and the Augustinian priory of Trianos near Sahagún which he set up in around 1185.[65] He was also responsible for the foundation of two leper-hospitals: one at Villamartín near Carrión in 1196, which he made over to the Military Order of Santiago; the other at San Nicolás del Real Camino near Sahagún, which was established some time before 1198.[66] Both of these hospitals lay squarely on the pilgrim-road to Compostela.

Pilgrimage

In common with the promotion of the cults of saints and the endowment of religious communities, the practice of pilgrimage was viewed by contemporaries as 'a means of assuaging guilt, demonstrating virtue and averting the wrath to come'.[67] Pilgrimage enjoyed a notable surge in popularity in most regions of the West from around the second half of the tenth century onwards. Influenced by changes in the penitential system administered by the church, the *peregrinatio* came to be widely regarded as a mechanism to expiate sin. In return for the absolution of his sins, a layman would vow to undertake a penitential pilgrimage to a sacred place. The major shrines of Christendom, Jerusalem, Rome and, from at least the tenth century, Santiago de Compostela, were the three greatest goals, but a pilgrimage might also be made to a humbler shrine associated with a popular local saint. In this way, pilgrimage began to be accepted as a means of spiritual cleansing by laymen who felt themselves otherwise unwilling or unable to devote the rest of their lives to the service of God.[68]

---

[64] There are some notes on his career in J. González, *El reino de Castilla en la época de Alfonso VIII*, 3 vols. (Madrid, 1960), I, 347–9; and P. Martínez Sopena, *La Tierra de Campos Occidental: poblamiento, poder y comunidad del siglo X al XIII* (Valladolid, 1985), pp. 393–4.

[65] On the foundation of Matallana, see V. A. Alvarez Palenzuela, *Monasterios cistercienses en Castilla (siglos XII–XIII)* (Valladolid, 1978), pp. 108–10. On the hospital at Cuenca, see J. González, *Repoblación de Castilla la Nueva*, 2 vols. (Madrid, 1975–6), II, 147–8. On Tello Pérez's support for the abbey of Trianos, see *Documentos del monasterio de Santa María de Trianos (siglos XII–XIII)*, ed. G. and J. Castán Lanaspa (Salamanca, 1992), nos. 21, 24, 32, 50 and 65.

[66] On the hospital of Villamartín, see Vázquez de Parga, Lacarra and Uría Riu 1948–9, *op. cit.* note 44, II, 216–17 and III, no. 55; Barton 1997, *op. cit.* note 62, p. 331. On San Nicolás, see G. Castán Lanaspa, 'San Nicolás del Real Camino, un hospital de leprosos castellano-leonés en la Edad Media (siglos XII–XV)', *Publicaciones de la Institución 'Tello Téllez de Meneses'* 51 (1984), 105–223.

[67] Fletcher 1984, *op. cit.* note 3, p. 95.

[68] On this trend see C. Vogel, 'Le pèlerinage pénitentiel', in *Pellegrinaggi e culto dei santi*

In Spain, the pilgrimage to Compostela appears to have become an increasingly popular and well-organised affair from the middle of the eleventh century onwards. The pilgrim road ran from four principal starting-points in France – Tours, Vezelay, Le Puy and St Gilles du Gard – and converged at Puente la Reina in the western Pyrenees from where the so-called *camino francés*, or French Road, wound its way westwards across northern Spain via Logroño, Burgos, Carrión, Sahagún, León and Astorga, and so on to its ultimate destination in Galicia.[69] The pilgrim road to Compostela left a lasting impression on the communities through which it passed. It was reflected in the innovative sculptural forms which came into vogue in places as far apart as Jaca in the Pyrenees and Sahagún in the Tierra de Campos, and in the buildings designed in the popular Romanesque style which sprang up in great numbers along the route.[70] Moreover, as the volume of pilgrim traffic steadily increased, so colonies of foreign merchants and artisans set up shop along the French Road in order to cater for the needs of the faithful who passed through in such numbers.[71] A case in point was the town of Sahagún near León, where a thriving mercantile district grew up some time before 1085, reportedly attracting craftsmen and traders from all parts of Europe, and of all manner of professions, including smiths, carpenters, tailors, furriers and shoemakers.[72] Meanwhile, kings, clerics and laymen competed to enhance the facilities that were available to the pilgrims: mending roads, building bridges and churches, and erecting hostels and hospitals for those in need. For example, it was Alfonso VI of León-Castile (1065–1109) who was remembered by Bishop Pelayo of Oviedo as the monarch who 'lest any moments of his life be lacking in good works commanded to be built all the bridges that there are from Logroño to Santiago'.[73] And it was the same monarch who in 1072 released

in Europa fino alla prima Crociata, Covegni del Centro di studi sulla spiritualità medievale 4 (Todi, 1963), pp. 39–92.
[69] The classic account of the pilgrimage remains Vázquez de Parga, Lacarra and Uría Riu 1948–9, *op. cit.* note 44. The vast literature that has been generated by the pilgrimage is usefully catalogued by M. Dunn and L. K. Davison, *The Pilgrimage to Santiago de Compostela: a comprehensive annotated bibliography* (New York, 1994).
[70] See S. Moralejo, 'The tomb of Alfonso Ansúrez (†1093): its place and the role of Sahagún in the beginnings of Spanish Romanesque sculpture', in *Santiago, Saint-Denis, and Saint Peter: the reception of the Roman Liturgy in León-Castile in 1080*, ed. B. F. Reilly (New York, 1985), pp. 63–100; W. M. Whitehill, *Spanish Romanesque Architecture of the Eleventh Century* (Oxford, 1941).
[71] L. G. de Valdeavellano, *Orígenes de la burguesía en la España medieval* (Madrid, 1969), pp. 103–76; J. Gautier-Dalché, *Historia urbana de León y Castilla en la Edad Media (siglos IX–XIII)* (Madrid, 1979), pp. 67–85; and J. I. Ruiz de la Peña Solar, 'Las colonizaciones francas en las rutas castellano-leonesas del camino de Santiago', in Ruiz de la Peña Solar 1993, *op. cit.* note 31, pp. 283–312.
[72] *Crónicas anónimas de Sahagún*, ed. A. Ubieto Arteta (Zaragoza, 1987), pp. 19–24.
[73] 'Ad hec autem, ne ulla tempore vite ipsius uacarent a bonis operibus, studuit facere omnes pontes qui sunt a Locronio usque ad Sanctum Iacobum': *Crónica del obispo Don Pelayo*, *op. cit.* note 19, p. 84.

pilgrims from the obligation of paying tolls when they passed by the castle of Autares in the mountains of León *en route* to Compostela.[74] Countess Teresa Ovéquiz, some time before 1077, completed the bridge across the River Pisuerga at Carrión which her husband Count Gómez Díaz had begun.[75] And another Castilian nobleman, Domingo, built a bridge over the River Oja and was responsible for laying out the pilgrim-road that eventually ran from Nájera, in the Rioja, as far as Redecilla, to the east of Burgos, and who was later to be canonized for his efforts as Santo Domingo de la Calzada.[76]

According to the author of the 'Pilgrim's Guide' contained within the *Book of Saint James*, a twelfth-century collection of texts relating to the cult of St James at Compostela, the major hospitals of Christendom, those of Jerusalem, Mont-Joux and Santa Cristina, were the three 'columns' which God had established for the support of the poor. The hospitals in question were described as 'holy places, houses of God, places of refreshment for holy pilgrims, of rest for the needy, of comfort for the sick, of salvation for the dead, of assistance to the living'.[77] Those who had founded these hospitals, the author added, would surely possess the kingdom of God. It was doubtless with just that end in mind that Count Nuño Pérez established his hospital at Puente de Itero prior to 1174 and Tello Pérez founded the leper-hospitals of Villamartín and San Nicolás del Real Camino in the 1190s. And these were far from being exceptional ventures. During the course of the eleventh and twelfth centuries scores of hostels and hospitals were erected to attend to the needs of pilgrims who made their way to Compostela, or to other major cult-centres such as Oviedo.[78] By the later medieval period, the city of Burgos alone could boast some thirty-two hospitals of one sort of another, while Astorga and León each had at least twenty.[79] Many others were situated in isolated rural areas: the hospital of San Isidro del Puerto, high up in the mountains between León and the Asturias, had been founded by the monks of Pardomino some time before 1118 to prevent pilgrims from perishing from the cold as they made their way across the treacherous mountain pass; and that of San Nicolás de Ortega, established by the Castilian nobleman Juan Vélaz prior to 1138, which lay in the Montes de

---

74 *Colección documental de León IV, op. cit.* note 4, no. 1182.
75 *Documentación de Carrión, op. cit.* note 57, no. 8.
76 'Le Livre IV', *op. cit.* note 31, p. 249; Vázquez de Parga, Lacarra and Uría Riu 1948–9, *op. cit.* note 44, II, 162–3.
77 'Loca sancta, domus Dei, refectio sanctorum peregrinorum, requies egentium, consolatio infirmorum, salus mortuorum, subsidium pariter ac vivorum': 'Le Livre IV', *op. cit.* note 44, p. 7.
78 See, in particular, the studies in *El Camino de Santiago, la hospitalidad monástica y las peregrinaciones*, ed. H. Santiago-Otero (Salamanca, 1992); J. Uría Ríu, 'Las fundaciones hospitalarias en los caminos de la peregrinación a Oviedo', in *Estudios de historia de Asturias* (Gijón, 1989), pp. 131–85; and M. E. García García, 'La hospitalidad y el hospedaje: fundaciones hospitalarias en Asturias', in Ruiz de la Peña Solar 1993, *op. cit.* note 31, pp. 211–46.
79 P. Martínez Sopena, *El Camino de Santiago en Castilla y León* (Salamanca, 1993), p. 48.

Oca east of Burgos, a notoriously perilous district where attacks by robbers on passing pilgrims were commonplace.[80]

The enthusiastic efforts that were made by secular patrons like Nuño and Tello Pérez is proof enough that the laity of León and Castile was far from indifferent to the pilgrimage to Compostela. Yet, somewhat surprisingly, explicit references to men and women of the region themselves undertaking a pilgrimage to Compostela, or indeed to any other Spanish shrine, remain few and far between. Indeed, apart from the Leonese noblewoman Fronilde Peláez, who is known to have made a pilgrimage to Compostela in 1045, and the Galician lady Urraca Fernández de Traba, who travelled to Oviedo 'for reasons of prayer' in 1192, our sources have next to nothing to tell us about the matter.[81] All the same, it is hard to believe that members of the Leonese court would not have chosen to visit the tomb of St James whenever the royal itinerary took in Compostela, particularly when it is known that numerous members of the Leonese royal family did undertake pilgrimages to Compostela. These include Fernando I, who is said to have turned to St James for assistance prior to his successful campaign to conquer the city of Coimbra in Portugal in 1064, also Count Henry of Portugal, the son-in-law of Alfonso VI, who travelled as a pilgrim to Compostela in 1097, and Queen Urraca who made the same journey in 1112.[82]

The deafening silence of our sources in this respect might be explained by the fact that by and large only long-distance pilgrimages, which involved a journey of at least several hundred miles, and carried a correspondingly higher degree of risk, were likely to give rise to situations which needed to be put into writing.[83] For example, it was common practice for those who were about to undertake a major pilgrimage to seek the intercession of a favoured local religious community by making a grant of land shortly before they set out. We have already referred to the case of the noblewoman Teresa, who promised a number of properties to the monks of San Millán de la Cogolla prior to going on pilgrimage to Rome in 1096.[84] Equally, a long-distance pilgrimage entailed a considerable expense and potential pilgrims might find

---

[80] *Colección documental del archivo de la catedral de León (775–1230): V (1109–1187)*, ed. J. M. Fernández Catón (León, 1990), no. 1364; Vázquez de Parga, Lacarra and Uría Riu 1948–9, *op. cit.* note 44, III, no. 4.

[81] On Fronilde Peláez, see *Colección documental de León IV, op. cit.* note 4, no. 1022; cf. M. R. García Alvarez, 'La Infanta Fronilde, peregrina a Compostela', *Compostellanum* 9 (1964), 173–95. For the pilgrimage of Urraca Fernández de Traba, see *El monasterio de San Pelayo de Oviedo. Historia y fuentes, I: colección diplomática (996–1325)*, ed. F. J. Fernández Conde, I. Torrente Fernández and G. de la Noval Menéndez (Oviedo, 1978), no. 42.

[82] *Historia Silense*, ed. Pérez de Urbel and González Ruiz-Zorrilla, *op. cit.* note 20, pp. 190–1, López Ferreiro 1898–1909, *op. cit.* note 32, appendix, no. x; *Historia Compostellana, op. cit.* note 32, p. 109.

[83] Bull 1993a, *op. cit.* note 14, pp. 210–17.

[84] *Cartulario de San Millán de la Cogolla, op. cit.* note 50, no. 263.

themselves having to sell or mortgage off some of their property to a religious community in order to raise the necessary funds. Thus, in 1100 the Leonese nobleman Muño Pérez pledged a number of his estates to the monks of Sahagún in return for a loan of 1000 silver shillings to enable him to undertake a pilgrimage to Jerusalem.[85] Conversely, for a layman living in, say, Lugo, León or Burgos, the journey to Santiago de Compostela, if not exactly comfortable or risk-free, was hardly comparable in terms of either difficulty or cost with a pilgrimage to a far-off shrine such as Rome or Jerusalem.

Jerusalem, of course, had a special resonance for the men and women of the Latin West. In the words of Hans Mayer, 'it was a keyword which produced particular psychological reactions and conjured up particular eschatological notions'.[86] Laymen had been undertaking pilgrimages to the Holy Land for centuries, but the numbers who did so appear to have increased markedly during the course of the eleventh century, influenced partly by heightened apocalyptic and millennial fears, but above all by the increasing popularity of the penitential pilgrimage.[87] And the steady stream of pilgrims eastwards became a flood after 27 November 1095 when, at the Council of Clermont, Pope Urban II called upon the knights of the West to undertake an armed pilgrimage to Jerusalem in order to liberate the oppressed Christian churches in the East. But although some contemporary commentators, such as Guibert of Nogent, were quick to portray the armed pilgrimage which Pope Urban promoted as a new way of salvation, the motives of those who travelled to the Holy Land appear to have been 'solidly embedded in contemporary spiritual anxieties and aspirations'.[88]

According to the chronicler Sigebert of Gembloux, knights from Spain were among those who responded to the pope's appeal and took part in the expedition to the Holy Land that we call the First Crusade.[89] Charter evidence similarly reveals the names of a number of peninsular knights who travelled to Jerusalem in the first half of the twelfth century, although whether they did so as members of the new Army of Christ or as pilgrims in the traditional sense it is mostly impossible to judge.[90] The case of Muño Pérez, who raised a loan from the monks of Sahagún in June 1100 to enable him to undertake a journey 'to visit the sepulchre of the Lord in Jerusalem', has been mentioned. Another

---

[85] *Colección diplomática del monasterio de Sahagún (857–1230): III (1073–1109)*, ed. M. Herrero de la Fuente (León, 1988), no. 1053.

[86] H. E. Mayer, *The Crusades*, trans. J. Gillingham, 2nd edition (Oxford, 1972), p. 11.

[87] See D. F. Callahan, 'Jerusalem in the monastic imaginations of the early eleventh century', *The Haskins Society Journal* 6 (1994), 119–27; cf. Bull 1993a, *op. cit.* note 14, pp. 209–10.

[88] C. J. Tyerman, 'Were there any crusades in the twelfth century?', *English Historical Review* 110 (1995), 553–77 (p. 555).

[89] Sigebert of Gembloux, 'Chronica', in *Monumenta Germaniae Historica: Scriptores*, ed. G. H. Pertz, *et al.* (Hanover, 1844), VI, 367.

[90] See, for example, A. Ubieto Arteta, 'La participación navarro-aragonesa en la primera cruzada', *Príncipe de Viana* 8 (1947), 357–83.

putative crusader was Pedro Gutiérrez who made over a collection of estates to Sahagún in November of the same year shortly before he set off for the East.[91] The *Historia Compostellana* reports that by 1120 large numbers of Galician knights were taking the cross in order to campaign overseas, and references to a number of other possible Galician crusaders crop up in subsequent years.[92] One magnate whose crusading credentials are beyond question was the Castilian Count Rodrigo González de Lara who, when exiled by Alfonso VII of León-Castile (1126–57) in 1137, travelled as a pilgrim to Jerusalem where he energetically campaigned against the Muslims.[93]

However, mounting concern that the popularity of the crusading ethic was leading excessive numbers of peninsular knights to abandon their own struggle with the Muslim Almoravids in order to travel to the Holy Land led Pope Urban II and his successor Paschal II to urge the would-be crusaders to stay at home.[94] In January 1125, nearly two years after Pope Calixtus II had made it abundantly clear that he regarded the campaigns that were being waged against the Muslims in the Iberian peninsula to have the same salvatory character as those in the Holy Land, Archbishop Diego Gelmírez of Santiago de Compostela issued a passionate call to arms in which he spoke of opening up a shorter and far less difficult path to Jerusalem through the regions of Spain.[95] Similarly, when some time in the 1130s the Galician knight Muño Alfonso declared his intention to go on a pilgrimage to Jerusalem, he was persuaded by the archbishop of Toledo and other leading churchmen that he could perform equal penance for his sins by waging war on the Muslims of al-Andalus.[96] The fact that so very few laymen from León and Castile are known to have journeyed as pilgrims to the Holy Land in the second half of the twelfth century strongly suggests that these appeals did not fall on deaf ears.[97] The road to Jerusalem had been seemingly closed off to the pious; but to the warrior aristocracy of León and Castile it may well have appeared that the way to salvation was now clearer than ever before.

---

91 *Colección diplomática de Sahagún III, op. cit.* note 85, no. 1060.
92 *Historia Compostellana, op. cit.* note 32, p. 253. The Galician magnate Count Fernando Pérez de Traba, for example, made two journeys to Jerusalem, the second of them in 1153: AHN, Clero, 527/6 and 1126/6.
93 'Chronica Adefonsi Imperatoris', *Chronica Hispana saeculi XII. Part I, Corpus Christianorum Continuatio Medieualis* 71, ed. A. Maya Sánchez (Turnhout, 1990), i, §47–8 and ii, §30. On the chequered career of Count Rodrigo González de Lara, see González 1960, *op. cit.* note 64, pp. 260–2; Barton 1997, *op. cit.* note 62, p. 116, n. 80 and pp. 292–3.
94 *Papsturkunden in Spanien: I Katalonien*, ed. P. Kehr (Berlin, 1926), pp. 287–8; *Historia Compostellana, op. cit.* note 32, pp. 24–6 and 77–8.
95 *Bullaire de Pape Calixte II*, ed. U. Robert, 2 vols. (Paris, 1891), II, 266–7; *Historia Compostellana, op. cit.* note 32, pp. 378–9.
96 'Chronica Adefonsi Imperatoris', *op. cit.* note 93, ii, §90.
97 For three exceptions, see AHN, Códices, 1439B, fol. 23v; *Colección documental de León V, op. cit.* note 80, no. 1512; *Tumbos de Sobrado, op. cit.* note 53, no. 484.

5

Jacques de Vitry and the Ideology of Pilgrimage

DEBRA J. BIRCH

Enthusiasm for pilgrimage amongst the peoples of Christendom remained unabated throughout the medieval period. Journeys to the tomb or shrine of a saint or martyr, or a visit to some other holy place, were readily undertaken by men and women, young and old, rich and poor alike. Some travelled only as far as a local holy place, while others ventured much further afield. For the majority of these people the decision to set out on pilgrimage was not the result of any duty or obligation. Rather it was a personal decision, each of them choosing for themselves both the time of their departure and their destination. The motivation behind the decision to go on pilgrimage was also personal. For some there was the hope of a cure for a disease or ailment; others were perhaps motivated by less worthy considerations, such as improved opportunities for begging. But, for the majority, pilgrimage is probably best understood as a manifestation of popular religious enthusiasm. These pilgrims believed that saints had the ability to intercede with God on their behalf and that prayers offered at their tombs, or at shrines, would secure the saints' intercession and so ease their road to the heavenly kingdom.

It was against this background of widespread popular enthusiasm for pilgrimage that Jacques de Vitry (c. 1160/70–1240), one of the greatest preachers of his time, composed the two sermons addressed to pilgrims, which are considered in this paper. The sermons are found amongst Jacques de Vitry's seventy-four *Ad status* sermons.[1] Also known as the *Sermones vulgares*, they were addressed to various social groups and were amongst the very first of the genre.[2] As yet unpublished, these sermons not only highlight Jacques de

---

1 J. B. Schneyer, *Repertorium der Lateinischen Sermones des Mittelalters für die Zeit von 1150–1350*, 9 vols. (Münster, 1969–1979), III, 220, lists fourteen manuscripts in which the *Sermones vulgares* can be found, although not every manuscript necessarily contains all seventy-four sermons. Transcriptions of some of these sermons can be found in J. B. Pitra, *Analecta novissima spicilegii solesmensis altera*, 2 vols. (Paris, 1885–1888), II.
2 Apart from pilgrims, recipients of other sermons include priests, prelates, canons, judges, preachers, crusaders, sailors, merchants, the poor and afflicted, labourers and widows. See for example, B. van den Hoven, *Work in Ancient and Medieval Thought* (Amsterdam, 1996), pp. 208–43 and D. L. d'Avray and M. Tausche, 'Marriage Sermons in *Ad status* Collections of the Central Middle Ages', in *Modern*

79

Vitry's skills as a preacher, which were widely admired by contempories, but also reveal his attitude towards pilgrimage and his more general concerns for the spiritual welfare of all men.

Jacques de Vitry was certainly recognised as one of the great popular preachers of his age[3] and contemporaries commented favourably upon his preaching skills. The Dominican, Vincent of Beauvais (died c. 1264), remarked upon his success in preaching the crusade against the Albigensians, a commission which had been laid upon him in 1213 by Raymond, bishop of Uzès. 'By the sweetness and charm of his eloquence', wrote Vincent of Beauvais, Jacques de Vitry was able to persuade an enormous multitude to take up the Cross.[4] Jacques de Vitry's success in 1213 brought another commission in the following year from Robert de Courçon, papal legate to France, to preach the Crusade to the Holy Land.[5] This commission took Jacques de Vitry to Brabant where Thomas of Cantimpré (died c. 1270) watched his performance, describing how Jacques de Vitry fell to the ground again and again, with eyes rolling and blood flowing from his mouth.[6] He presented his audience, Thomas of Cantimpré wrote, 'with a great spectacle of horror'. Then as all were weeping, Jacques de Vitry got to his feet as if nothing had happened.[7] Perhaps such dramatic displays were what another Dominican, Stephen of Bourbon (died c. 1260), had in mind when he wrote that no one either before or after Jacques de Vitry could so move the crowd to religious fervour.[8]

The fame which these important preaching commissions engendered may well account for Jacques de Vitry's election as bishop by the canons of the church of St John at Acre c. 1215.[9] Consecrated by Honorius III, he set out for Acre in September 1216, arriving there in the November of the same year.

Questions about Medieval Sermons, ed. N. Bériou and D. L. D'Avray (Spoleto, 1994), pp. 77–134.

[3] On the life of Jacques de Vitry, see P. Funk, *Jacob von Vitry: Leben und Werke* (Leipzig and Berlin, 1909); A. P. Bagliani, *Cardinali di curia e 'familiae' cardinalizie dal 1227–1254*, 2 vols., Italia Sacra 18 and 19 (Padua 1972), I, 98–109; A. Forni, 'Giacomo da Vitry, predicatore e sociologo', *La cultura. Rivista di filosofia letteratura e storia* 18 (1980), 34–89; B. M. Bolton, 'Faithful to whom?: Jacques de Vitry and the French Bishops', unpublished paper given at the 3rd Conference for the Study of the Crusades and the Latin East (Syracuse, July 1991); Jacques de Vitry, *Historia occidentalis*, ed. J. F. Hinnesbusch (Fribourg, 1972), pp. 3–7; Monica Sandor, 'The Popular Preaching of Jacques de Vitry (d.1240)' (unpublished Ph.D. thesis, University of Toronto, 1993).

[4] Vincent of Beauvais, *Ex speculum historiale*, MGH.SS 24, pp. 164–7 (pp. 165–6).

[5] Jacques de Vitry, *Historia occidentalis*, op. cit. note 3, p. 5. See also J. J. van Moolenbroek, 'Signs in the heavens in Groningen and Friesland in 1214: Oliver of Cologne and crusading propaganda', *Journal of Medieval History* 13 (1987), 251–72.

[6] Thomas of Cantimpré, *Vitae Mariae Oigniacensis supplementum*, AASS June IV, pp. 666–78 (p. 677).

[7] Cantimpré, op. cit. note 6.

[8] E. W. McDonnell, *The Beguines and Beghards in Medieval Culture* (New Brunswick, 1954), p. 28, note 74.

[9] Funk 1909, op. cit. note 3, pp. 37–45.

During the next few years he seems to have concerned himself with the spiritual needs of his diocese and with the crusade against the Saracens, spending the years 1218 to 1221 with the army of the Fifth Crusade.[10] However, after the forced surrender of Damietta in 1221, Jacques de Vitry may have grown disheartened. He resigned his bishopric at some point, although the exact chronology of events remains unclear. He certainly left Acre in 1225, never to return, although this did not mark the end of his career. He was created Cardinal Bishop of Tusculum by Gregory IX in 1229, a position which he retained until his death in 1240.[11]

As well as enjoying a life of intense activity as bishop and crusade preacher, Jacques de Vitry was also a prolific writer. His surviving works include an historical work in two books[12] and a Life of the ascetic Mary of Oignies, his spiritual patroness, which was written at the request of his friend, Foulques, bishop of Toulouse.[13] There are also seven letters[14] and numerous sermons, including, amongst the *Sermones vulgares*, the two addressed to pilgrims which will be referred to here as sermons A and B.[15] As bishop of Acre and then as cardinal bishop of Tusculum, it is likely that Jacques de Vitry was in frequent contact with pilgrims. Indeed, it may well have been his own personal associations with and observations of these travellers which provided the inspiration for the two sermons he addressed to them. Unfortunately it is impossible to tell when these two sermons were written. It may be that the early period of Jacques de Vitry's career, taken up with preaching commissions, responsibilities as bishop of Acre and participation in the Fifth Crusade, would have provided less time and opportunity for writing than his later years as cardinal. Nor can we know with any certainty whether these sermons were ever actually delivered in the form in which we have them. It is quite possible that they were in fact intended as model sermons, containing themes which Jacques de Vitry had found to be effective and which he had then written down for use by other preachers.[16] What does seem likely, however, is that these two sermons, as we have them, were intended for very different audiences.

---

10 On the course of the Fifth Crusade, see J. M. Powell, *Anatomy of a Crusade 1213–1221* (Philadelphia, 1986), pp. 123–93; Funk 1909, *op. cit.* note 3, pp. 45–51.

11 Alberic de Tre Fontaneis, *Chronica, MGH.SS* 23, pp. 631–950 (p. 923).

12 For a brief summary of the contents of the *Historia Hiersolomitana abbreviata*, see Jacques de Vitry, *Historia occidentalis, op. cit.* note 3, pp. 9–10.

13 Jacques de Vitry, *Vitae B. Mariae Oigniacensis*, *AASS* June IV, pp. 636–66.

14 Jacques de Vitry, *Lettres*, ed. R. B. C. Huygens (Leiden, 1960).

15 The labelling of these sermons denotes nothing beyond the order in which they are found in the manuscript. Manuscript references are to Paris, Bibliothèque Nationale, Latin MS 3284. Also on these sermons, see D. J. Birch, 'Medieval Pilgrimage: with particular reference to Rome in the period from Paschal II to Innocent III' (unpublished Ph.D. thesis, University of London, 1994), pp. 297–319 and 324–62.

16 P. J. Cole, *The Preaching of the Crusades to the Holy Land 1095–1270* (Cambridge, Mass., 1991), p. 133. Other preachers certainly made use of Jacques de Vitry's sermons. See for example, Guibert of Tournai, *Sermones ad omnes status de novo correcti et emendati*

Sermon A

Sermon A was probably written for an audience of ordinary men and women. The metaphors and examples used, such as references to the cultivation of vines, the making of bread and the weaving of shirts, would have been familiar to such an audience.[17] In addition, *exempla*, or illustrative stories, intended to reinforce the message of the sermon, are extensively used to help keep the audience's interest and to assist them in understanding the argument.[18]

It was his use of *exempla* when preaching in France, Stephen of Bourbon argued, that had enabled Jacques de Vitry to move the people in a way that no other preacher had been capable of previously.[19] The practice of including *exempla* in sermons had probably not begun much earlier than 1200 and although Jacques de Vitry was not the first preacher to employ them, he successfully popularised their use.[20] The appeal of Jacques de Vitry's *exempla* with other preachers is clearly demonstrated by the numerous manuscript collections which contain different numbers and combinations of his illustrative stories. The irregular form and contents of these manuscript collections, Crane has argued, suggest that they were put together by different preachers at various times for their own individual use, and that the selections reflect these preachers' own particular tastes and purposes.[21]

In his Life of Mary of Oignies, Jacques de Vitry had himself noted the usefulness of *exempla*, arguing that men were moved more by examples than by precepts.[22] He developed this idea further in the introduction to his *Sermones vulgares*, arguing that rough preaching would convert more laymen than the elaborate sword of a subtle sermon. For the edification of ordinary and simple people one must present tangible and concrete examples with which they are familiar through experience. For they are moved more, he argued, by strange illustrations than by authorities or profound observations. Examples, he continued, should always be edifying and purposeless tales should be omitted. The conclusions of philosophers might also be included where they are useful and should be introduced not merely for edification but also to excite attention.[23] Here Jacques de Vitry recalled a personal experience:

(1510). See also M. Papi, 'Crociati, pellegrini e cavalieri nei sermones di Gilberto di Tournai', *Studi Francescani* 73 (1976), 373–409, especially pp. 396–402 for Guibert's sermon addressed to pilgrims.

[17] MS Latin 3284, fol. 129v.
[18] Jacques de Vitry, *The Exempla or Illustrative Stories from the Sermones Vulgares*, ed. T. F. Crane, *The Folk Lore Society* 26 (1878).
[19] McDonnell 1954, *op. cit.* note 8, p. 28.
[20] McDonnell 1954, *op. cit.* note 8, p. 28.
[21] Crane 1878, *op. cit.* note 18, p. xlvii.
[22] Jacques de Vitry, *op. cit.* note 13, p. 636.
[23] McDonnell 1954, *op. cit.* note 8, p. 29.

Once when I had been preaching a sermon for some time, I noticed that a great number of people were overcome by tiredness and sleep, so with one word I woke them up and made them listen. I remember saying that he who sleeps or dozes will not disclose my secrets or counsel. Everyone then opened their eyes and having made a noise, afterwards listened attentively in silence to my useful and serious words.[24]

As well as *exempla*, Jacques de Vitry made use of Biblical quotations. In Sermon A he tells the story of Abraham,[25] instructed by God to leave behind his country, his kindred and his father's house to go in search of the promised land.[26] He was commanded to exchange all that was familiar for the life of an exile, a wanderer in foreign places. In return for obeying God's command and undertaking this exile, however, Abraham enjoyed God's help and was promised great rewards: 'And I will make of thee a great nation and I will bless thee and magnify thy name and thou shalt be blessed.'[27] He was promised that his seed would be multiplied as the stars in heaven and that the promised land would be found. Jacques de Vitry chose to begin the sermon with an account of Abraham's exile because he considered Abraham to be the 'first pilgrim'.[28] By sending Abraham into exile, Jacques de Vitry explained, God had given man '*exemplum peregrinationis*' or example of pilgrimage.[29] Pilgrims were the imitators of Abraham, exiles astray in unfamiliar lands. According to Jacques de Vitry, those who, like Abraham, left behind home and family for the love of God would be similarly rewarded.[30] They would receive the promised land, a land flowing with milk and honey. The argument is reinforced through quotation of the text of Matthew 19. 29: 'Everyone that hath left house, or brethren, or sisters, or father, or mother, or wife, or children, or lands for my name's sake shall receive an hundredfold and shall possess life everlasting.'

Jacques de Vitry explained to his audience, however, that to imitate Abraham by departing from home and family was not enough on its own to earn these rewards. The pilgrim's journey had to be a penitential one, an opportunity for him to atone for his misdemeanours. For it was through his labours that the pilgrim was cleansed of his sins. Jacques de Vitry then cited a host of unlikely situations from which good might emerge. From the putrid

---

24 Pitra 1885–1888, *op. cit.* note 1, II, p. 193. See also McDonnell 1954, *op. cit.* note 8, p. 29: '. . . cum aliquando protrahem sermonem, et viderem populi multitudinem affectam taedio et dormitantem, uno modo dicto verbo, omnes incitati sunt et innovati ad audiendum. Exempli gratia, aliquando memini me dixisse: "ille qui (modo) dormitat, secreta mea vel consilium meum non revelabit" '.
25 MS Latin 3284, fols. 128v–129r.
26 Genesis 12. 1.
27 Genesis 12. 2.
28 MS Latin 3284, fol. 128v.
29 MS Latin 3284, fols. 128v–129r.
30 MS Latin 3284, fol. 129r.

egg the chicken is hatched, from burnt hay comes pure glass and, thus, from his labours the pilgrim is purged of his sin and earns his celestial reward.[31]

Having established that the pilgrimage is to be a period of expiation, Jacques de Vitry went on to provide his audience with a model of how the pilgrim should conduct himself on his journey. Quoting St Bernard, he warned that the pilgrim must not stray from his path.[32] He must turn neither to the left nor to the right. All distractions should be ignored. The pilgrim, Jacques de Vitry continued, should wear only light clothing. He should not stay more than one night in a particular place and his ultimate destination should be ever in his mind. He should not delight in the sight of beautiful things nor should he rejoice until he returned to his homeland.[33] The penitential nature of the pilgrim's journey is a theme to which Jacques de Vitry returned repeatedly. 'Nothing', he instructed his audience, 'is more efficacious or satisfying than the labour of the pilgrimage.'[34] 'For just as a man sins with all his limbs', he warned, 'so too must he make reparation by labouring with all of them.'[35] If the pilgrim was accustomed to sleep on a soft bed, then he must make reparation during his pilgrimage by sleeping on a hard one. If he habitually rose late in the morning, then during his pilgrimage he had to make reparation by getting up early. If he had sinned by showing too much love and affection to his family, he must make reparation by leaving them behind.[36] To reinforce his message, Jacques de Vitry included an *exemplum* here concerning a certain knight about to depart 'beyond the sea', perhaps on crusade to the Holy Land. Before his departure he ordered his two sons, whom he dearly loved, to be brought before him, so that his departure might be made all the more difficult for him and his merit thereby increased.[37]

In this sermon Jacques de Vitry also warned that the pilgrim should not take many possessions with him on his pilgrimage. He should carry his scrip and staff, but he should not be burdened down by other unnecessary items. Nor should he willingly show or exhibit his wealth to thieves.[38] In warning the pilgrim to refrain from displaying his wealth, Jacques de Vitry was implying

---

[31] MS Latin 3284, fol. 129r.

[32] MS Latin 3284, fol. 129r–129v. See St Bernard, *Sermones de tempore*, PL 183, cols. 35–360 (col. 183).

[33] MS Latin 3284, fol. 129v.

[34] MS Latin 3284, fol. 129v. 'Nulla autem efficatior quam labor peregrinationis.'

[35] MS Latin 3284, fol. 129v. 'Nam sicut omnibus membris homo peccavit ita cunctis membris laborando satisfacit.'

[36] MS Latin, 3284, fol. 129v.

[37] MS Latin 3284, fol. 129v. This idea that the pilgrim should leave behind all that was familiar and dear to him is reminiscent of the early Irish Cambray Homily, which refers to pilgrimage as 'white martyrdom'. Red martyrdom is death, but white martyrdom is the separation from everything that an individual loves for the sake of God. See *Thesaurus Palaeohibernicus. A Collection of Old-Irish Glosses Scholia Prose and Verse*, ed. W. Stokes and J. Strachan, 3 vols. (Cambridge, 1901–1910), II, 246–7.

[38] MS Latin 3284, fol. 129v.

Jacques de Vitry and the Ideology of Pilgrimage

that the pilgrim who remained true to the ideal of simplicity and poverty would not attract the interest or attention of thieves and bandits. Assaults on pilgrims are a recurrent theme in our sources.[39] An indication of just how commonplace such incidents were is provided by the laws designed to offer some form of protection to pilgrims, which were passed in many countries and by the Church throughout the medieval period.[40] In Jacques de Vitry's view perhaps, pilgrims who carried large sums of money and then fell foul of robbers had only themselves to blame.

Jacques de Vitry's insistence on the poverty of the pilgrim and the penitential nature of his journey might have been a response to his own observations of pilgrims and the way they conducted themselves. While many pilgrims may well have set out with good intentions, Jacques de Vitry knew that it was all too easy for them to fall into temptation along the way, hence his insistence on the pilgrim's single-mindedness concerning his journey and purpose. He had probably also had occasion to see numerous pilgrims burdened down by the worldly goods which he insisted that they should be able to do without.

Jacques de Vitry, however, was not alone in his concern over the way in which many pilgrims conducted themselves. Criticism of pilgrimage had been building during the twelfth century. What use were pilgrimages, Maurice of Sully, bishop of Paris (1160–1196) was moved to ask, if those who undertook them left behind their villages but not their vices?[41] Most criticism, however, was levelled against the money spent on such journeys. Honorius of Autun had suggested that money expended on pilgrimages might be used instead for works of charity. Such money, he believed, was better spent on the poor than upon a visit to Jerusalem.[42] A similar suggestion was made by Lambert le Bègue in an apology addressed to the antipope Calixtus III (1168–1178). In this he reckoned that money spent upon pilgrimages might be used instead for nourishing the hungry and thirsty, clothing the naked, helping strangers and ransoming captives.[43]

It was also the penitential nature of the pilgrim's journey and the ideal of poverty that the author of the *Veneranda dies* sermon wanted to impress upon his audience. Contained in Book 1 of the *Codex Calixtinus*, and written in the twelfth century to be read to pilgrims to Compostela on 20 December, the second feast day of St James, this sermon stated that the pilgrim's scrip should

---

39 Birch 1994, *op. cit.*, note 15, pp. 107–10.
40 F. Garrisson, 'A propos des pèlerins et de leur condition juridique', *Etudes d'histoire du droit canonique dediées à Gabriel le Bras* 2 (Paris, 1965), 1165–89; H. Gilles, 'Lex peregrinorum', *Cahiers de Fanjeaux* 15 (1980), 161–89.
41 C. A. Robson, *Maurice of Sully and the Medieval Vernacular Homily* (Oxford, 1952), pp. 108–9. See also G. Constable, 'Opposition to Pilgrimage in the Middle Ages', in *Religious Life and Thought (11th–12th Centuries)* (Variorum Reprint, London 1979), pp. 125–46.
42 Honorius of Autun, *Elucidarium*, PL 172, cols. 1109–1176 (col. 1152).
43 Constable 1979, *op. cit.* note 41, p. 144.

be made from the hide of a dead animal.[44] This was a sign that the pilgrim should mortify his own flesh with cold, hunger, thirst, fasting and many other labours.[45] The pilgrim's scrip, the author also noted, should only be of a small size, and moreover, it should always be open. The small size of the scrip indicated that the pilgrim carried only a very modest sum with him, placing his trust in the Lord for his daily bread. The fact that it was always open was a sign that the pilgrim should spend his money on the needy and ought then to receive and to give when need arose.[46] The sermon's author insisted that since the disciples had been sent into the world bearing nothing, neither bag nor staff, neither bread nor money, the pilgrim should carry no money beyond what he intended to distribute to the poor. The author asked his audience to consider what would become of those who carried gold and silver, spent their time eating and drinking and gave nothing in alms. The same message was reiterated several times, contrasting in particular the wealth of pilgrims with the poverty of the apostles. If Blessed Peter departed from Rome without shoes and, following his crucifixion, went straight to heaven, why was it that so many pilgrims travelled with large sums of money, two sets of clothing and ate rich food and drank strong wine? The pilgrim who died with money in his pocket, the sermon's author warned, would be forever excluded from the kingdom of heaven.[47] In his own sermons, therefore, Jacques de Vitry was addressing concerns which were probably the result of his own experience and contact with pilgrims, but which clearly had also been widespread for some time.

The skill of Jacques de Vitry as a preacher is apparent in the next section of Sermon A. He had been telling his audience that the road of the pilgrim was a hard and difficult one, emphasising the need for penance and hard work. Presumably he realised that on hearing this message, many would have grown disheartened and perhaps disinclined to undertake a pilgrimage. Immediately, therefore, he reminded them that this labour was the only way to achieve salvation and that those who shied away from the task were stupid and foolish. 'He who wishes to rest in the next world must labour in this.'[48] Here Jacques de Vitry asked his audience to consider how much labour must be put into viticulture or the weaving and production of a shirt. He then expected them to appreciate how much more effort must be put into the achieving of eternal life. Quoting Seneca, he reminded his audience that, 'great things

---

[44] *Liber sancti Jacobi, codex Calixtinus*, ed. M. M. Whitehill, 2 vols. (Santiago de Compostela, 1944), I, 141–76. See also T. Coffey, L. Davidson and M. Dunn, *The Miracles of Saint James: Translations of the 'Liber Sancti Jacobi'* (New York, 1996).
[45] Whitehill 1944, *op. cit.* note 44, I, 152–3.
[46] Whitehill 1944, *op. cit.* note 44, I, 152.
[47] Whitehill 1944, *op. cit.* note 44, I, 156–7.
[48] MS Latin 3284, fol. 129v. 'Laborare igitur oportet in hoc seculo qui quiescere vult in alio.'

cannot be bought for small sums'.[49] It was the weak and the lazy who did not have the courage for the task and in seeking to escape punishment for sins in this world they would find themselves damned in the next. Seeking to escape Scylla, Jacques de Vitry warned, one was all too likely to be caught by Charybdis.[50]

Jacques de Vitry's direct appeal to his audience continued as he stirred them yet again with the reminder that each of them had the opportunity to decide for themselves whether to follow the path to heaven or hell. Each must choose between eternal life or eternal damnation; whether they would hang on the cross of salvation to Christ's right or the cross of damnation to his left.[51] Again Jacques de Vitry roused his audience reminding them that when lying on a hard bed, they should remember that Christ too, young and small also lay on a hard bed, a manger in a stable.[52] When tired from the labours of the journey, they were to remember that Christ too was tired out by his journey. When their feet grew weary, they were to remember that Christ's feet were pierced by nails for their salvation. When lacking a pillow for the head, they were to remember the pillow which Christ had, a crown of thorns.[53]

The pilgrim, therefore, according to Jacques de Vitry, had to expect to suffer as Christ had once suffered. As the suffering Christ mopped the sweat from his brow on the way to Calvary, so too the pilgrim had to wipe the sweat from his brow as he suffered, he told his audience, in the furnace of tribulation and in the anguish of labours.[54] Yet he assured his listeners that all those who partook of this suffering would be present at the resurrection. Like the saints, the pilgrim had to bear and even delight in the hardships of this world, knowing that his reward awaited him in the life to come.

In the last part of Sermon A, Jacques de Vitry continued to develop the theme that the pilgrim's road is the road to salvation. The pilgrim should have no fear of death, rather he should seek death willingly, in the certainty that all who die in the service of Christ will be rewarded. To emphasise this message he likened the pilgrim's fear of death to young boys' fears of ghosts. They feared when there was nothing to fear, he said, for what awaited the pilgrim in heaven was infinitely better than his present life on earth.[55] 'The world is burning with the fire of vices', he warned his audience, 'yet miserable and obstinate sinners, although daily they hear the words of God, prefer to be

---

[49] MS Latin 3284, fol. 129v. Seneca, *Ad Lucilium epistulae morales*, trans. R. M. Gummere, 3 vols., Loeb Classical Library (London, 1917–1925), I, 126–7. 'Non potest parvo res magna constare.'
[50] MS Latin 3284, fol. 129v.
[51] MS Latin, fol. 129v.
[52] MS Latin 3284, fol. 130r.
[53] MS Latin 3284, fol. 130r.
[54] MS Latin, fol. 130r.
[55] MS Latin 3284, fol. 130r.

burned by fire in this world than to leave it.'[56] Jacques de Vitry compared these sinners to the crocodile through whose scales the Word of the Lord was unable to penetrate. They would rather be burnt in this world than depart from it and were, therefore, like the ass which stubbornly refused to leave the mill even though it was on fire. According to Jacques de Vitry's sermon, man was like an ape. For the ape discarded the nut because its shell was bitter to the taste. However, had the ape persisted to the centre, he would have found that the kernel was sweet. Just as the stupid and ignorant were put off by the bitter labours of this world, so they would never experience the rewards.[57]

This sermon ends with an *exemplum*, which cleverly encapsulates the serious message of the sermon, that the undertaking of hard and difficult labours in this world will be rewarded in the next. A hermit living in a cell had to make a long journey each day to collect water. To reduce the amount of daily labour he decided to rebuild his cell nearer to the water supply. One day, however, an angel appeared holding a wax-tablet and a stylus. The astonished hermit asked the angel what he was doing. The angel replied that God Himself had sent him to note down the number of steps the hermit had to take each day to fetch his water, so that he could be rewarded for his efforts in heaven. Thereupon the hermit promptly returned to his original distant cell. In conclusion, Jacques de Vitry reminded his audience, 'that God will note down all our steps in his book so that we can be rewarded'.[58]

Sermon A exhibits the skill of Jacques de Vitry as a sermon writer and preacher. He knows how to communicate his message to his audience and to keep their attention. He knows when and how to warn, to exhort and to encourage. He also succeeds in making the sermon work at more than one level and thereby renders it applicable to a wider audience. In one sense Jacques de Vitry is preaching to the pilgrim, an individual intent on making a pilgrimage to a tomb or shrine. He refers to the discomforts that must be borne on this journey if it is to be of any spiritual benefit. Specific instructions are given as to what the pilgrim should wear and what he should and should not take with him. Emphasis is placed on the positive response which should greet hard beds and early starts, with the pilgrim firmly instructed to shun all distractions and resist all temptations encountered on the journey.

Yet the sermon also works at another level. It not only deals with those about to depart to some holy place, but can also be seen to refer to the life of all men. For pilgrimages undertaken by individuals imitated the life of man on

---

[56] MS Latin 3284, fol. 130v. 'Mundus iste undique succensus est igne viciorum et miseri atque obstinati peccatores licet quotidie verbis dei stimulentur maluit igne conburi in hoc mundo quam recedere ab illo.'

[57] MS Latin 3284, fol. 130v.

[58] MS Latin 3284, fols. 130v–131r. '... omnes passus vestros in libro suo dominus scribet ad remunerandum.'

earth which was itself seen to be a pilgrimage.[59] This theme, the ideology of life as a pilgrimage, is more fully developed in the second of Jacques de Vitry's sermons addressed to pilgrims, referred to here for convenience as Sermon B.

Sermon B

The more sophisticated structure and scholarly content of this sermon suggests that it is unlikely to have been intended for the same kind of audience as Sermon A. Nor would this be uncharacteristic of Jacques de Vitry, as studies of the two sermons addressed to crusaders, suggest that one was intended for those about to set out on crusade, while the other was written for non-combatants, including wives, children and aged parents.[60] Of the two sermons addressed to pilgrims, Sermon A, as has been seen, was probably intended for ordinary men and women. Sermon B, on the other hand, was probably intended for a more select audience than the first, and perhaps a clerical one.

A major difference between the two sermons is that there are no *exempla* within the text of Sermon B. Presumably the intended audience did not need stories to retain their interest or to understand the arguments. The only *exempla* are to be found in a long list at the end of the text, included there perhaps only in case they should prove useful to others at some stage as preaching aids. The subject matter of this sermon also has a different emphasis. Jacques de Vitry was less concerned with the actual physical undertaking of a journey to a particular shrine or holy place, than with the more general theme of man as a pilgrim on earth. In a sense every man was a *peregrinus*, an exile, waiting until death brought release, allowing him to return to his real home in heaven. The origins of this theme are Scriptural. 'We are confident', wrote St Paul to the Corinthians, 'and have a good will to be absent rather from the body and to be present with the Lord.'[61] It was a theme taken up by the early Christian Fathers. St Ambrose (339–397) described life as a three-stage pilgrimage,[62] while St Augustine (354–430) interpreted it as either a pilgrimage to the city of God, Jerusalem, or to the city of man, Babylon.[63] St Columbanus (c. 550–615) in a penitential on the transitory nature of earthly life, wrote, 'Let us ever ponder on the end of the road, that is our life, for the end of our roadway is our home ... on the road we live as travellers, as pilgrims, as guests of the world.'[64]

---

[59] G. B. Ladner, '*Homo viator*: Medieval Ideas on Alienation and Order', *Speculum* 42 (1967), 233–59.
[60] Cole 1991, *op. cit.* note 16, pp. 138–9.
[61] II Corinthians 5. 1–2 and 7–8.
[62] See C. K. Zacher, *Curiosity and Pilgrimage: The Literature of Discovery in Fourteenth Century England* (Baltimore and London, 1976), p. 44.
[63] St Augustine, *Confessions*, PL 32, cols. 659–868. See for example, cols. 703, 780, 782 and 834.
[64] St Columbanus, *Opera*, ed. G. S. M. Walker, *Scriptores Latini Hiberniae* 2 (Dublin,

Man's pilgrimage on earth was Jacques de Vitry's main preoccupation in this sermon and he selected for his protheme, Psalm 118. 19, 'I am a sojourner on the earth: hide not thy commandments from me.'[65] He continued by explaining how Ishmael, far from home and thirsting, called upon the Lord for help and so was led to water. Here Jacques de Vitry tried to show how man, an exile on earth, can call upon the Lord to have his thirst quenched by sacred scripture. It was only the lovers of the temporal world, he wrote, who had no desire for this spiritual refreshment.[66]

As in Sermon A, the themes of penance and salvation are of major importance. The treatment of these themes in Sermon B, however, is very different. Taking as his text Zechariah 14. 18, 'there shall be destruction wherewith the Lord will strike all nations that will not go up to keep the Feast of the Tabernacles', Jacques de Vitry explained that the feast of the Tabernacles was the 'feast of the pilgrims', to which all men were invited as guests.[67] Just as the Israelites offered gifts to the Lord from their harvest during the Feast of the Tabernacles, so pilgrims too should offer gifts to God and labour with joy in his service. Indeed this should be a joyful task because all those who died in the service of God would be rewarded with eternal happiness. The sermon shows that Jacques de Vitry regarded the Feast of the Tabernacles as three feasts together in one.[68] It was the feast of affliction, through which the bodies of those participating underwent suffering. It was also, however, the feast of expiation and of propitiation; so that through their suffering, pilgrims were purged and cleansed, and through the great mercy and propitiation of the Lord, the remission of all sins could be gained. For just as the Feast of the Tabernacles was the celebration of the gathering in of the harvest, this was also the appropriate feast at which to celebrate the gathering in of nations to the Lord. Jacques de Vitry's emphasis, therefore, fell once more upon man as a pilgrim. All men were *peregrini*, and all possessed the free will to choose whether they would undertake hardships and toil in this life in the service of God, and thus achieve salvation, or whether they would neglect this Feast of the Tabernacles and suffer eternal ruin.

The remainder of Sermon B is concerned with ensuring that the pilgrim is properly equipped for the labour and toil of this world, so that he will be able to achieve the spiritual rewards of his undertaking. He must have a contrite heart and must confess his sins. For in this way the pilgrim will have the strength to cross over from Egypt to Israel and to make the spiritual transition from vice to virtue. Pilgrims must also receive the cross of Christ. As in his crusade sermons, here Jacques de Vitry emphasised the protective powers of

1957), 96–7. Also K. Hughes, 'The Changing Theory and Practice of Irish Pilgrimage', *Journal of Ecclesiastical History* 11 (1960), 143–51.
[65] Other biblical references include Genesis 47. 9 and I Peter 2. 11.
[66] MS Latin 3284, fol. 131r.
[67] MS Latin 3284, fol. 131r: 'festum peregrinorum'.
[68] MS Latin 3284, fol. 131r.

Jacques de Vitry and the Ideology of Pilgrimage

the cross, a theme also taken up again in the list of *exempla* at the end of Sermon B. A nun, who chanced to eat a lettuce without crossing herself beforehand, swallowed a devil together with its leaves. When a holy man tried to exorcise this evil spirit, the devil complained that it was not his fault that the nun had not crossed herself and so had swallowed him too.[69] A second *exemplum* concerns a certain Jew who was spending the night in a cemetery, to which an evil spirit came. Although the Jew had no faith in the cross, he still made the sign. The spirit fled and the Jew, experiencing the efficacy of the cross, became a Christian.[70]

In the tradition of the *Rule of St Benedict*, Jacques de Vitry also used images of warfare which showed that the pilgrim's life consisted in large measure of a battle against evil. In the same way as a soldier without weapons was not safe in battle, he wrote, so no one could fight against the devil without the cross.[71] Whoever bore the 'sign of the emperor', that is the cross of Christ, he told his audience, could perform the labour of his pilgrimage in safety.[72] Having taken up the cross, however, the pilgrim had to persevere in his pilgrimage. Many pilgrims saved themselves from their sins but later returned to their debauchery and so ruined their pilgrimage. For just as a horse which lost a shoe was useless, Jacques de Vitry wrote, the same could also be said of a pilgrimage where there was no perseverance.[73]

Jacques de Vitry stressed how easy it was for the pilgrim to give way to temptations and to lose the battle against evil. Many, tired out by the journey, drank so much that they became intoxicated. Others were not thirsty, but seeing their companions drinking, weakly followed their example.[74] It was when the pilgrim was drunk that he was in danger and then even lives were not safe. Pilgrims should drink and eat only for the refreshment of their bodies and not to excess. Yet wine, Jacques de Vitry insisted, was but one example of the temptations, of which the pilgrim had to beware. There were many harlots and evil women awaiting the unwary. It was safer by far, Jacques de Vitry reckoned, to sleep amongst demons, who fled at the sign of the cross, than amongst women of this kind. Samson slept among the Philistines and nothing evil befell him. When he lay with Delilah, however, he lost his hair.[75] The pilgrim, Jacques de Vitry warned, would also find evil men along the way and thus the pilgrim should choose his companions carefully. To emphasise his point he quoted Proverbs 13. 20: 'he who walketh with the wise shall be wise; a friend of fools shall become like to them'.

In this sermon Jacques de Vitry employs a two-part model similar to that

---

[69] MS Latin 3284, fol. 134r.
[70] MS Latin 3284, fol. 134r.
[71] MS Latin 3284, fol. 134r.
[72] MS Latin, fols. 133v–134r.
[73] MS Latin, fol. 132r.
[74] MS Latin 3284, fol. 132r.
[75] MS Latin, fol. 132v.

used by St Augustine. He shows that man may take one of two paths. He may ascend to the Feast of the Tabernacles, thus stepping out on the road to Jerusalem, on the road towards salvation and the city of God. On the other hand, he shows that there are those who prefer not to attend the Feast of the Tabernacles, and will try to tempt the pilgrim to take a different route, the road to Babylon, the city of sinful man and damnation. Such people, he said, retained the evil infusion of wine and desired the taste and smell of vices, and grew in strength when pilgrims gave in to the temptations which they offered.

In the last part of Sermon B, therefore, Jacques de Vitry is keen to stress the importance of making sure that the pilgrim remains properly equipped and stays firmly on the road to Jerusalem. This was obviously the responsibility of the Church and presumably the task of the clergy, for whom this sermon may have been intended. The folly of departing from the road to Jerusalem should be explained to all. Quoting Isaiah 31. 1, Jacques de Vitry showed how futile it was to put one's trust in men.[76] The pilgrim should put his hope not in man, but in God, not in the courage of the multitude, but in the mercy of the Saviour.[77] Then, he reminded his audience, the pilgrim should be made to consider the labours and effort which had already been put into his pilgrimage. Returning to a theme used earlier in the sermon, he emphasised that the pilgrim had to be made to persevere on his chosen course. The pilgrim ought not to have wasted all the efforts he had already made by giving into some whim or carnal desire. It was only the senseless and mad who did so. Indeed, the foolishness of such people is well illustrated in this sermon, where they are compared to a farmer who toils all year in his field and then after harvesting his crops, sets fire to them.[78] Finally, Jacques de Vitry argued that the pilgrim had to be made to understand the futility of not accepting what the Lord had offered. The Lord saved mankind through the cross and it was the foolish who did not accept what he offered, remission of sins and entry to the celestial kingdom.[79] It was only the foolish traveller who bought a sack of chaff when he could have had a sack of corn for the same price or less.[80] Pilgrims ought, therefore, to consult the wise merchants, the archbishops, bishops, priests and scholars, for advice as to the best purchase.[81] Perhaps Jacques de Vitry sought to humour his audience here.

Many people, Jacques de Vitry explained, did not understand the profit to be gained from the undertaking of a pilgrimage. Such people were like those suffering from a fever, who mocked the doctor attending them. Once cured,

---

[76] MS Latin 3284, fol. 132v. Isaiah 31. 1: 'Woe to them that go down to Egypt for help trusting in horses and putting their confidence in chariots... and have not trusted in the Holy One of Israel and have not sought after the Lord.'
[77] MS Latin 3284, fol. 132v.
[78] MS Latin, fol. 133r.
[79] MS Latin, fol. 133v.
[80] MS Latin, fol. 133v.
[81] MS Latin 3284, fol. 133v.

however, they offered him thanks.[82] The pilgrim, therefore, had to suffer and undertake the hardships of this world if he was to rest in the next. If he was to taste the sweet fruit of the cross, Jacques de Vitry concluded, he had also to taste the bitterness of the root.[83]

Both of these sermons addressed to pilgrims illustrate the skills of Jacques de Vitry as a preacher which were frequently admired and praised by his contemporaries. Written against a background of popular enthusiasm for pilgrimage, the sermons may well have been inspired by the pilgrims Jacques de Vitry would have observed at different times in the course of his career, especially in the Holy Land and Rome. Criticism of pilgrimage and the way some pilgrims conducted themselves, as well as questions about the spiritual value of such journeys, had been growing during the twelfth century. These concerns were obviously shared by Jacques de Vitry, who insisted throughout these two sermons on the penitential nature of pilgrimage. It was not enough to set out with good intentions; the whole journey should be a time for atonement, suffering and hardship. Yet Jacques de Vitry's sermons show that he was not only concerned with the conduct of pilgrims making their way to some holy place. As befitted his role as bishop and cardinal, he was concerned with the spiritual welfare of all men. Taking up a theme found in the Scriptures and in the writings of the early Church Fathers, Jacques de Vitry developed extensively the idea that a journey to a holy place was the metaphor for man's life on earth. To achieve salvation man had to remain on the right path and it was the duty of the Church to ensure that every individual was properly equipped for his pilgrimage so that he did not stray from the road to the city of God and the reward of salvation which awaited him.

Acknowledgements I am most grateful to Miss Brenda Bolton, Professor Diana Greenway and Dr Philip de Souza for their comments on earlier versions of this paper.

---

[82] MS Latin 3284, fol. 133v.
[83] MS Latin 3284, fol. 133v.

6

The Medieval Experience at the Shrine

BEN NILSON

The great shrines of medieval cathedrals, and the pilgrims who attended them, are one of the clichés of historical accounts. They are often brought into a historical discussion to add colour, with many references to golden caskets, teeming throngs of unwashed pilgrims and fervent, sometimes fanatical, devotion. Surprisingly, this important medieval experience has rarely been described in full and that is the purpose of this paper.

A medieval shrine could be experienced in several ways: as an insider, from the privileged position of the clergy, or from the outside, as a pilgrim or tourist. This study will view the shrine through the eyes of pilgrims, examining their activities within the cathedral, but ignoring other important aspects of pilgrimage, such as the making of vows or the journey itself. The word shrine will be used to refer to the large monuments in English cathedrals or abbeys which held the remnants of saints. These monuments consisted of a stone base supporting an elaborate casket, or *feretrum*, the whole being contained (in the most prestigious cases) within a chapel behind the high altar. In English the casket, base or entire chapel could be called a feretory, and the cathedral officer in charge of the shrine was often called a feretrar. It is not known whether these larger shrines were more important in the devotions of pilgrims than smaller, more local ones. However, they are necessarily the focus of this study because information about them has survived through records kept by the cathedrals.

The most important sources for pilgrim activities are the accounts of miracles at the shrine, or *miracula*. These often have the advantage of being pilgrims' own stories (although seen through the filter of the clerical recorder) and thus provide a valuable insight into the mentality and behaviour of ordinary pilgrims. Nevertheless, the information these sources give about medieval pilgrim practices is small compared to the total quantity of hagiographic literature. *Miracula* are generally limited to the twelfth and thirteenth centuries, and are much more concerned with details of a malady and its miraculous cure than with how the pilgrim gave thanks at the shrine. Many other and very different types of document can shed light on pilgrim activities, three of the more useful being bishops' registers, church accounts and chronicles. Bishop's registers and chronicles begin for most cathedrals at the Conquest. Church accounts begin in the late twelfth century for Canterbury, and at later dates for other churches. Despite this variety of sources, the

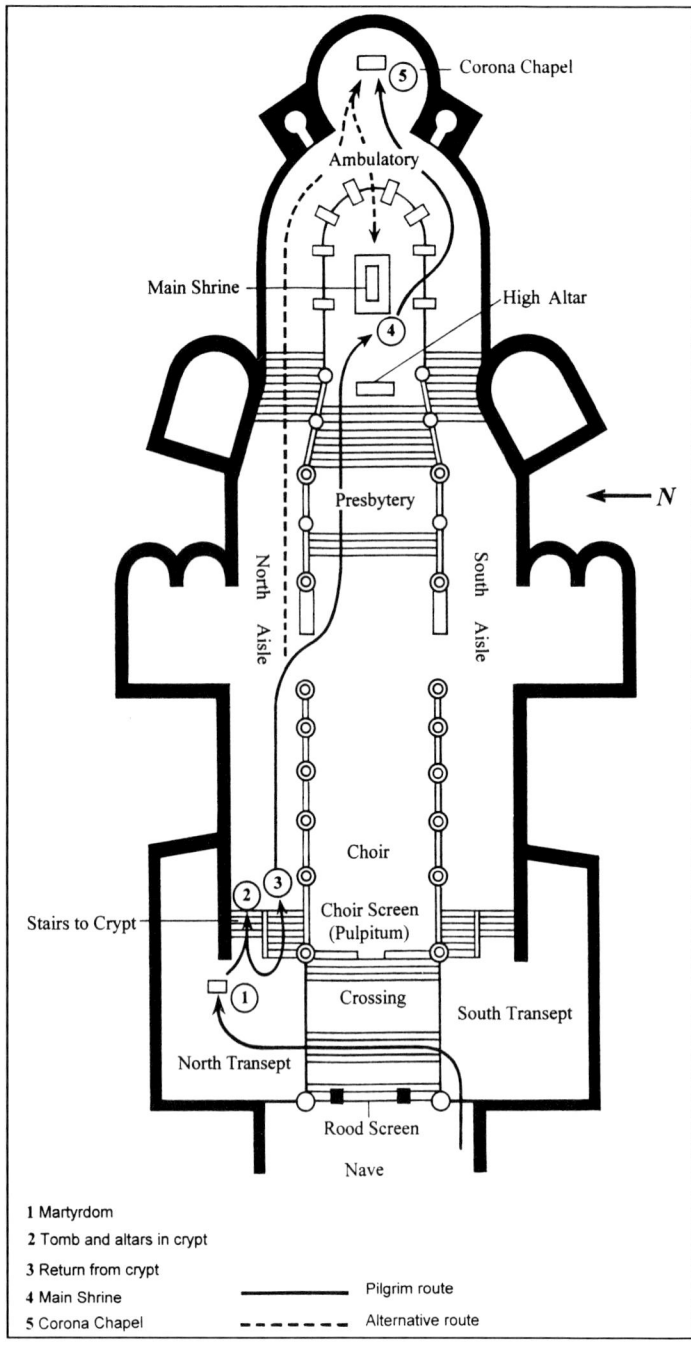

Fig. 1 The East End of Canterbury Cathedral.

amount of information contained in any one of them is small. References to shrines are a rarity. The medieval view seems to have been that everyone knew what happened at a shrine, and therefore it needed no description. For this reason a large number of sources must be consulted.

The Pilgrim at the Cathedral

When pilgrims arrived at a great English church, how did they get in? There is a tradition common to several cathedrals that pilgrims entered by way of a special door on the north side. T. D. Atkinson held that the north transept door at Ely was reserved for pilgrims, and perhaps was replaced later by doors in the north choir aisle.[1] It has also been assumed that pilgrims to Westminster and Winchester entered via doors in the north transepts.[2] In at least one case a door on the north side of a cathedral was named after the saint who was particularly venerated at that site: the north door of the nave at Winchester, located in the westernmost bay of the north aisle, is known as St Swithun's door, probably because it opens towards Swithun's original grave site.[3] Nevertheless, hard evidence that pilgrims entered any cathedral exclusively from the north, or from any other direction, is non-existent. One might expect pilgrims to be given a more impressive entry, through the large doors at the west end of the church, but perhaps their use was reserved for special occasions.

In any case, pilgrims probably entered the nave first, the only public part of the church, and the area where lay people could gather and perhaps take part in services. Admission to the nave was easy, since it was open during regular daylight hours. The sites of lesser and unofficial cults, such as miracle-working images, or tombs with saintly occupants like that of Archbishop Robert Winchelsey at Canterbury, were often in the nave. The most formidable obstacle separating pilgrims from the tomb-shrines in the nave would have been the iron grill or fence which surrounded most examples of this type of shrine, at least in the later Middle Ages. More popular tombs, like that of St William in York, had a clerk to watch over them and keep pilgrims at bay.

To visit a greater shrine the pilgrim needed to penetrate further into the church, passing a series of screens one by one and entering the domain largely reserved for the clergy. In the more important English churches there was a choir screen, usually of stonework of considerable height, separating the nave and choir. In monastic churches there was also a rood screen, one or more bays

---

[1] T. D. Atkinson, *An Architectural History of The Benedictine Monastery of Saint Etheldreda at Ely*, 2 vols. (Cambridge, 1933), I, 28.
[2] 'They would probably enter the north transept by the small doorway of the western aisle, which we may call the Pilgrims' doorway.' F. B. Bond, *Westminster Abbey* (London, 1909), p. 67. G. W. Kitchin claimed that pilgrims to St Swithun were not allowed in the choir, nave or south transept: *Compotus Rolls of the Obedientiaries of St Swithun's Priory, Winchester*, ed. G. W. Kitchin (London, 1892), p. 44.

further west (see Figure 1). The status of laymen beyond the choir screen is uncertain. There is some evidence that secular, or non-monastic, cathedrals allowed lay people limited access to choir services and to the choir aisles and altars.[4] Records of the secular canons at Lincoln state that on ordinary Sundays the presiding clerics should, after asperging the clerics (sprinkling them with holy water), do the same for the laity standing in the presbytery.[5] Benedictine cathedrals were more restrictive, and in theory laity were not allowed beyond the nave since the choir was technically part of the convent.[6] This prohibition must not have been rigidly followed, especially if there was a shrine somewhere beyond the rood screen. *Miracula* give the impression that shrines in monastic cathedrals were open at all times, as in the case of a man who spent a vigil at the shrine of Etheldreda, right behind the high altar of Ely Cathedral Priory, 'all night and day'.[7]

Monastic cathedrals certainly restricted the entrance of women to a greater degree than men. St Cuthbert's supposed aversion to women, and their resultant restriction to points west of a line drawn on the nave floor of Durham cathedral, is well known.[8] Presumably this denied women access to, and even a view of, the shrine of St Cuthbert far to the east. Yet eleven women are still

---

[3] C. R. Peers and H. Brakspear, 'Architectural Description of Winchester Cathedral', *Victoria County History: Hampshire and the Isle of Wight*, ed. W. Page, 5 vols. (Folkstone, 1912), V, 58.

[4] W. St J. Hope, 'Quire Screens in English Churches, with Special Reference to the Twelfth-Century Quire Screen Formerly in the Cathedral Church of Ely', *Archaeologia* 68 (1917), 44.

[5] *Ceremonies and Processions of the Cathedral Church of Salisbury*, ed. C. Wordsworth (Cambridge, 1901), p. 20: 'Post aspersionem clericorum, laicos in presbiterio hinc inde stantes aspergat.'

[6] H. Braun, *English Abbeys* (London, 1971), p. 97; Benedictine chapter statutes of 1444, for example, state that outsiders should not pass through any part of the convent and should be kept out during breakfast and dinner when the monks were absent: *Documents Illustrating the Activities of the General and Provincial Chapters of the English Black Monks, 1215–1540*, ed. W. A. Pantin, Camden Society 3rd Series 45, 47 and 54 (1931–7), II, 208.

[7] *Liber Eliensis*, ed. E. O. Blake, Camden Society 3rd Series 92 (1962), 306.

[8] Bishop Hugh made the chapel, 'in quo mulieberis licite fieret introitus; ut quæ non habebant ad secretiora sanctorum locorum corporalem accessum, aliquod haberent ex eorum contemplatione solatium': Geoffrey of Coldingham, in *Historiæ Dunelmensis Scriptores Tres*, ed. J. Raine, Publications of the Surtees Society 9 (London, 1839), 11. See also Reginald of Durham, *Reginaldi Monachi Dunelmensis Libellus de Admirandis Beati Cuthberti Virtutibus quae Novellis Patratae sunt Temporibus*, ed. J. Raine, Publications of the Surtees Society 1 (London, 1835), 152–3. H. Colgrave stated that 'The legendary dislike of women which was later attributed to [Cuthbert] belonged to the Norman period, when the belief in the inferiority and impurity of women caused admirers of the saint to bestow on him the fashionable prejudice.' H. Colgrave, *St Cuthbert of Durham* (Durham, 1947), p. 15. V. Tudor believed that the Benedictines introduced the belief shortly after their arrival in order to strengthen their position against the married clergy they replaced: V. Tudor, 'The Misogyny of St Cuthbert', *Archaeologia Aeliana* 5th Series 12 (1984), 158–64.

mentioned as givers of gifts to the shrine, and some are described as pilgrims, in a pair of shrine inventories from 1397 and 1401.[9] In 1300 the bishop of the monastic cathedral at Ely issued a statute banning female access to the cathedral choir (containing Etheldreda's shrine) except on special occasions.[10] This, of course, could be taken to suggest that women had been frequenting the choir freely before this time. A partition was ordered to be erected in the south choir aisle of the same cathedral 'lest frequent access of lay people, and especially women, hinder the contemplation of the monks'.[11]

Monastic views on the admission of women are further illustrated in a passage from the Chronicles of Meaux Abbey. Miracles apparently occurred after a rood, or crucifix, was placed in the convent's choir in 1339, upon which the Cistercian monks sought licence to admit women. After permission was granted, the chronicler complained that women often entered the monastery, yet their devotion was cool and they cost the abbey much in hospitality:

> It was then thought that if women had access to the said cross the devotion of the community would be augmented, and would redound with many advantages to our monastery. Concerning which the Abbot of the Cistercian Order, having been asked by us, gave us licence so that honest men and women could approach the said cross, although women would not be permitted to enter through the cloister and dormitory or other office, unless they were a foundatrix, wife or daughter [of a founder], or wife of a son of a founder; the which would also not be permitted either to stay over night within the limits of the abbey, nor to linger before prime or after compline. And also if we have them among us, then he will revoke the aforementioned licence. On account of this licence, to our misfortune, women often came to the said cross, but in them devotion is particularly cool and they came as much to get a look at the inside of the church, and our wealth was spent in their hospitality.[12]

The monks' hopes that admitting women would increase local devotion had not gone according to plan. In practice, women were probably granted much freer access to monastic shrines than the statutes ordained. Miracle stories in particular seem to show that women could come and go at all hours. For example, a very ill woman entered Reading Abbey while the monks were singing matins and writhed all night at the shrine before being healed by means of a bout of vomiting.[13] It should be remembered that the fact of its

---

[9] Durham Dean and Chapter Archives (hereafter DDCA), 'Feretrars' Rolls', 1397, 1401.
[10] *Ely Chapter Ordinances and Visitation Records, 1241–1515*, ed. S. J. A. Evans, in *Camden Miscellany* XVII, Camden Society 3rd Series 64 (1940), 11.
[11] *Ely Chapter Ordinances, op. cit.* note 10, p. 23: 'Ne frequens accessus secularium et maxime mulierum contemplationem impediat monachorum.'
[12] T. Burton, *Chronica Monasterii de Melsa*, ed. E. A. Bond, Rolls Series 43, 3 vols. (London, 1866–8), III, 35–6.
[13] 'The Miracles of the Hand of St James', ed. B. Kemp, *Berkshire Archaeological Journal* 65

being recorded in the *miracula* shows that this type of behaviour was not only tolerated but celebrated in at least some circles.

While the *miracula* suggest little regulation of pilgrims, fourteenth-century and later sources indicate that viewings of the shrine were more controlled. Access through the choir was generally organised under the supervision of the shrine-keeper, with his clerk or servants acting as guides. Erasmus, who visited Canterbury in the early sixteenth century, was given a personal tour by the prior, but such a high-ranking escort must have been a rare privilege. Shrines were generally closed during mass or when the guardians were obliged to be absent.[14] The opening of the shrine was announced through the church. At Durham this was by means of bells attached to the rope suspending the cover of the shrine which would ring when it was lifted.[15] At Ely the almonry schoolboys were given 3s. at the time of the fair to call pilgrims, while some Lincoln servants were paid out of shrine funds for 'arousing the people'.[16] Before the morning mass at the shrine of Thomas Becket one of the two shrine-keepers opened the doors of the church and rang a bell three times to tell pilgrims and travellers that the service was about to begin.[17] The Canterbury shrine was then closed for lunch, during which time the junior clerk was to attend to any pilgrims at 'the doors in the forward part of the church' (probably at the rood screen).[18] After noon the doors were again opened, and the keepers received pilgrims and ensured that all showed proper reverence.[19] In the *Tale of Beryn* (an anonymous fifteenth-century continuation of Chaucer's

---

(1970), 7. The situation was more pronounced in secular cathedrals. At Lincoln a group of matrons of the city appear to have been in the habit of holding vigils together at the tomb of St Hugh shortly after 1200: Giraldus Cambrensis, *Vita S. Remigii et Vita S. Hugonis*, in *Opera*, ed. J. F. Dimock, Rolls Series 21 (London, 1877), VII, 132–3.

[14] This may have been less true in the twelfth and thirteenth centuries. A pilgrim approached the shrine of St Cuthbert while Bishop Hugh Pudsey was saying mass at the high altar: Reginald of Durham, *Libellus de Admirandis Beati Cuthberti, op. cit.* note 8, p. 209.

[15] The bells were six, and of silver: *Rites of Durham, Being a Description or Brief Declaration of All the Ancient Monuments, Rites and Customs Belonging or Being within the Monastical Church of Durham before the Suppression*, ed. J. T. Fowler, Publications of the Surtees Society 107 (Durham, 1903), 4.

[16] At Ely, for example, in 1425/6, 'For four scholars' helping in the time of the fair, for calling pilgrims and minding wax – 2s.' Cambridge University Library, MS Ely Dean and Chapter (hereafter CUL, MS EDC) 5/12, Feretrar's Roll 4. At Lincoln, 'Duobus exitantibus populum .xij.d.', 'Capellano custodi inferiori excitandi populum sicut superius.' *Liber Niger, Statutes of Lincoln Cathedral*, ed. H. Bradshaw and C. Wordsworth, 2 vols. (Cambridge, 1892), I, 336–7.

[17] 'Customary of the Shrine of St Thomas', London, British Library, MS Additional 59616, fol. 1.

[18] 'Customary of the Shrine of St Thomas', BL MS Add. 59616, fol. 4.

[19] 'Customary of the Shrine of St Thomas', BL MS Add. 59616, fol. 2. The time after matins was apparently also the most popular time for pilgrims to assemble at the tomb of St Hugh: Giraldus Cambrensis, *Vita S. Hugonis, op. cit.* note 13, p. 133.

Canterbury Tales), the pilgrims headed to the church after arranging their lodging. At the church door a question of courtesy arose, which was settled by the Knight putting the Parson and Friar to the fore. Once in and aspersed by a monk, the Knight hurried to the shrine while the others stopped to gaze at stained glass windows.[20] In general, it appears that fourteenth-century and later pilgrims assembled in the nave and were summoned forward at an appropriate time. Of course, those of particularly high status could command the opening of the shrine at any time. At Durham, the clerk of the shrine was instructed to rush to the feretrar (shrine keeper) as soon as 'any man of honor or worshippe' wished to see the shrine. The feretrar then brought the keys and oversaw the clerk as he unlocked and uncovered the shrine.[21]

Important shrines were usually in a chapel behind the high altar, surrounded by stone screens or iron fencing. Since most feretory chapels were limited in space, pilgrims would have had to file in one entrance and out the other in order to view the various relics and marvels, all the while under the supervision of the clerk. Alternatively, they might have been marshalled in groups, each one consecutively assembled before the shrine and given a dissertation, much as with modern tours and as seems to have been the case when Erasmus toured Canterbury (see below). Indeed, the only time the sacrist of Westminster Abbey was supposedly allowed to speak in church was to draw a layman's attention to relics.[22] In summary, *miracula* suggest frenetic activity around shrines that were relatively free of access in the twelfth and thirteenth centuries. Later and more worldly sources suggest a sober and controlled atmosphere in the fourteenth and fifteenth centuries.

The route that pilgrims took from the nave to a shrine behind the high altar doubtless varied from church to church. The most probable path involved passing through the choir and/or rood screens, going through the crossing, and then moving down the north or south choir aisle before entering the shrine-chapel from the side. More information on the route taken by pilgrims has survived for Canterbury than for anywhere else.[23] The path taken by dignitaries and monks for their offerings at the 1420 Jubilee was probably typical and is shown in Figure 1: they went first to the Martyrdom (a shrine set up on the spot where Thomas Becket was murdered) in the north transept, then to his empty tomb and the altar of St Mary in the crypt. They returned to

---

20 *The Tale of Beryn*, ed. F. J. Furnivall and W. G. Stone (London, 1887), pp. 5–6.
21 *Rites of Durham*, op. cit. note 15, p. 94.
22 H. F. Westlake, *Westminster Abbey*, 2 vols. (London, 1923), II, 291: no original source cited.
23 There are minor clues from various sources. For example, A. Klukas, from an analysis of the *Decreta Lanfranci*, has posited that eleventh-century pilgrims entered the cathedral by the west door, passed through gates in the aisle south of the rood and choir screens, and then moved down to the crypt by way of axial stairways situated just before the presbytery: A. W. Klukas, 'The Architectural Implications of the *Decreta Lanfranci*', *Anglo-Norman Studies* 6 (Woodbridge, 1984), 148.

the transept and passed through the choir, moving progressively further east, visiting the high altar and the main shrine to the saint before arriving at the far east end, the Corona Chapel, where another shrine held the severed top of Thomas' skull. Finally, they returned to the presbytery to visit the relics and the tombs of SS Alphege, Blaise and Dunstan.[24] This was probably a more convoluted route than that at many churches due to the number of separate sites that functioned as shrines to St Thomas (the Martyrdom, the tomb in the crypt, the Corona Chapel and the main shrine right behind the high altar).

The route taken through Canterbury Cathedral by Erasmus in the early sixteenth century is also illustrative. He left the nave by doors in the south aisle then passed through the tunnel under the choir steps to the Martyrdom in the north transept. From there he took the stairs to the crypt before ascending to the choir where he visited the high altar, Corona Chapel and the main shrine of St Thomas. Finally, he descended into the crypt for a second time to see the altar of St Mary in the undercroft.[25] While Erasmus was by no means a typical pilgrim, the main pattern of his visit was probably similar to the standard tour. Pilgrims began in the nave and made their way to the closest shrine; in this case the Martyrdom in the north transept. Next, they descended the nearby steps to the crypt, re-ascended and probably either passed beside the high altar or took the north choir aisle and ambulatory to the Corona and then the main shrine. In the late fourteenth century, Prior Chillendon rebuilt 'the rooms of the three petty sacristans which at that time were in the north aisle of the Church, obstructing in very unseemly fashion the way, that is to say the passage leading to the shrine of St Thomas'.[26] This suggests that pilgrims usually moved down the north aisle, or at least tried to. In most other churches the existing evidence, if there is any, also seems to support a route for pilgrims down the north rather than south choir aisle. Architectural remains at Norwich, for example, show that the south choir aisle was effectively blocked by a number of chapels.[27]

Once the area behind the high altar was reached, entrance into the feretory chapel itself depended on its precise situation. A shrine in a retrochoir (an extension of the cathedral to the east of the high altar), especially one at or near the height of the surrounding aisles, was most easily entered through a gate in

---

[24] Contained in the treatise on the jubilee, printed in R. Foreville, *Le Jubilé de Saint Thomas Becket* (Paris, 1958), pp. 140–1.

[25] Desiderius Erasmus, *Pilgrimages to Saint Mary of Walsingham and Saint Thomas of Canterbury*, trans. J. G. Nichols, 2nd edition (London, 1875), pp. 42–50.

[26] 'A Monastic Chronicle Lately Discovered at Christ Church, Canterbury, with Introduction and Notes', ed. C. E. Woodruff, *Archaeologia Cantiana* 29 (1911), 62 and 65: 'Et cameras trium parvorum sacristarum, que tunc in ala boriali ecclesie in via viz. qua itur ad fferetrum Sci Thome multum inhoneste dictum viam accloyantes.'

[27] W. H. St J. Hope and W. T. Bensly, 'Recent Discoveries in the Cathedral Church of Norwich', *Norfolk Archaeology* 14 (1901), 111: 'From the cuts in the walls it is clear that the aisle was crossed by a number of screens.'

The Medieval Experience at the Shrine

the encircling fence or screen. This was certainly the case at Ely, where an iron grating around the shrine was penetrated by a door to the north.[28] The grate around the shrine of St Erkenwald at St Paul's cathedral also had locking doors which, if a representation in Dugdale is correct, were on the east side.[29] If the shrine-chapel was raised on a platform above the level of the ambulatory (a common enough arrangement) then steps of some sort would be needed. The shrine platform at Chichester, for example, was apparently reached by a flight of stairs to either side of the platform.[30]

In a few instances the barriers around shrines suggest that they were approached by way of the presbytery, passing immediately to one side of the high altar. A view of Canterbury's choir, painted in 1657, shows clear abrasions in the pavement at the position of the two doors in the missing reredos (screen behind the altar), possibly caused by pilgrims going to and from the shrine.[31] These pathways are to either side of the original altar position. At York, after renovations in 1472, the shrine was almost certainly approached only by going past the high altar.[32] A 1728 plan by B. Willis, the earliest information we have for Durham, does not show any steps to the north or south of the feretory platform.[33] It is probable that medieval access in these instances was restricted to the two doors in the altar screen.[34] Perhaps a shrine was made holier because it was only accessible by passing the high altar. This would accentuate the *sanctum sanctorum* aspect of later shrines and give the process of entry an added degree of solemnity. This necessitated the closure of shrines during mass but, as we shall see, this was probably the case anyway.

---

[28] The sacrist roll for 1349/50 mentions a door in the feretory fence at Ely: 'Item in j pare garnet pro le Wyket versus feretrum.' E. M. Hampson and T. D. Atkinson, 'The City of Ely', in *Victoria County History: Cambridge and the Isle of Ely*, ed. R. B. Pugh (London, 1953), IV, 70 ('Garnet' is given as a hinge on p. 70, n. 15). Also an undated feretrar's roll which places his chamber 'opposito hostii feretri S. Ethaldr' ex parte boreali'. Note that the latter (CUL, MS EDC 5/12/6) is not a regular feretrar's account but appears to be a fabric roll for that officer's various tenements and buildings.

[29] W. Dugdale, *The History of St Paul's Cathedral in London from its Foundation*, 2nd edition (London, 1716), p. 114.

[30] 'The Early Statutes of the Cathedral Church of the Holy Trinity, Chichester, with Observations on its Constitution and History', ed. M. E. C. Walcott, *Archaeologia* 45 (1877), 173.

[31] W. D. Caröe, 'Canterbury Cathedral Choir during the Commonwealth and After, with Special Reference to Two Oil Paintings', *Archaeologia* 62/2 (1911), 359.

[32] C. Wilson, *The Shrines of St William of York* (York, 1977), pp. 19–20.

[33] B. Willis, *A Survey of the Cathedrals of York, Durham, Carlisle, Chester, Man, Lichfield, Hereford, Worcester, Gloucester and Bristol* (London, 1727), p. 223.

[34] There are examples of this means of access from outside England as well. At St Andrews, after the reconstruction sometime prior to 1443, the shrine was reached by going through the reredos doors. D. McRoberts, 'The Glorious House of St Andrew', in *The Medieval Church of St Andrews*, ed. D. McRoberts (Glasgow, 1976), p. 67.

The Pilgrim's Devotions

The object of pilgrimage was to adore the saint, and the pilgrim's goal was to get as close to the relics as possible. By the later Middle Ages, the only tangible part of the shrine was the stone monument that served as a base for the golden reliquary. Pilgrims caressed, kissed and pressed against the stonework, sometimes prying or scraping pieces off for use in healing potions.[35] Without exception, shrine bases were provided with niches in which pilgrims could kneel, an accommodation toward an apparant desire to be virtually *inside* the shrine.

Whether ensconced in a niche or gazing up at the golden chest, the pilgrim prayed to the saint for intercession or thanked him or her for help already given. In the prologue to the *Tale of Beryn* the pilgrims knelt before the shrine and prayed.[36] In the *miracula* stories some pilgrims appear to have given very brief thanks while others remained for days: one blind woman stayed near the tomb of St Hugh of Lincoln for a year.[37] Yet, the shrine was more than just a convenient spot to honour the powers of a saint. It was also a space to experience that power, a holy place where miraculous healings took place. Some pilgrims came to the shrine specifically to be healed. Perhaps the most common method of accomplishing this was through the process familiar to all pilgrims of praying, offering and departing in hope. This method did not really make use of the numinous qualities of a shrine, but rather expected help through the saint's intercession with God. However, it was also believed that intimate contact with a shrine or its objects could bring about healing of a more thaumaturgic or miraculous nature. For example, touching one's head to the place of the first burial of St Etheldreda was said to cure maladies of the eyes.[38]

The offering, particularly if it was of a votive nature (made in fulfilment of a vow), was crucial to any miracle of healing. A vivid illustration of the variety and number of votive objects can be seen in an inventory of the non-monetary

---

[35] Scrapings from the tomb of St William of Norwich were reportedly a commonly used cure, see Thomas of Monmouth, *The Life and Miracles of St William of Norwich*, ed. A. Jessopp and M. R. James (Cambridge, 1896), miracles on pp. 135–6, 150, 162 and 190. Dust scraped with a knife from the mortar of the tomb of St Hugh was used as a healing plaster: Giraldus Cambrensis, *Vita S. Hugonis, op. cit.* note 13, p. 141. At York a piece of the tomb of St William, broken off by a man to take home for his sick wife, turned into bread while crossing Ousebridge: *Miracula Sancti Willelmi*, in *Historians of the Church of York and Its Archbishops*, ed. J. Raine, Rolls Series 71, 3 vols. (London, 1879–94), II, 539.

[36] *Tale of Beryn, op. cit.* note 20, p. 6.

[37] Giraldus Cambrensis, *Vita S. Hugonis, op. cit.* note 13, p. 139.

[38] Richard of Cirencester, *Speculum Historiale de Gestis Regum Angliæ*, ed. J. E. B. Mayor, 2 vols., Rolls Series 30 (London, 1863 and 1869) I, 209: 'Qui cum suum caput eidem loculo apponentes orassent, mox doloris sive caliginis incommodum ab oculis amoverunt.'

offerings collected at the shrine-tomb of Thomas Cantilupe at Hereford. Made in 1307 by the commissioners investigating Thomas' canonisation, the inventory's contents include:

170 ships in silver and 41 in wax
129 images of men or their limbs in silver, 1424 in wax
77 images of animals and birds of diverse species
108 crutches
3 vehicles in wood and 1 in wax, left by cured cripples
97 night-gowns
116 gold and silver rings and brooches
38 garments of gold thread and silk[39]

The number of wax eyes, breasts and ears could not be counted in their 'multitude', yet investigators were told that the wax offerings on view were only a small fraction of the total, the rest having been sold or having deteriorated with age.[40] Two similar lists exist for the tomb of Richard Scrope in York Minster, which attracted a short but intense cult in the early fifteenth century. These included whole bodies, heads, limbs and other assorted body parts, rings, crosses, buckles, anchors, oars, belts, sheep, ships, bulls, arrows, and horses, all of silver.[41]

The type of object left was symbolic of the miracle sought. The night-gowns mentioned at Hereford, for example, were given by formerly infertile women who had been granted a child.[42] Unneeded crutches were often left at shrines, such as those found when the shrine of St Mary at Caversham was pulled down in 1538.[43] A gift could also be left in the hope of a cure not yet worked, usually in the form of a wax image of whatever needed the miraculous attentions of the saint. As we have seen at Hereford, limbs, eyes and whole figures of people were common.[44]

The tale of John Combe, recorded in 1414, can be taken as a case study. During a sporting dispute he was struck with a large stick so that his head was broken open and his shoulder blade smashed. Made deaf and blind, he had been bedridden for three months when he had a vision of a man in shining white who told him to make a head and shoulders of wax and give them the same wounds as his, then go to the tomb of Bishop Osmund at Salisbury where

---

[39] *AASS*, Oct., I, 594–5.
[40] Some offerings were collected even as the commissioners counted them, including eighty-five of wax and one of silver: *AASS*, Oct., I, 594–5.
[41] *Historians of the Church of York*, op. cit. note 35, III, 389–90.
[42] *AASS*, Oct., I, 595.
[43] In a letter to Cromwell Dr London reported: 'I have also pullyd down the place sche stode in, with all other ceremonyes, as lightes, schrowdes, crowchys, and imagies of wex, hangyng abowt the chapell.' *Three Chapters of Letters Relating to the Suppression of Monasteries*, ed. T. Wright, Camden Society Old Series 26 (1843), 221.
[44] For a general discussion of votives see R. C. Finucane, *Miracles and Pilgrims: Popular Beliefs in Medieval England* (London, 1977), pp. 96–9.

he was to pray and offer the image. Combe obeyed the instructions and was cured.[45] Such methods were not limited to the lower classes. Edward I employed the same type of cure for his gerfalcons, an image of one of the birds being offered at the shrine of St Thomas.[46] Wax images were generally left on the shrine or its altar, or hung from a beam. At Richard Scrope's tomb the offerings seem to have been either hung on rods labelled A to F, or attached to three cloths hanging nearby.[47] Some votive images offered to the tomb of Bishop Edmund Lacy at Exeter were found walled into a screen. All were made in moulds and show signs of having been hung by wick-like threads.[48]

Offerings of a candle were more common even than images, and are often mentioned in *miracula* and other records, sometimes being made to match the proportions of an invalid in some way.[49] A typical example of such descriptions is the order of one man that 'a candle be made to his measure in length and width'.[50] For Hereford we are lucky to have the personal account of a devotee of St Thomas Cantilupe in 1307. Hugh le Barber, who had been barber to Thomas, appealed to his deceased master when his eyesight left him in old age, sending two wax eyes to Hereford, twice making and sending his measurements (presumably converted into wax) and finally going there on pilgrimage. With each donation his eyesight improved until he was able to play chess and read the pips on dice.[51]

The details of how 'measuring' was carried out are not absolutely clear, but the practice has implications for the size of candles at shrines.[52] If the descriptions are literally correct, then there were candles over five feet tall around shrines, which seems unlikely. In an extreme example, a man surrounded his sick oxen with a thread and offered a candle 'to the measure of the thread' to the tomb of St William of Norwich.[53] Obviously, the candle was not the width or length of a group of oxen. Normally, the measuring threads were used as

---

[45] *The Canonization of Saint Osmund*, ed. A. R. Malden (Salisbury, 1901), pp. 171–2.
[46] At a cost of 4s. 8d. (in addition to 4d. in monetary offering): *Records of the Wardrobe and Household, 1285–1286*, ed. B. F. Byerly and C. R. Byerly (London, 1977), no. 368, p. 2239.
[47] *Historians of the Church of York, op. cit.* note 35, III, 389–90.
[48] U. M. Radford, 'Wax Images Found in Exeter Cathedral', *Antiquaries Journal* 29 (1929), 164.
[49] For a fuller description of this practice see Finucane 1977, *op. cit.* note 44, pp. 95–6.
[50] Thomas of Monmouth, *Life of St William, op. cit.* note 35, p. 210.
[51] See the testimony of Hugh in E. M. Jancey, 'A Servant Speaks of his Master: Hugh le Barber's Evidence in 1307', in *St Thomas Cantilupe, Bishop of Hereford: Essays in his Honour*, ed. M. Jancey (Hereford, 1982), pp. 200–1.
[52] See discussion in J. Fowler, 'On a Window Representing the Life and Miracles of S. William of York, at the North End of the Eastern Transept, York Minster', *Yorkshire Archaeological and Topographical Journal* 3 (1875), 304–6. In one example the candle is made to the length of the saint's tomb: Thomas of Monmouth, *Life of St William, op. cit.* note 35, p. 151.
[53] Thomas of Monmouth, *Life of St William, op. cit.* note 35, pp. 153–4.

wicks, usually doubled back upon themselves.[54] A candle offered to the shrine of St Cuthbert was made of sixty-six folded threads.[55] Another option was to make the candle very thin and coil it in upon itself until it formed a roll. Candles of this type may be depicted on St Thomas's tomb in stained glass windows at Canterbury.[56] An unusual offering, taking this practice to an extreme, was the 'candela in rota', a taper wound around a drum which was donated to the shrine of St Thomas at Canterbury and renewed each year by the city of Dover 'which contained in its length the circuit or border of the said city'.[57] This candle was lit during the mass of St Thomas and on other occasions of note in the shrine-chapel, and lengths were cut from it to supply tapers for the funerals of Canterbury paupers.

On occasion a candle or image was said to be of the same weight as an invalid. In 1443, for example, some wax images made to the weight of John Paston were sent to Walsingham by his mother-in-law when he was ill.[58] This type of offering would have been affordable only for the wealthy. Most cathedrals paid about 6d. per pound for wax, at which rate an image or candle made to the weight of a man would have cost over £4. Nevertheless, we can be certain that candles approaching this weight were occasionally made. Henry, duke of Lancaster, willed that his funeral should be 'nothing vain or extravagant' yet should include five candles weighing one hundred pounds each.[59]

While the exact nature of these offerings remains a mystery, their use is clear; both wax images and measured candles had very potent symbolic and magical aspects. It is possible that burning the offering was symbolically equated with the disappearance of the disease.[60] Certainly, sympathetic magic using wax images could be employed in other contexts to curse or harm as well as heal.[61]

If healing did not happen instantaneously, then a sick pilgrim was usually prepared to remain within the holy emanations of the shrine as long as

---

54 'The normal practice was to use the measuring thread (sometimes doubled back on itself) to form the wick of a candle of standard proportions; or alternatively to coat it thinly with wax and twist it into a "trindle", a coil shaped like a Catherine wheel': 'Miracles of St Osmund', ed. D. Stroud, *Hatcher Review* 23 (1987), 112–13. See also Finucane 1977, *op. cit.* note 44, p. 95.
55 Reginald of Durham, *Libellus de Admirandis Beati Cuthberti, op. cit.* note 8, p. 134.
56 See plates XIV and XV in M. D. Anderson, *A Saint at Stake* (London, 1964).
57 'Customary of the Shrine of St Thomas', BL MS Add. 59616, fol. 9.
58 *Paston Letters and Papers of the Fifteenth Century*, ed. N. Davis, 2 vols. (Oxford, 1971), I, 218: 'My moder hat be-hestyd a-noder ymmage of wax of [th]e weytte of yow to Oyur Lady of Walsyngham.'
59 *A Collection of All the Wills, Now Known to be Extant, of the Kings and Queens of England*, ed. J. Nichols (London, 1780), p. 84.
60 Anderson 1964, *op. cit.* note 56, p. 188.
61 See C. Hole, 'Some Instances of Image-Magic in Great Britain', in *The Witch Figure*, ed. V. Newall (London, 1973), pp. 83–8. For contintental examples and a general discussion of candles used in the cult of saints, see D. R. Dendy, *The Use of Lights in Christian Worship* (London, 1959), pp. 108–19.

permitted. Vigils at the shrine extended into lengthy residences and could lead to the permanent presence of pilgrims day and night, in monastic as well as secular churches. Churches employed night watchmen and their posts were often at or near the shrine.[62] Pilgrims, nestled in the niches and holes of the shrine base, often (according to the *miracula*) received healing visions in their sleep. The mentally deranged had to be chained to the shrine by well-wishers and relatives. What effect a screaming, chain-rattling demoniac had on the other pilgrims, or indeed on the services at the nearby high altar, is worth wondering.[63]

If pilgrims were not healed by their own efforts at the shrine then they could resort to other relics presented by the cathedral clergy for that purpose. Water, most famously that of St Thomas Becket, was used as a healing potion, as was the oil which occasionally flowed from tombs. The oil which came from the tomb of St William of York, for example, cured several pilgrims in the early fourteenth century.[64] A miracle was treated as a great event: a woman whose cure at Lincoln was judged to be a true miracle was led in procession to the tomb of St Hugh.[65]

By no means all offerings were votive. An offering was an indispensable part of any pilgrimage regardless of whether or not a miracle was sought. Although probably not mandatory, later shrine-keepers exerted considerable pressure on visitors to pay. At Walsingham Erasmus noted that a priest stood and watched and, although no force was employed, he believed that 'a kind of pious shame' caused some to give more than they otherwise would.[66] One standard type of gift was a wax candle or taper similar to those seen in some saints' shrines today. These were sometimes on sale to pilgrims in the cathedral; the revenue from candles given to the relics at Ely, for example, was recorded by the shrine keeper.[67] Wax was fairly expensive at about 6d. per pound, partly due to a preference for costly bees' wax, which was fragrant and was given mystic significance by the death of the bee during its labour.[68] The

---

[62] The waiting pilgrims' constant presence 'made it necessary for the monastic wardens of the shrine to sleep alongside of their charge': D. Knowles, *The Monastic Order in England*, 2nd edition (Cambridge, 1963), p. 481. He cites miracle stories including that of a soldier, cured during a vigil, who woke up the monks there, in *Memorials of St Edmund's Abbey*, ed. T. Arnold, 3 vols., Rolls Series 96 (London, 1890), I, 78.

[63] A demoniac who was not chained down tore off his clothes and terrified other worshippers at the tomb of St William: Thomas of Monmouth, *Life of St William, op. cit.* note 35, p. 225. Another was chained at the tomb of St Hugh for a week: Giraldus Cambrensis, *Vita S. Hugonis, op. cit.* note 13, p. 127.

[64] *Miracula Sancti Willelmi*, in *Historians of the Church of York, op. cit.* note 35, II, 282, 284 and 537–40.

[65] Giraldus Cambrensis, *Vita S. Hugonis, op. cit.* note 13, p. 126.

[66] Erasmus, *Pilgrimages to Saint Mary and Saint Thomas, op. cit.* note 25, pp. 14–15.

[67] For example, the Feretrar's roll for 1422/3: CUL, MS EDC 5/12, Feretrar's Roll 1.

[68] Anderson 1964, *op. cit.* note 56, p. 184; Prior William More, for example, spent 13d. on

Plate 1 Detail of window from York Minster showing the life and miracles of St William of York. A man offers a model of a leg and foot at the shrine. Other offerings hang from a rail.

volume of costly candles and wax votive offerings both deposited and burnt at shrines made wax a sort of currency, with the accountants sometimes making two accounts: one for money and one for wax.

Offerings in money were the most common and best recorded. In the twelfth and thirteenth centuries it was probably usual to place coins directly on the altar or shrine top, and in some places this continued at later dates. The early fifteenth-century 'Customary of the Shrine of St Thomas' advises that the paraphernalia for mass be tidied up promptly so that pilgrims could give their offerings.[69] In most instances, however, one or more strong boxes, or 'pyxes', were eventually used. By the fifteenth century the usual description of money from an offering site, for example, was 'from the pyx'.[70] Canterbury Cathedral had many such pyxes besides those connected with St Thomas; the Sacrist's

---

renewing two tapers at St Wulfstan's shrine in 1528: Worcester Cathedral Archives, 'Prior William More's Journal', fol. 106.
69 'Customary of the Shrine of St Thomas', BL MS Add. 59616, fols. 1–2.
70 'De Pyxide', for example DDCA, Feretrar's roll 1381–2.

rolls of the late fifteenth century mention boxes in the nave and crypt, at SS Sythe and Appollonia, and the shrines of SS Dunstan and Alphege.[71] Iron bound and provided with coin slots and locks, a pyx had an obvious advantage for security over offerings left on an altar. It might even be fixed in place, as was the iron box attached to the pillar below the image of the Virgin in the nave of St Paul's.[72] The chests and their keys were frequent items of expense in the shrine accounts. At Canterbury, for example, 4d. was paid towards making a pyx in the crypt in 1487/8.[73] Those in great shrines might be more than plain oak and iron: a 1520 relic list from Westminster Abbey includes 'a lytle box of sylver enamelyd to putt in the offryng money'.[74]

Cathedral accounts occasionally tell us of the types of coins, sometimes rare, sometimes illegal, used by pilgrims. In the Durham accounts of the early fifteenth century we see Scottish and foreign money, even after the former was banned from England in 1423.[75] A form of receipt appearing in several shrine accounts over a long range of time is 'broken money' (or more rarely 'broken silver'). In 1423/4, for example, the Worcester sacrist received 'for broken silver sold 13s. 4d.'[76] Broken money or silver could be one of, or a combination of, three things. Firstly, it could represent the remains of coins halved or quartered to make small change, and so damaged or cut that they were no longer passable currency.[77] Secondly, it might signify coins that had been bent or folded to dedicate them to a saint, a reasonably common practice.[78] This or similar mutilation, such as piercing holes in a coin, could accompany a vow of pilgrimage and so ensure that the promised money was not spent before it was offered.[79] Thirdly, 'broken silver' could represent silver gifts or shrine paraphernalia that were not fine or whole enough to preserve at the shrine or sell as

---

[71] CCA, MS DCc/MA 7, fols. 36r, 69 and 92r among other references.
[72] Dugdale, *St Paul's, op. cit.* note 29, p. 21.
[73] CCA, MS DCc/MA 7, fol. 69.
[74] Westlake 1953, *op. cit.* note 22, II, 500. All the offering pyxes that survive (universally from the fifteenth century and none known to have been from a shrine) are of oak, except one of iron at St George's chapel, Windsor; J. C. Cox and A. Harvey, *English Church Furniture* (London, 1907), p. 240.
[75] This income appeared from 1417/18 to 1431/2. In 1418/19 it was worth 27s. 9d. J. Raine, *St Cuthbert, With an Account of the State in Which his Remains were Found Upon the Opening of his Tomb in Durham Cathedral, in the Year MDCCCXXVII* (Durham, 1828), p. 148, n. †.
[76] *Compotus Rolls of the Priory of Worcester of the XIVth and XVth Centuries*, trans. S. G. Hamilton (Oxford, 1910), p. 64.
[77] Raine 1828, *op. cit.* note 75, p. 149, n. †.
[78] See R. C. Finucane, 'The Use and Abuse of Medieval Miracles', *History* 1.198 (1975), 1, n. 5; Finucane 1977, *op. cit.* note 44, pp. 94–5. For an example, see Reginald of Durham, *Libellus de Admirandis Beati Cuthberti, op. cit.* note 8, p. 231.
[79] E. Duffy, *The Stripping of the Altars: Traditional Religion in England, c. 1400–c. 1580* (London, 1992), pp. 183–4.

an item.[80] In each of these cases the silver would no longer be usable in its original form and would have to be sold by weight.

Gold coins were another variant and a somewhat rare offering. Before they came to be commonly circulated in medieval England they were generally reserved for shrine offerings. P. Spufford has written:

> Just as in France, a certain amount of gold coin was available in England in the mid-thirteenth century, and, as in France, it was treated as a commodity and not yet as a part of the currency. Instead it was used for such strictly uncommercial purposes as prestigious alms-giving by the king. Those gold coins that were used as royal alms at once ceased even to be objects of commerce. They were given on the great festivals of the Church and ended up, along with similar offerings by other great men, in the treasuries of monasteries and cathedrals, or attached to shrines, such as that of St Thomas of Canterbury, or those of St Lawrence and St Ethelbert in London. They remained there until they were melted down and turned into ornamental goldsmith's work.[81]

In a record of 1171, some had found their way from Muslim Spain to the shrine of St Lawrence in London.[82] Gold coins of Arabic origin were called 'obols of musca'; a later medieval example being the £12 collected at Westminster over the six years before 1476.[83] D. A. Carpenter has argued convincingly that the, mainly Arabic, gold coins acquired by the wardrobe under Henry III were at first only intended to fund royal offerings.[84]

When gold coins became part of English currency, in the middle of the fifteenth century, they began to be recorded in the financial accounts. In 1456, for example, a chest of St Osmund contained 37s. 4d. in gold, £9 in groats (silver coins), £2 in half groats and £6 6s. 8d. in pennies (these proportions are not necessarily the same as those received at the shrine since larger and more valuable coins were no doubt preferentially retained).[85] The Lincoln records of the fifteenth and early sixteenth centuries occasionally have separate reckonings for gold in the possession of the shrine, including florins, angels and

---

[80] At Durham in 1433/4 some silver spoons were sold at the same time as broken money and to the same person, although they were different enough to deserve separate mention: 'Et de 25s. rec. de Thome Nesbytt pro fracta pecunia et duobus coclearibus.' DDCA, Feretrar's Roll 1433–4.
[81] P. Spufford, *Money and its Use in Medieval Europe* (Cambridge, 1988), p. 183.
[82] Spufford 1988, *op. cit.* note 81, p. 185.
[83] Westminster Abbey Muniments (hereafter WAM), MS 19723.
[84] 'The story of Henry III's gold treasure begins on his return from Gascony in September 1243. Before that, the Wardrobe only acquired gold to fund the king's pious oblations.' D. A. Carpenter, 'The Gold Treasure of Henry III', in *Thirteenth Century England I*, ed. P. R. Coss and S. D. Lloyd (Woodbridge, 1986), p. 62; see also p. 71.
[85] *Canonization of St Osmund*, *op. cit.* note 45, p. 174.

Portugese cruzados.[86] The same coin can sometimes be followed through several accounts. A particularly long-lasting example was the 10s. double cruzado which survived five accounts.[87] The adoption of gold coins as real currency did not stop their traditional use as a royal gift. In 1485 the keeper of the shrine of St Hugh had in his possession 'a certain gold noble attached by king Richard III of England on the head of St Hugh'.[88]

The most valuable of offerings were gifts of jewellery, among which rings played a special role. In 1441, for example, the widow Joan Denys willed to the shrine of St Thomas her profession ring and to the shrine of St Augustine her wedding ring.[89] Bishops seem to have been partial to willing their pontifical rings to shrines. In 1436 Bishop Robert Fitzhugh left his pontifical ring 'to be fixed on the shrine of St Erkenwald and there to remain in perpetuity'.[90] Rings and other jewellery were frequently fixed directly to the surface of a shrine, and sometimes even placed inside. A Lichfield inventory of 1345 states that there was 'Also one morse of pure gold and two gold rings, which were offered that they may be placed in the shrine of St Chad, by Dan Thomas de Berkeley and his wife, and one other (ring), as catalogued above, replaced in the coffer; and Richard, the Sacrist, now says that they are in the shrine of St Chad'.[91]

Gifts in kind to shrines are rarely mentioned in the documents, but do continue until late in the Middle Ages. At Hereford Cathedral in 1490/1 8s. were received as the price of an ox given to the shrine and sold.[92] The *Valor Ecclesiasticus* records £6 6s. received in one year for wool given to St Kenelm at Winchlecombe.[93] Other, rarer offerings might be in the same category. For example, gifts from shipwreck survivors to St John of Beverley included a silk cloth, possibly part of a rescued cargo.[94]

---

[86] For example, 1341: Lincoln County Archive, Dean and Chapter (hereafter LCA, D&C), Bj/5/16/1, fol. 50; The last mentioned coins, 'crusidors', were probably Portuguese *cruzados*, minted after 1457 from African gold obtained by Henry the Navigator. Portugal was, at that time, the most important source of gold for England: Spufford 1988, *op. cit.* note 81, pp. 321–2 and 370.

[87] LCA D&C Bj/5/16/2b, fols. 6–7.

[88] LCA D&C Bj/5/16/1, fol. 36.

[89] 'Some Early Kentish Wills', ed. C. E. Woodruff, *Archaeologia Cantiana* 46 (1934), 34.

[90] *Registrum Statutorum et Consuetudinum Ecclesiae Cathedralis Sancti Pauli Londiniensis*, ed. W. S. Simpson (London, 1873), p. 398: 'Quem super Capsam Sancti Erkenwaldi figi et ibidem remanare in perpetuum volo.'

[91] The entry concludes that 'it is well to enquire of John, his predecessor, as to the truth of this': 'Sacrist's Roll of Lichfield Cathedral Church, AD 1345', ed. J. C. Cox, *Collections for a History of Staffordshire* 6/2 (1886), appendix 1, 208–9.

[92] 'Clavigers' Accounts', Hereford Cathedral Archive, MS R585, fol. 22.

[93] *Valor Ecclesiasticus, Tempore Henrici VIII*, ed. J. Caley, 6 vols. (London, 1814), II, 461.

[94] *Miracula Sancti Johannis, Eboracensis Episcopi*, in *Historians of the Church of York, op. cit.* note 35, I, 319–20.

Other Activities

Pilgrims could avail themselves of various services in the cathedral. The most important of these were masses, often performed at the shrine altar. One of the two Canterbury shrine-keepers, called the spiritual feretrarian, was dedicated to performing mass at the shrine of St Thomas.[95] Sometimes specific chantries (an endowment for a priest to sing masses) were set up at a shrine. For example, there were chantries organised at both the head shrine and altar of St Richard of Chichester, and in 1311 a chantry was founded at the altar attached to the shrine of St Erkenwald of London.[96] Chantry masses might have been watched, if not attended, by pilgrims. Pilgrims could also take advantage of masses performed at other altars. One woman was cured at the tomb of St Hugh while mass was performed at the nearby altar of St John the Baptist, with others present 'as much clerics as laity'.[97] It was only on rare occasions that sermons were preached. One such was the 1420 jubilee of St Thomas Becket, when an Augustinian doctor of theology giving a sermon on the theme of the Jubilee had to repeat his performance three times because those who were unable to hear it earlier demanded encores.[98] Sermons were occasionally given in the event of a miracle, such as that delivered at Lincoln after the cure of a woman at St Hugh's tomb.[99]

In the later Middle Ages one of the major attractions of shrines were the indulgences attached to them. In 1215 Innocent III limited the indulgence power of bishops to forty days for most occasions, and one hundred for the dedication of a church.[100] However, indulgences were cumulative, and often many bishops would grant indulgences to the same shrine, especially if they were present on the translation of the saint. The pope could grant further and much more potent indulgences. In 1472–1473, for example, Sixtus IV granted twelve years plus twelve lents of penance to those who visited Salisbury cathedral on the memorial service and translation of St Osmund.[101] The subject of indulgences is a complex and detailed one for which there is much evidence of a legal nature. The process by which they were sought and obtained does

---

95 'Customary of the Shrine of St Thomas', *op. cit.* note 17, fol. 1.
96 *The Chartulary of the High Church of Chichester*, ed. W. D. Peckham, Sussex Record Society 46 (1942 and 1943), 308; G. H. Cook, *Old St Paul's Cathedral: a Lost Glory of Medieval London* (London, 1955), p. 54.
97 Giraldus Cambrensis, *Vita S. Hugonis, op. cit.* note 13, p. 123.
98 *Le Jubilé, op. cit.* note 24, p. 142.
99 Giraldus Cambrensis, *Vita S. Hugonis, op. cit.* note 13, p. 122: 'Unde et præcentor Willelmus, qui paulo post episcopus Lincolniensis effectus est, eodem palmarum die, in sermone suo ad populum, solemniter hoc miraculum promulgavit.'
100 This was canon 61 of Lateran IV: *Le Jubilé, op. cit.* note 24, p. 36.
101 *Ceremonies and Processions of the Cathedral Church of Salisbury*, ed. C. Wordsworth (Cambridge, 1901), p. 43.

not need to be dealt with here. However, the means by which indulgences were promoted by the local clergy and granted to pilgrims are much less clear.

There are at least two instances where indulgences connected with English shrines were directly advertised. In the Westminster sacrist's accounts of 1364/5 a monk was paid 2s. for riding to London to proclaim an indulgence on the day of the relics and St Peter.[102] There was also some effort to advertise the 1420 Jubilee of St Thomas and its plenary indulgence. The author of the treatise on the Jubilee saw a poem and letter fixed to the door of St Paul's, London, proclaiming the indulgence along with a schedule of previous indulgences, while another poem on the subject was composed and posted about the church.[103] A letter confirming the indulgence was also placed on the door of the church of the Domus Dei in Ospringe, Kent, on the pilgrim route from London to Canterbury.[104] It seems likely that most shrine indulgences were advertised in a similar manner.

A pilgrim who knew the power of remission granted to a shrine might consider him or herself to have received it merely by performing the usual devotions. It is to be expected, however, that pilgrims would have sought out some sort of confirmation of the blessing, and certainly conditions were attached to most indulgences. The pilgrim often had to visit the shrine at a required time, be properly confessed and leave offerings. For example, indulgences were given to those who celebrated the first feast of St Thomas of Hereford in October.[105] Canterbury needed special provisions to give confession to large numbers of pilgrims. In a letter of Pope Martin V to Christ Church in 1426 the priory was granted the right to ordain monks at a younger age than usual in order to minister to the frequent pilgrims.[106] An indulgence generated revenue that made up for the inconvenience of giving confessions: offerings at the three chief altars at Norwich, for example, increased greatly in 1400 due to the seven-year indulgence of Boniface IX.[107]

The last act of a pilgrim in a great church, like that of today's tourist, was

---

[102] WAM, MS 19630.

[103] *Le Jubilé, op. cit.* note 24, pp. 129–35: 'Ecce patent annis Thome jubilacio flexis./Quintupla pontificis duplaque nunc comitis./Henrici regis quinti stant bis quatuor annis./Anglia gaudeat hiis conjubilando sacris.'

[104] *Le Jubilé, op. cit.* note 24, p. 136.

[105] *Registrum Ade de Orleton, Episcopi Herefordensis, AD mcccxvii–mcccxxvii*, ed. A. T. Bannister, Canterbury and York Society 5 (1908), 142–3. Two letters, granting indulgences from Popes Nicholas IV (1291) and John XXII (1328) to Canterbury, order that confession be made; the indulgence granted to the shrines of Canterbury by Boniface IX in 1395 was only for certain feast days and only on condition that gifts were made to the fabric of the church.

[106] *Le Jubilé, op. cit.* note 24, pp. 182–3.

[107] H. W. Saunders, *An Introduction to the Obedientiary and Manor Rolls of Norwich Cathedral Priory* (Norwich, 1930), p. 103; N. P. Tanner, *The Church in Late Medieval Norwich 1370–1532*, Studies and Texts 66 (Toronto, 1984), 88.

often to obtain a souvenir. Badges are the best known medieval shrine momentos.[108] In the *Tale of Beryn* the pilgrims all bought badges 'ffor men of contre shuld[e] know whom [th]ey had[de] sou[gh]te', except for the miller and pardoner who filled their pockets with stolen badges.[109] Despite being made of fragile lead or pewter about 1,300 have been found in England, indicating that they were once exceedingly numerous.[110] They generally carried an image of the saint, the shrine or instruments of martyrdom, and had an open-work design set off by a background of coloured parchment, paper, or mirror, plus clips or pins for fixing them to the traditional pilgrim's hat.[111]

At many shrines pilgrims could also obtain a small lead ampulla filled with holy water or oil. A sealed ampulla found in Yorkshire contained an infusion of aromatic herbs and spices.[112] The earliest surviving ampullae, from the thirteenth century, are large and adorned with images,[113] but later examples lost their pictorial role to badges and became smaller so that they could be stitched on a hat rather than worn suspended from the neck.[114]

Paper or parchment souvenirs may have been on sale at some shrines, but only one example survives: a vellum leaf from Bromholm, showing an image of the sacred cross over prayers that were probably meant for recitation in front of the relic.[115] If necessary a document could be obtained to prove that one had performed a pilgrimage. A certificate of pilgrimage dated 1312, and sealed by Prior Eastry, affirmed that someone with the initials N. de L. had gone in pilgrimage to the lights of St Thomas of Canterbury and other sanctuaries which he personally visited.[116] Other souvenirs were specific to the shrine. During the fair at Ely a pilgrim could purchase brightly coloured silken necklaces called 'Etheldreda's Chains'.[117] C. W. Stubbs claimed, on unstated authority, that the monks originally gave tiny shackles of iron as souvenirs, in

---

108 See B. Spencer, 'Pilgrim Souvenirs', in *Medieval Waterfront Development at Trig Lane, London*, ed. G. and C. Milne, London and Middlesex Archaeological Society, Special Paper 5 (1982), 304.
109 *Tale of Beryn*, op. cit. note 20, p. 7.
110 There is written evidence for badges being made of precious metals: B. Spencer, 'Medieval Pilgrim Badges', in *A Contribution to Medieval Archaeology*, ed. J. G. N. Renaud, Rotterdam Papers 1 (Rotterdam, 1968), pp. 137 and 139.
111 Spencer 1968, op. cit. note 110, p. 138. See also *Tale of Beryn*, op. cit. note 20, p. 7.
112 Spencer 1968, op. cit. note 110, p. 139.
113 For example, a surviving ampulla of St Wulfstan is a wide-mouthed vessel surrounded by a narrow circular band and having on one side a figure of Wulfstan, on the other St Mary: B. Spencer, 'A Thirteenth-Century Pilgrim's Ampulla from Worcester', *Transactions of the Worcester Archaeological Society* 3rd Series 9 (1984), 7.
114 B. Spencer, 'Two Leaden Ampullae from Leicestershire', *Transactions of the Leicestershire Archaeological and Historical Society* 55 (1979–80), 88–9.
115 F. Wormald, 'The Rood of Bromholm', *Journal of the Warburg Institute* 1 (1937–8), 34.
116 *Le Jubilé*, op. cit. note 24, p. 171.
117 D. J. Stewart, *On the Architectural History of Ely Cathedral* (London, 1868), p. 190; Nicholas Harpsfield, *Historia Anglicana Ecclesiastica*, ed. E. Campion (London, 1622),

commemoration of a famous miracle, and only later replaced them with plaited ribbands.[118]

Apart for these, which show up as sales of silk in the Ely feretrar's rolls, income from badges and other souvenirs does not appear in cathedral accounts. Perhaps the usual practice was for cathedrals to lease a stall in the cathedral close to a private merchant. In any case, the cathedral did not have a monopoly on souvenirs, as badges were often sold in town shops. The duke of Norfolk bought badges from a Bury townsman in 1483, for example, and they are known to have been displayed in shops outside the gates of Canterbury Cathedral in the fifteenth century.[119]

Numbers and Patterns

These, then, are the documented activities of pilgrims at great shrines. It is important to our perception of a medieval shrine, however, to know how many pilgrims were there. *Miracula* give the impression of great crowds. The tomb of St Erkenwald was said to be surrounded by 'an innumerable crowd'.[120] After a miracle of St Milburga in 1101 the sick were reported hardly to fit in the church and cemetery.[121] Certain other sources give equally grand impressions. The Worcester Chronicler declared that in 1201 fifteen to sixteen people were miraculously cured by St Wulfstan each day, suggesting that the total number of pilgrims was much higher.[122] Pilgrims at Canterbury were said to number in the hundreds of thousands.[123] All of the above are valuable contemporary statements, but as estimates of special events they could be extreme exaggerations of the numbers of pilgrims more usually expected.

There is a simple exercise that can be used to estimate the number of pilgrims arriving at the shrine of St Hugh of Lincoln. It is based on the idea that

p. 86: 'Solent Angliæ nostræ mulieres torquem quendam tenui et subtili serico confectum collo gestare, quem Etheldredæ torquem appellamus.'
[118] C. W. Stubbs, *Historical Memorials of Ely Cathedral* (London, 1897), p. xiii.
[119] Spencer 1968, *op. cit.* note 110, p. 141.
[120] *The Saint of London: The Life and Miracles of St Erkenwald*, ed. E. G. Whatley (Birmingham, New York, 1989), p. 134.
[121] Odo of Ostia, 'An Early Twelfth-Century Account of the Translation of St Milburga of Much Wenlock', trans. A. J. M. Edwards, *Transactions of the Shropshire Archaeological Society* 57 (1961–64), 146.
[122] *Annales de Wigornia*, in *Annales Monasticii*, ed. H. R. Luard, Rolls Series 36 (London, 1869), 391.
[123] S. Heath, *In the Steps of the Pilgrims*, 2nd edition (London, no date), p. 21, no reference given. At the 1420 jubilee of St Thomas numbers were so great that they almost filled the nave. While the doors were opened private mass could only be said at the shrine with difficulty, and solemn mass with singing not at all, because the confluence of people was so great: *Le Jubilé, op. cit.* note 24, p. 142.

one coin, usually a penny sterling, was the standard and indeed traditional offering to an English shrine. If this assumption is accurate, the number of coins ought roughly to equal the number of pilgrims. An account from Lincoln for 1335 gives the amount of offerings at St Hugh's shrine as £28 3s. 10d., plus 13s. 9d. in farthings and halfpennies.[124] The smaller coins may have been recorded separately because a shrine box was sometimes used by cathedrals as a convenient source of small change. At Durham the feretrar gave an average of 7s. per year towards 'the prior's obols', which were probably a gift of small coins, perhaps literally halfpenny pieces, to the prior for his almsgiving. There was a general shortage of small-denomination coins for charity giving in England in the later Middle Ages, a situation described as injurious to beggars and other recipients.[125]

Because the smaller coins were recorded separately at Lincoln, and because no coins larger than a penny were in common circulation in 1335, it is clear that the vast bulk (almost 97%) of the offerings recorded was given in the form of sterling pennies. It can then be calculated that about 8,000 individual coins were offered to St Hugh in 1335. If one makes the probably unjustified assumption that the few pilgrims who got away without paying cancelled out the effect of those who gave more than one coin at the shrine, then the above number can be taken as a rough estimate of the number of pilgrims to the Lincoln shrine over the accounting year 1334/5. This works out to a daily average of about twenty-two pilgrims. The same exercise performed using a part-term account of 1409 which also records small coin separately results in 408 pilgrims, or about twelve per day for that period.

If the Lincoln conditions held true elsewhere then each pound of yearly offerings represents about 240 pilgrims. A small income of £5 yearly therefore required over 1,000 pilgrims, while £100 was produced by 240,000. Obviously, these figures should only be seen as a very approximate estimate. They would be greatly reduced if many rich pilgrims gave large amounts of money, or increased if there were hordes of non-paying 'tourists'. However, they do at least give an order of magnitude. They show, for example, that the claims of Canterbury to have hosted hundreds of thousands of pilgrims on special occasions are probably not gross exaggerations, yet also that, on an average day, a shrine like Lincoln's was not exactly thronging with pilgrims.

These are average numbers, however, and more detailed analysis shows that in fact they varied greatly according to the time of year. An indication of seasonal fluctuation can be derived from the accounts of Ely, Hereford, Durham and the Shrine of the Martyrdom at Canterbury, all of which have some detailed records showing offerings at different times. In the late fourteenth century, for example, the Durham shrine box was emptied at intervals by the feretrar's colleague (*socius*) and the money recorded in a receipt

---

[124] LCA, D&C, Bj/5/16/1, fols. 46v–50.
[125] Spufford 1988, *op. cit.* note 81, p. 331.

indenture made between him and the feretrar.[126] They record periods of irregular length, from two weeks to a year, each of which had multiple and apparently random dates of collection. Dividing the receipts by the days between collection dates results in an average daily income, which in turn can be averaged between indentures to give an approximate estimate of how much money could be expected on any one day of the year. Three or four dates, spread over the times of best weather, accounted for one third to one half of the yearly income to St Cuthbert's shrine. The most profitable was the feast of the Translation of St Cuthbert, the major festival of the saint, on 4 September. The other exceptional dates were the Deposition of St Cuthbert, Pentecost and Corpus Christi. The latter two, during which a great procession passed through the shrine-chapel,[127] fall so closely together that it is difficult to separate their effects using the method described above. Movable feasts, they could occur on any date between 17 May and 24 June. The usual income on any one of the main offering days was £4, compared to an average of about 1s. per day in summer, and half that in winter. The period from Christmas to late January was unseasonably profitable, often over 10d. per day. The periods immediately after the main feast days were also above average; for example, the offerings after the feast on the fourth of September remained high well into October.

The data for Hereford, Ely and Canterbury bear out the Durham findings, and show, not surprisingly, that offerings to shrines were subject to seasonal variation. This suggests that the bulk of the money came from pilgrims travelling from out of town, since they would have been more influenced by weather and travelling conditions than would townsmen or cathedral clerics. The accounts also show that activity centred strongly around the feasts of the saints, and the days of Pentecost and Corpus Christi. Combining this evidence with the estimated average pilgrim numbers given above, it is conceivable that only three or four pilgrims arrived on most days at shrines like that of St Hugh of Lincoln, but that many hundreds arrived on the days close to major feasts. It should be noted that these figures are for established shrines in the fourteenth and fifteenth centuries. Newer cults probably received much more attention.

In only one instance is there a direct record of the income received on different days of the week. The early sixteenth-century records of the Shrine of the Martyrdom of St Thomas give day by day accounts for some periods, thereby allowing averages of the receipts for each weekday.[128] This exercise

---

[126] While only nineteen of these pyx indentures survive, most of the feretrar's accounts state that the yearly offerings were 'as shown by indentures', so they must originally have been at least as numerous as the account rolls.

[127] *Rites of Durham, op. cit.* note 15, pp. 107–8.

[128] For this purpose I have disregarded the rare days when incomes were over 2s. because a special feast day or the visit of a generous dignitary happening to fall on that day would disturb the overall result.

shows that Sunday was the most profitable day with an average income of a little more than three pence. Although 60% better than the income of Saturdays, Sundays averaged under 10% (only 0.3d.) more than Thursdays (the second most profitable day). This difference is noticeable but hardly dramatic.

Royal, Noble and Ecclesiastical Pilgrims

So far this paper has been concerned with ordinary pilgrims. However, chroniclers were always proud to describe the attentions paid to their churches by illustrious devotees, particularly royal visitors. As a result, the known pilgrimages of English kings are too numerous to mention in detail. Royalty visited shrines for the same reasons as other pilgrims, including the fulfilment of a vow of pilgrimage. King John, for example, fulfilled a vow to St Edmund by visiting the shrine at Bury immediately after his coronation, and in 1343 Edward III went to Canterbury, Walsingham and Gloucester 'after many vows' on account of surviving a shipwreck.[129] Kings sometimes sought aid in battle from shrines. In 1283 Edward I gave thanks for subjugating Wales at the shrine of St Wulfstan, 'because he had a special love for it'. Before leaving for France he sent gold necklaces to the shrine of St Wulfstan, at Worcester, where the monks performed three weekly masses until his return in 1297, after which he sent the shrine another necklace, nine candles and 14s.[130] Henry V prayed, kissed the relics and made an offering at both Canterbury and St Paul's on his return from Agincourt.[131] At least one royal act of thanksgiving was related to marital rather than martial conquests. Henry III put an image of a queen on the shrine of Edward the Confessor to commemorate his wedding in 1236.[132] The Confessor's shrine often benefited from coronations in Westminster Abbey; in 1400 it received £16 in gold during the coronation of Henry IV.[133]

Although performed for much the same purpose as a regular pilgrimage, a royal visit understandably received much more attention. The 1447 visit by Margaret of Anjou to Canterbury when she was only sixteen years old exemplifies the great planning and solemnity involved. The queen was met by the prior at the entrance to the cathedral, then waited on her knees in the nave

---

[129] John came 'voto et deuocione tractus': Jocelin of Brakelond, *The Chronicle of Jocelin of Brakelond*, ed. H. E. Butler (London, 1949) p. 116; *Adae Murimuth Continuatio Chronicorum*, ed. E. M. Thompson, Rolls Series 93 (London, 1889), 135.
[130] *Annales de Wigornia*, op. cit. note 122, pp. 488, 514 and 536.
[131] Jehan de Waurin, *Recueil des croniques et anchiennes istoiries de la Grant Bretaigne, a presente nommé Engleterre*, ed. W. Hardy, 5 vols., Rolls Series 39 (London, 1868), II (1399–1422), 223–4.
[132] *Calendar of Close Rolls of the Reign of Henry III, AD 1234–1237*, ed. H. C. Maxwell-Lyte (London, 1908), p. 278.
[133] WAM, MS 19659.

while the choir sang verses. When the antiphon began she set out for the presbytery, and when she reached the high altar the prior said a collect. After the queen made an offering at the altar, the precentor began the antiphon *Pastor Cesus*, and the convent processed with her to the shrine. There the prior said a second collect, and the queen offered first at the shrine altar and then at the Corona. Finally, she went down to the palace through the cloister.[134]

By the fifteenth century major ecclesiastics were treated in much the same way as kings and queens, but with correspondingly less pomp and ceremony. On the unexpected arrival of Archbishop Chichele at Canterbury Cathedral he was ceremoniously brought into the church, where he visited the choir during mass. At the response of St Thomas he went to the shrine where the prior said a collect while the archbishop prayed. When finished, the archbishop gave his blessing, received amen and went on to the Corona.[135] The archbishop of York came to Canterbury in 1469 and made a pilgrimage to SS Thomas and Augustine, but caused a dispute when he at first refused to give a jewel to the shrine of St Thomas as a sign of his obedience.[136]

The royal and wealthy had several advantages over other pilgrims, one being the ability to perform pilgrimage by proxy. In 1502 Elizabeth of York sent two men on round-robin pilgrimages to various shrines. The first, a priest, was gone for twenty-seven days and distributed 48s. 4d. to several shrines including those at Reading, Hales, Worcester and Walsingham, for which labour he received 10d. per day. The other man was gone for thirteen days, visiting seven places including Canterbury and London.[137] Powerful individuals could also ask for relics. In 1315 a letter from Archbishop Walter Reynalds to Prior Eastry warned of Queen Isabelle's imminent arrival at Canterbury. She had specially asked the archbishop whether she could have any particle ('aliquam particulam') of St Thomas's bones, which Reynalds ordered the convent to give her when she arrived.[138]

Royal and noble offerings were, of course, much greater than others in value. In 1285 Edward I gave statues and jewellry worth £355 10s. 11½d. to the shrine of St Thomas.[139] Cloth of gold was frequently used as a royal gift, as

---

134 William Glastynbury, 'The Chronicle of William of Glastynbury, Monk of the Priory of Christ Church, Canterbury, 1419–1448', ed. C. E. Woodruff, *Archaeologia Cantiana* 37 (1925), 126–7.
135 William Glastynbury, 'Chronicle', *op. cit.* note 134, pp. 131 and 134.
136 John Stone, *The Chronicle of John Stone*, ed. W. G. Searle, Cambridge Antiquarian Society 34 (1902), 109 and 111.
137 Windsor, Eton, Reading, Caversham, Cokthorp, Hayles, Tewkesbury, Worcester, Northhampton, Walsingham, Sudbury, Woolpit, Ipswich and Stokeclare. *Privy Purse Expenses of Elizabeth of York*, ed. N. H. Nicolas (London, 1830), pp. 3–4.
138 Printed in *Le Jubilé*, *op. cit.* note 24, pp. 171–2, from Lambeth, *Register of Walter Reynolds*, fol. 64.
139 C. E. Woodruff, 'The Financial Aspect of the Cult of St Thomas of Canterbury', *Archaeologia Cantiana* 44 (1932), 29, n. 1; A. J. Taylor, 'Edward I and the Shrine of St

for example by Edward I to the shrine of St Richard at Chichester in 1299.[140] Any item of value would be gratefully accepted by the clerics in charge of shrines, whether it was sent or brought in person. The Annals of Worcester for 1293 record that when the king sent St Wulfstan a gold necklace before he went to France the chapter duly ordered three masses to be sung daily for his safe return.[141] There are even some instance of spoils of war being offered at a shrine. The Crown of Llewelyn II was offered to the shrine of St Edward at Westminster by Prince Alphonse in 1285, two years after it was surrendered to his father.[142] Richard I gave the banner of the emperor of Cyprus, taken in 1192, to the shrine of St Edmund.[143]

The most common form of offering made by kings was gold coins. Edward I placed gold florins on the shrine altar at Canterbury for 'the foetus then existing in the queen's belly' in 1300.[144] Royal offerings often appear to have been formalised. When the same king and his family visited Canterbury fifteen years earlier, the cost of an offering, whether by the king, his wife or his children, was consistently 7s.[145] The king made twelve separate donations in the cathedral worth a total of £4 4s., while three offerings by the queen came to 21s. This price of a royal offering prevails in other wardrobe accounts as well.[146] No single coin or multiple thereof was worth exactly 7s. It is possible that this was a token value assigned to a special coin used for royal oblations. The *Book of the King's Chapel* records that Henry VI daily offered a special gold talent equivalent to five nobles in weight that was redeemed each time by the clerk of the jewels for 7d.[147] In the late thirteenth century one of the king's oblations in France was described as 'for the king's offerings at high mass which he heard at St Eutrope's for his great penny, 7d. sterling'.[148] Similarly, in

---

Thomas of Canterbury', *Journal of the British Archaeological Association* 132 (1979), 24–5.
140 Walcott 1877, *op. cit.* note 30, p. 174.
141 *Annales de Wigornia, op. cit.* note 122, p. 514: 'Decimo sexto die Februarii venit clericus regis cum oblatione regali, et obtulit beato Wlstano monile aureum et ad magnum altare duos pannos aureos, quia tunc rex cogitavit quod transiret in Franciam festinanter.'
142 E. M. R. Ditmas, 'The Cult of Arthurian Relics', *Folklore* 75 (1964), 28; *Annales de Wigornia, op. cit.* note 122, p. 490.
143 W. T. Mitchell, 'The Shrines of English Saints in Wartime before the Reformation', *Pax* 30 (1940), 79.
144 M. Prestwich, 'The Piety of Edward I', in *England in the Thirteenth Century*, ed. W. M. Ormrod (Grantham, 1985), p. 124.
145 Taylor 1979, *op. cit.* note 139, pp. 22–3.
146 For example, the Wardrobe Accounts for 25 Edward I (1296/7), London, British Library, Additional MS 7965.
147 *Liber Regie Capelle*, ed. W. Ullmann, Henry Bradshaw Society 92 (1961), 61 and 63; B. Wolffe, *Henry VI* (London, 1981), p. 11.
148 *Records of the Wardrobe and Household, 1286–1289, op. cit.* note 46, no. 2532, p. 288.

1286 the wardrobe paid 'for the price of the great penny of the king 7d.'[149] The 'great penny' of Edward I may have been equivalent to the gold talent of Henry VI. If so, then perhaps the frequent oblations worth 7s. represent a traditional multiplication of the value of the single coin, since its worth was arbitrary in any case. The coin would be redeemed later by the king's clerks to be given again at the next shrine.

The pilgrim's experience at a cathedral or great abbey shrine was complex, involving many layers of spiritual and economic interaction. It is important to note that these activities were governed not by law or theology, but by tradition and custom, and were not therefore proscriptive. Many of the practices, such as bending pennies or using prayer niches, have much to do with magic and medieval perceptions of the universe. The substance of these beliefs did not change with social status, only the scale and style with which they were acted out. Thus the actions of a king, whether visiting a shrine with his court, or offering a wax image of his falcon, were directed with the same hopes and expectations as the average supplicant.

---

[149] 'Wardrobe Accounts for 25 Edward I', *op. cit.* note 146, fol. 6.

7

The Perils, or Otherwise, of Maritime Pilgrimage to Santiago de Compostela in the Fifteenth Century

WENDY R. CHILDS

The impulse to pilgrimage was strong in the late medieval west and in England, as elsewhere, there were numerous shrines of either local or national importance which made satisfactory goals for devotional journeys. However, the more devout, penitential or more adventurous pilgrims yearned to go further afield, to cross the sea and visit the great Christian shrines on the continent, whatever the difficulties. This paper examines some of the physical aspects of such journeys, specifically comparing travel by land and sea to Santiago de Compostela in Galicia.

Together with the holy cities of Jerusalem and Rome, St James's Compostela was one of the three great medieval pilgrim centres of western Europe.[1] From the twelfth through to the sixteenth century English pilgrims of varied social rank were attracted there. By the late fourteenth and fifteenth centuries, as well as nobles and churchmen, the visitors included men such as William Wey (a scholar), and women such as Margery Kempe (the wife of a merchant from Lynn), as well as thousands of other ordinary lay folk of 'middling sort'.[2] The majority of these people were carried by ship from England, arriving in Galicia at Coruña.

All English pilgrims to European shrines had, of course, to face a sea journey and maritime discomfort in some proportion, since they had at least to cross the Channel. But once in France, they could, if they wished, choose to remain on land for the remainder of their route. Only pilgrims going to Jerusalem would have been unable to avoid a further long sea journey from Bari, or Venice, to Jaffa. The deliberate choice of the voyage to Coruña, which

---

1 For the origins of the shrine at Compostela, see R. A. Fletcher, *St James's Catapult: the Life and Times of Diego Gelmirez* (Oxford, 1984) and S. Barton, 'Patrons, pilgrims and the cult of saints in the Medieval Kingdom of León', this volume, pp. 64–8.
2 *The Itineraries of William Wey, fellow of Eton College, to Jerusalem AD 1458 and AD 1462 and to St James of Compostella AD 1456*, ed. G. Williams (London, 1857), pp. 153–60; *The Book of Margery Kempe, 1436*, ed. S. B. Meech, EETS OS 212 (Oxford, 1940), I, 105–110; *Calendar of Patent Rolls 1367–70*, 140.

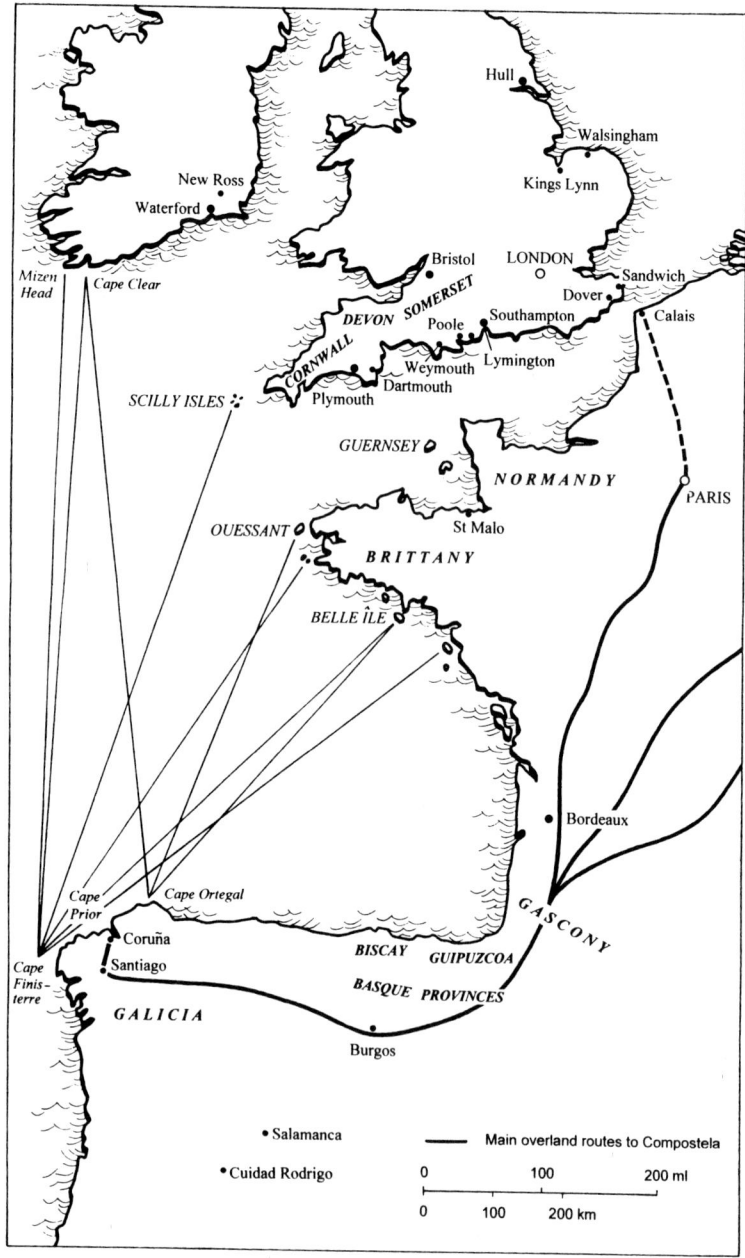

Figure 1 Sites mentioned in the text and routes between England and Galicia in the fourteenth and fifteenth centuries. The sea routes marked are the longest Bay of Biscay crossings given in the Sailing Directions (see page 141).

involved some 500 miles across the Bay of Biscay, is interesting and makes the advantages and disadvantages of the sea route worth further examination (Figure 1). English pilgrims were not the only ones to travel by sea; some of the richer German pilgrims also made this choice.[3] So, too, did Irish pilgrims, but this is not surprising given their geographical position.[4]

There were three main ways for English pilgrims to get to Compostela. The first was to take a short sea crossing from south-eastern England to northern France. This was normally from Dover to Calais (which became safely English after 1347).[5] From Calais they could join the major overland roads through France and northern Spain to Santiago de Compostela. The land routes, though arduous and over difficult terrain, were well-defined, regularly trodden, and lined with hostels and hospitals. The second possibility was to take a longer sea voyage to Bordeaux (in English hands from 1152 to 1453, and the centre of a lively wine trade with England). From here they could join the land route from Paris to the Pyrenees which passed through Bordeaux. The third possibility was to take a direct sea passage to Spain. This could be to any northern Spanish commercial port, or directly to Coruña, which then entailed only a journey of about forty miles to Compostela. In the late fourteenth and early fifteenth centuries it is clear that many English men and women deliberately chose the dangers and discomforts of a long sea route to Coruña rather than enduring the overland journey for anything more than the shortest of distances. Why was this?

The dangers of medieval sea journeys are well known. They could involve storm, wreck, seizure by the enemy in time of war, and piracy. The last two should not have been major problems for pilgrims, who were under the protection of both the church and lay authorities. If inadvertently arrested at sea during war-time they should have been released, although this obviously caused them delay and further expense. Pilgrims of 'middling sort' were unlikely to be of much interest to pirates. They would have yielded relatively little money and, in a ship carrying only pilgrims, there would have been little other cargo to plunder. The sole case in which pilgrims are known to have been seized and put to ransom seems to have been a special one. In 1473 the *Mary* of London, returning to Ireland with 400 pilgrims, was seized off Waterford. On

---

3   See M.-L. Favreau-Lilie, 'The *reys ad Sanctum Jacobum in Ghalecia* from Northern and Northwestern Germany', in *Actas del II Congreso Internacional de Estudios Jacobeos: Rutas Atlánticas de Peregrinación a Santiago de Compostella*, Ferrol, Septiembre 1996, 2 vols. (Xunta de Galicia 1998), I, 119–33.

4   See R. Stalley, 'Sailing to Santiago: maritime pilgrimage from Ireland', in *Actas del II Congreso Internacional de Estudios Jacobeos: Rutas Atlánticas de Peregrinación a Santiago de Compostella*, Ferrol, Septiembre 1996, 2 vols. (Xunta de Galicia 1998), I, 255–75.

5   Access to Norman ports should also have been straightforward, especially in the periods when Normandy was in English hands (up to 1204 and again in 1419–1450 under Henry V and Henry VI), but there is no evidence for English pilgrims using this route.

the outward voyage the pilgrims had been picked up in Ross by the *Mary* after it had unloaded a general commercial cargo brought from London. It is possible that the *Mary* pre-empted the local ship owners, who had expected to carry the pilgrims, and that, irritated at losing their profits, they lay in wait for her return and demanded compensation from the pilgrims.[6]

Storm and wreck were much more compelling fears during the age of sail. Indeed, sailors and merchants, caught in severe storms, not infrequently swore to undertake pilgrimages if God or the saints brought the ship home. Understandably enough, the shrines they then visited were safely on home shores. In several such cases Yorkshire men headed for Our Lady of Walsingham in Norfolk. In the later fifteenth century Nicholas Palmer of Hull set off for Walsingham as soon as his ship docked from Iceland, and in 1457 the York Mercers recorded payments for journeys to Walsingham which had been promised in the face of danger to the *Katherine* of York.[7] Wreck was an everpresent fear, since neither the north-west coast of Spain nor the south-west coasts of England, are easy in bad weather. Although no specific references to the wreck of pilgrim ships survive, it is likely that some sank. Later descriptions show how horrifying sailing-ship wreck was, as vessels, caught in mountainous seas and gale force winds, were driven helplessly onto rocks. In the Middle Ages there was the further risk of being murdered after staggering ashore. Under English law, if any living thing (including the ship's cat or dog) survived the wreck, the vessel was legally judged not wreck and owners of goods salvaged could claim them back. This sometimes provided an incentive for local people to kill those who finally reached the shore.

Storms were terrifying and debilitating but even in good weather there was poor accommodation, poor food, nowhere to lie down, overcrowding and the danger of theft by fellow travellers in the crush. The problems are displayed in several well-known literary texts. The Bohemian baron, Leo of Rozmital, travelling in Europe between 1475 and 1477 as ambassador rather than pilgrim, had a terrible time crossing the English Channel in both directions.[8] Coming from Calais to Sandwich his first ship sprang a leak and returned, he was nearly drowned boarding the second, and he and his men were so distressed by seasickness that 'they lay on the ship as if they had been dead'. On the return journey from Poole to St Malo they took sufficient supplies for four days but the journey took seventeen. They were blown to Guernsey, losing their mast, and were caught by a squall so sudden that the bows of the ships were forced under and water poured through the hatchways before the sails could

---

[6] *Calendar of Patent Rolls 1475–85*, 78; and see R. Stalley 1998, *op. cit.* note 4, pp. 265–6.
[7] Public Record Office, London, C1/37/26: the petition is undated but must belong to either 1465–1470 or 1480–1483; *York Mercers and Merchant Adventurers 1356–1917*, ed. M. Sellars, Publications of the Surtees Society 129 (Durham, 1917), pp. 59–63.
[8] *The Travels of Leo of Rozmital through Germany, Flanders, England, France, Spain, Portugal and Italy 1465–1467*, ed. M. Letts, Hakluyt Society 2nd Series 108 (Cambridge, 1957 for 1955), pp. 32, 42, 59–60 and 62–4.

be furled. When it was over, Schaseck wrote 'we thanked God on our knees'. This is of course the landsman's view, a seaman might say that the crew's experience and skill, and the ship's seaworthiness, were clearly sufficient to cope with a sudden squall.

An anonymous poem of the fifteenth century described the problems even in good weather, and emphasised hardship from the start; 'men may leve alle gamys, that saylen to Seynt Jamys'.[9] Passengers were pushed around by the crew raising the sails ('what, howe, mate! thow stondyst to ny'), suffered seasickness ('our pylgryms have no lust to ete'), were bored, had little shelter or bedding and suffered from the stink of the bilge-water ('for when that we shall go to bedde, the pumpe was nygh oure beddes hede, a man were as good to be dede, as smell therof the stynk').

Despite these dangers and discomforts English pilgrims used the longer sea routes. The use of the route to Coruña becomes increasingly well-recorded from the mid fourteenth century, and in the first half of the fifteenth century it appears to be particularly popular with ordinary lay people. Between 1361 and 1484, some 329 licences were issued to ship owners for pilgrim transport, the vast majority falling between 1400 and 1456. During these years over 15,000 pilgrims might have been carried, and in each of the Jubilee years of 1428 and 1434 licences for over 3,000 pilgrims were issued.[10] These numbers appear to be much higher than those for pilgrims known to have visited Rome[11] and are probably the result not only of Compostela's spiritual standing but also of its greater accessibility. They show that large numbers of people were prepared to confront a longer sea journey rather than face a lengthy trek overland. Four factors suggest themselves as being influential in this decision: the difficulty of the land routes themselves, the speed of the sea route, possible improvements in the organisation of the sea route, and the increasing regularity (and perhaps safety) of sea travel in the period.

The land routes were clearly not an easy option. Indeed, they became politically more difficult for the English from the mid fourteenth century because of war between England and France (of whom Castile was an ally). Although pilgrims should have been unmolested, the fear of spies made harassment

---

[9] *The Stacions of Rome and the Pilgrims Sea-voyage*, ed. F. J. Furnivall, EETS OS 25 (London, 1867), pp. 37–40; also printed in R. and R. C. Anderson, *The Sailing Ship* (London, 1926), pp. 92–3.

[10] Jubilee years, in which pilgrims obtained a greater number of indulgences for the pilgrimage, were declared when the feast of St James (25 July) fell on a Sunday. For further information on the licences see below, pp. 130–2.

[11] The evidence is admittedly fragmentary and incomplete but it suggests far fewer lay people visited Rome. Nearly 400 individual licences were issued for the Jubilee year in Rome in 1350, but thereafter available evidence generally shows only twenty to seventy-five a year, although this rose to over 100 a year in the 1490s and reached 750 in the Jubilee year of 1500; G. B. Parks, *The English Traveler to Italy* (Rome, 1954), I, 351–57 and 373–4. More churchmen are likely to have visited Rome in the course of their work.

likely.[12] The land routes were also physically difficult. They covered long distances in sometimes harsh terrain, and in the thirteenth century the journey to Rome and to Compostela had both been reckoned to take about the same time – sixteen weeks.[13] Again, literary sources illustrate the problems. Leo of Rozmital's party, which did not use the normal pilgrim route but went via Salamanca, Ciudad Rodrigo and Portugal, and Arnald von Harff, who did travel the normal pilgrim road, all emphasised poor food, worse wine, scant shelter, evil inns, harsh and stony terrain and the murderous hostility of the natives. Rozmital's men found the stretch from Biscay to Burgos especially frightful. It was unsafe, they needed weapons at all times, there was no water, no shade and bridge tolls were high. Von Harff's criticism was more measured, but he recorded the murders of two pilgrims in his group on the return journey and was driven to conclude, 'all in all Spain is an evil country'. An anonymous English poem of 1425 which described the land journey from Bordeaux to Compostela was less condemning. The author wrote of fair towns, a good country, and seems to have quite liked Spain except that the people were ungodly, the wine was evil, there was no bedding, nor tables and natives sat on the floor as in Ireland.[14]

A strenuous journey was not, of course, unfitting. Pilgrimage was meant to be difficult, to be a penance or to offer a spiritual experience through facing and overcoming austerity and hardship. An unusual illustration of the hunger and weariness expected to accompany pilgrimage is found in the criticism of Edward II for hurrying his men without rest to meet the Scots at Bannockburn in 1314, 'not as if he was leading an army to battle but as if he was going to St James's'.[15] Sufficient deprivation to serve the purpose of pilgrimage was apparently provided by either sea or land travel. The attraction of the sea route may have been that it had the advantage of great speed if all went well.

The huge variations between medieval vessels and the lack of good technical information about them makes estimates of average speed difficult. One of the best estimates suggested a possible average speed in fair weather of three to six knots.[16] But journey time depended less on the speed of the ship than on the state of the weather, and much time could be lost waiting for

---

[12] The treaty between the duke of Lancaster and Enrique Trastamara in 1388 specifically asked for free passage for pilgrims as well as merchants.

[13] *Statutes of Lincoln Cathedral*, ed. H. Bradshaw and C. Wordsworth (Cambridge, 1897), part 2, 57.

[14] *Leo of Rozmital*, op. cit. note 8, pp. 78–108; *The Pilgrimage of Arnald von Harff*, ed. M. Letts, Hakluyt Society 2nd Series 94 (London, 1946), pp. 262–77; *Hakluytys Posthumus or Purchas His Pilgrimes*, ed. S. Purchas, 20 vols. (Glasgow, 1905–07), VII, 527–70: the Spanish part is reprinted in *Two Pilgrim Itineraries of the Later Middle Ages*, ed. R. B. Tate and T. Turville-Petrie (Xunta de Galicia, 1995), pp. 35–48.

[15] *Vita Edwardi Secundi*, ed. N. Denholm-Young (London, 1957), p. 51.

[16] D. Ellmers, *Frühmittelalterliche Handelsschiffahrt in Mitten- und Nord-Europa* (Neumünster, 1972), p. 250, cited in G. Hutchinson, *Medieval Ships and Shipping* (London, 1994), p. 169; see also I. Friel, *The Good Ship* (London, 1995), pp. 84–6.

favourable winds. For the route to Coruña we have some examples of total voyage times and it is clear that, once the ship had put to sea, some were fast, and that a speed near to five or even six knots could be maintained over several days. In 1456, William Wey, scholar of Eton College, left Plymouth on Monday, 17 May, and arrived in Coruña five days later, on Friday, 21 May. If the prevailing winds allowed ships to travel the minimum distance between Plymouth and Coruña, a journey of five twenty-four-hour days would indicate an average speed of about 4.5 knots. But Wey's journey began and ended in daylight and so cannot have been more than 4.5 days, which indicates an average of over five knots. If the route taken was not the shortest, then the average speed would be higher still.

Wey spent the weekend in Santiago, was back in Coruña by Tuesday or Wednesday, and attempted to leave on Friday, 28 May. The ship was blown back to Coruña and did not finally leave until 5 June, arriving back in Plymouth on 9 June. Wey was away for twenty-four days, but if winds had been good he might have been away for only sixteen. A similar speed was recorded by Margery Kempe from Bristol in 1417. Her narrative is less precise, but it is clear that her outward journey took seven days, her return journey five days and that she spent fourteen days in Spain. She appears to have been away overall for twenty-six days. Both had to wait some time for their ships to leave England, but that could equally happen on short Channel crossings as shown by the description of Rozmital's followers, waiting for wind in Sandwich.[17] Thus, in favourable circumstances, the whole voyage, there and back, with several days in Santiago, could be completed in about three weeks.

A shorter journey almost certainly meant a cheaper journey for pilgrims. The only information about costs for the sea voyage comes from 1473 when the Irish pilgrims aboard the *Mary* of London were charged 7s. 6d. each (presumably return).[18] If the land journey of over 1,000 miles was completed at twenty miles a day (a reasonable to good speed for a mixed group of pedestrians and riders), it would take at least fifty days each way. An allowance of 2d. per day (which might cover simple fare and accommodation)[19] would amount to at least 8s. 4d. each way, a total of 16s. 8d., and to this must be added the cost of crossing the Channel. Begging and staying in pilgrim hostels would reduce the amount required, but better fare or a longer time would increase it. The evidence for comparative costs is fragile, but is probably sufficient to indicate that the land journey was likely to be at least twice as expensive as the sea journey.

Our information on the organisation of passenger transport to Coruña is partial, because it is largely drawn from English government licences

---

[17] *William Wey, op. cit.* note 2, pp. 153–5; *Margery Kempe, op. cit.* note 2, p. 110; *Leo of Rozmital, op. cit.* note 8, p. 50.
[18] *Calendar of Patent Rolls 1475–85*, 78.
[19] See G. C. Coulton, *Social Life in Britain* (Cambridge, 1919), pp. 421–2.

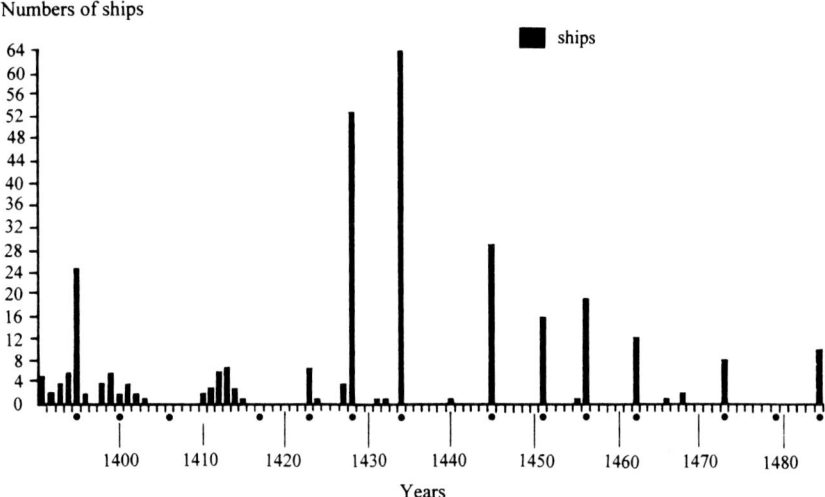

Figure 2 Ships licensed to carry pilgrims to Compostela, 1391–1448. Details of sources are in note 20 to the text. Jubilee years are marked with •.

permitting overseas travel. These show interesting changes of pattern, which suggest that travel arrangements for the route became increasingly well organised in the fifteenth century. It was probably a case of two developments reinforcing one another. As the route became more popular, so the ship owners geared up to accommodate the greater demand, and this in turn attracted more pilgrims to the sea route. Licences were issued because, in the second half of the fourteenth century, fear of spies and dislike of the export of bullion led governments to prohibit foreign travel to all except merchants, unless the travellers acquired special permission. At first pilgrims acquired individual licences, but examples of ship owners applying for general licences to transport groups of pilgrims to Spain soon appear in the records. A few group licences were recorded as early as the 1360s. They increased after 1391 when regulations were tightened, and increased further in the early fifteenth century, when the government made attempts to enforce the regulations. Copies of the licences were often registered centrally.[20] It is unlikely that registration was complete,[21] but sufficient information survives, especially for 1400–1456, to indicate the patterns of pilgrimage by sea and to show how

---

[20] Up to 1400 licences are found mainly on the patent rolls; thereafter almost exclusively on the treaty rolls. Some are printed in *Foedera, Conventiones, Litterae*, ed. T. Rymer, 3rd edition, 10 vols. (The Hague, 1739–45). Fuller lists are to be found in C. M. Storrs, 'Jacobean pilgrims from the early twelfth to the late fifteenth century' (unpublished MA thesis, University of London, 1964), and in E. Ferreira Priegue, *Galicia en el comercio marítimo medieval* (Santiago de Compostela, 1988), pp. 587–610.

[21] Government investigations in 1428 and 1435 showed that even then not all ship

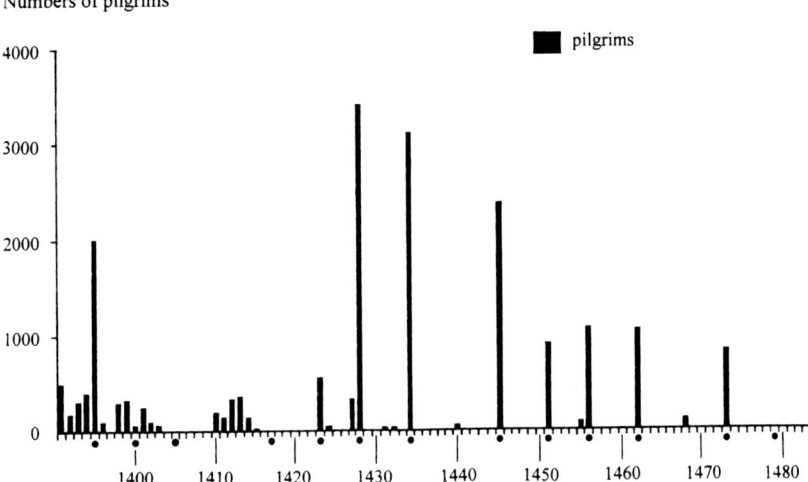

Figure 3 Pilgrims licensed to go to Compostela, 1391–1473. Details of sources are in note 20 to the text. The records for the ten ships licensed in 1484 do not provide information on the numbers of pilgrims to be carried. Jubilee years are marked with •.

English ship owners exploited a profitable market.[22] The licences recorded the name of the ship owner or master or both, the name of the ship, its home port and the number of pilgrims it might carry. They probably included the ship's tonnage and certainly included conditions of carriage, but these are only occasionally copied on the rolls.[23]

The issue of the licences shows a change of pattern in the fifteenth century (see Figures 2 and 3). Until the mid 1420s licences were registered for a few ships each year (perhaps with a slight increase in Jubilee years) but after that date licences were issued for very large numbers in Jubilee years and for few or

---

owners complied with the regulations and after the end of the Hundred Years War there was less attempt to enforce the regulations. The system decayed after 1456.

[22] Licences for 329 voyages are recorded for the whole period 1361–1485. Sixty-eight were recorded up to 1399, 228 (69%) for 1400–1456, and 33 for 1457–1484. They covered well over 20,000 pilgrims. Numbers of pilgrims are not always recorded in the first and third periods, but between 1400 and 1456 some 14,381 pilgrims might have been carried. Slight differences between my totals and those of Storrs and Ferreira are due to variant readings.

[23] Conditions from time to time stated that the pilgrims should be 'of the middling sort' and not of high status, that they should be the king's own subjects, that they should not carry bullion, that they should not plan to emigrate and that they should do nothing to harm the king nor reveal any secrets. Some, and possibly all, ship owners had to pay a levy on pilgrims carried: in 1395 Thomas Knap of Bristol paid the king six pence for each passenger; *Calendar of Patent Rolls 1391–6*, 572.

none in other years. For example, in the period 1410 to 1415 between one and seven ship owners bought licences each year for up to 340 pilgrims a year. Between 1416 and 1422 no licences were recorded, either through change of Chancery practice, or because none was issued (which would be possible given Henry V's naval expeditions and demands on shipping). In 1423, 1424 and 1427, again one to seven licences a year were recorded, and none in 1425 and 1426. But then there was a dramatic rise to fifty-three licences in the Jubilee year 1428, for 3,425 pilgrims. This was followed by only two licences in the next five years before another surge to sixty-four licences for 3,150 pilgrims in the Jubilee year of 1434. This pattern continued until the system of licences decayed. Taken with descriptions, such as William Wey's, of fast journeys on special pilgrim ships, this change of pattern suggests that ship owners were evolving something close to a 'package tour'. On their ships pilgrims could expect special voyages with a fast turn-round time in Coruña, allowing just sufficient time to visit Santiago. The practice was similar to the regular annual 'package tours' run in the fifteenth century by Venetians for pilgrims to Jerusalem.[24]

As mentioned above, this development was probably prompted by a combination of an increase in popularity of the sea route (which is suggested by the sheer numbers involved) and the desire by seamen to exploit any profitable opportunity. Ships were expensive and owners needed to keep them at sea and earning as much as possible. Many cargo voyages, even to fairly close destinations, could take two or three months. Additional quick voyages to slot in between freight voyages would be attractive. Ship owners might therefore be encouraged by apparently rising demand to buy licences speculatively, confident that they would fill their ships in Jubilee years. If it worked once, they did it again, and pilgrims returning from Coruña took home the news to other pilgrims that ships were easy to find simply by going to the appropriate ports.

The matter of how pilgrims and ships were matched, of how pilgrims knew where to find ships, is poorly documented. Undoubtedly some ships were chartered by self-constituted groups – possibly by a lord and his followers or by a cleric for his parish. These groups were likely to appoint an organiser who went well in advance to the nearest sea port and chartered a suitable vessel, the owner of which would then apply for a licence. This would explain the occasional sailings from Hull and Newcastle and other ports in the north and east of England. But not all pilgrims went in organised groups. Both Kempe and Wey were making individual journeys. For individual travellers, it was commonplace to join merchant routes and merchant groups. When Arnald

---

[24] *William Wey, op. cit.* note 2, pp. 4–25 and 56–102. Modern accounts of the 'packages' can be found in R. J. Mitchell, *The Spring Voyage: A Jerusalem Pilgrimage in 1458* (London, 1964) which is based on Wey's account, and in H. F. M. Prescott, *Jerusalem Journey* (London, 1954), based on the journeys of Felix Faber in 1480 and 1483.

von Harff set out on the early part of his journey from Cologne for Italy, he joined a group of merchants because, he said, they were good company and because they knew the way and the language. For the English, it was easy to discover which were the main western commercial ports and thus where to look for a cargo ship sailing in the right direction. Margery Kempe in 1417 chose to go to Bristol and met others there who had also made no prior arrangements. When no shipping was immediately available she wrote of these others scurrying from port to port looking for ships, but she stayed in Bristol and eventually took a Breton ship to Coruña.[25] Others who travelled on cargo ships were Lord Dusa, who persuaded a Guipuzcoan ship master to take him from Bristol to northern Spain, probably around 1462,[26] and the anonymous English poet who started his pilgrimage from Bordeaux.[27] It is not difficult to suppose that some ship owners responded to these arrivals by obtaining licences in advance and offering special voyages. Once this became known, other individuals could go to western ports with every expectation of finding ships waiting. This was undoubtedly the case with William Wey. He set out for Plymouth and found, as no doubt he expected to find, six specialist pilgrim transports waiting in harbour. William Purchas, the London mercer who set out for Plymouth in 1479, might also have been expecting to join a pilgrim ship.[28] In some cases masters may have managed in some way to publicise outside the ports that they had ships ready to sail. Certainly as early as 1391 Thomas Ashenden of Dartmouth had a licence 'whereof he may make proclamation throughout the realm', although how he did this is not recorded.[29]

The suggestion of a move to 'package tours' is not without problems. It is not clear why it started in the late 1420s, and indeed it could be argued that the surge of recorded licences in 1428 might have been partly due to the government's determined effort to enforce the regulation of overseas travel (certainly there were government inquiries that year into breaches of the licensing system). But that does not explain the similar pattern in subsequent years. On balance a change in organisation is the likely explanation. The later decline in numbers, as shown in Figures 2 and 3, is easier to explain. The end of the Anglo-French war weakened governmental worries, and by 1466 the first full treaty for a century was concluded with Spain. Some doubt about the validity

---

[25] *Margery Kempe, op. cit.* note 2, pp. 106–8. Although this was a Jubilee year no licences were given to English ships, probably because of expected heavy naval demands in the year of Henry V's second campaign in France. It is likely that the Breton cargo ship took advantage of there being numbers of pilgrims waiting to cross to Coruña, in much the same way as the *Mary* of London took advantage of pilgrims waiting to leave Ross in 1473. See above pp. 125–6.

[26] PRO, London, C1/27/44/.

[27] *Two Pilgrim Itineraries, op. cit.* note 14, pp. 35–48.

[28] PRO, London, C1/64/167, 1123.

[29] *Calendar of Patent Rolls 1388–92*, 390.

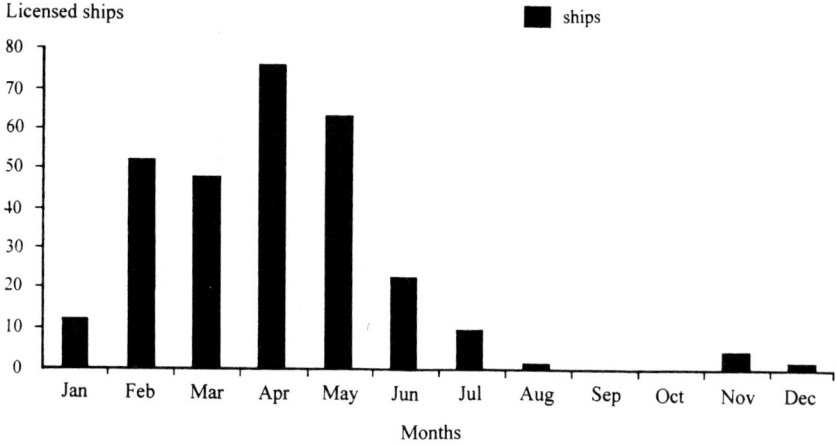

Figure 4 Licences for pilgrims' ships, 1391–1473, by month of issue. Details of sources are in note 20 to the text.

of the treaty in 1472–1473, and again at the change of English monarch in 1483, may have prompted a few ship owners to take the precaution of buying licences and ensuring that they were enrolled in 1473 and 1484, but the licence system had largely decayed by then. Already in 1456, when William Wey recorded thirty-two English ships at Coruña in May and June, only nineteen licences had been registered for the whole year. Other, minor, factors which may have contributed to the lower numbers of licences after 1434 could be an over-supply of shipping provided by owners in that year, leading to greater caution, and perhaps the beginning of a decline in interest in Compostela.

Not only does the change in the pattern of licences suggest that ship owners were taking the initiative in creating a 'package tour' in response to passenger demand, but the dates of issue of the licences seem to be more in the interest of ship owners than of pilgrims. Since St James's feast day falls on 25 July and the best weather for crossing the Bay of Biscay is in May and June (when both Kempe's and Wey's fast voyages took place), one might have expected licences to be issued in April, May and June for use in May, June and July. However, between 1400 and 1456 only 50% were issued in April, May and June, while 44% were acquired in January, February and March (see Figure 4). We do not, of course, know exactly when the licences were used. Owners might have taken out licences early simply to be ready to start a voyage as soon as it was needed, but it is possible that those acquiring licences in January and February intended to use them fairly soon, perhaps within a month or two, rather than to wait for June or July. This is strongly suggested when owners obtained two or three licences in a year for the same ship. In 1434, for example, Robert Coil and John Wenard bought three licences in February, May and July for their ship *Margaret* of Topsham, and there can therefore be little doubt that the first was used before May. Since most owners bought only one licence early in the year there is less indication of when they used it, but early spring would be attractive. It could be a fairly slack time commercially and it would be convenient to fit in a short passenger voyage between the main cargo voyages to Bordeaux, Andalusia or Iceland. It may also be significant that the acquisition of licences becomes earlier over the years. Those acquired in January to March rise from 28% of the total issued before 1400, to 44% between 1400 and 1456. There is also a perceptible shift towards acquiring licences in February between 1428 and 1456, when the pattern changes to the surge of licences in Jubilee Years. Licences acquired in April, May and June fell from 69% to 50% over the same period (between 1400 and 1456), again with a significant shift towards April rather than May after 1428. This suggests that the interests of the ship owners were taking priority over those of the pilgrims, but might also be an indication of the increase in the perceived safety of sea transport at this time.

There is no reason to suppose that owners would not have dared to use their licences to cross the Bay of Biscay in February and March, since a number did this regularly for trading voyages. Customs accounts for Bristol, which provide the most precise indications of destinations, show regular winter crossings of the Bay at the end of the fourteenth century. Between 1376 and 1391 about one quarter of outward bound ships were loading in January, February, and March for Portugal and Spain. At the end of the fifteenth century, between 1485 and 1493, 20% of departures for Portugal and Andalusia and 30% of arrivals from there were recorded in January, February and March, and further incoming ships in early April must have been sailing across the Bay of Biscay in late March. It seems, in the event, that pilgrims were happy with the early dates which provided them with a pilgrimage during Lent, Easter or Pentecost and there is no evidence that they made any effort to be there in July. Wey returned by 9 June without expressing any disappointment at missing St James's feast day, and Margery Kempe, who may in fact have been in Compostela for 25 July, does not seem to have made special arrangements to ensure it.

The number of licences issued to ships sailing from the south-west of England seems to confirm the suggestion of speculative ventures by ship owners. Seamen from the east coast were as familiar with the route at least as far as Bordeaux, as were seamen from the south-west, but 57% of the licences were issued to ships from the south-west, from Bristol and Somerset and especially from Devon and Cornwall. There is no doubt that pilgrims were expected to arrive in south-western ports in large numbers, and, as already shown, individual travellers from as far away as King's Lynn and London did indeed come to seek ships in the south-west. The precise ports of embarkation are only occasionally specified in the licences for the 1390s and are either the home port of the ship or its nearest major customs port. This was probably the pattern throughout the period, with ships from the smaller ports congregating in Plymouth, Dartmouth or Bristol to pick up passengers. Of the major west country customs ports, Plymouth seems to have been the one most often used. It was the government's preferred port of exit in the west of England for all travellers other than merchants, and it had an exceptionally large and safe harbour where many ships could anchor and wait. Like Dartmouth, it was a port much used by shipping of all types and nationalities for shelter just before or just after crossing the Channel. It is not surprising that intending pilgrims, such as Wey and Purchas, headed there and that ships from other ports congregated there. Wey tells us that in May 1456 there were six vessels waiting for pilgrims; two were local from Plymouth and Cargreen, and the four others came from Bristol, Weymouth, Portsmouth and Lymington.[30] All the major customs ports were used to handling seasonal influxes of seamen and merchants and would have had little difficulty in finding sufficient facilities for putting up pilgrims while they waited for ships.

The ships were in no way specialised passenger transports. They were normal commercial ships of all sizes. Probably three-quarters of the ships used for pilgrims were under 100 tons portage,[31] but those used ranged from the small *Katherine* of Penzance of thirty tons, licensed to carry thirty pilgrims, to the large *Trinity* of Newport in Wales of 400 tons, licensed to carry 300 pilgrims. We also know that the *Mary* of London which carried 400 pilgrims in 1473 was of 320 tons. The smallest would be simple one-masted ships, but by the mid fifteenth century the largest would carry three masts. These would have a covered hold and might have a superstructure of permanent cabins for the master and important merchants and a forecastle for defence. The accommodation and conditions for the pilgrims would depend on the size of the ship, what facilities the owner would put in, and what the pilgrims could pay for bedding and food. The better off might have arranged to sleep in the permanent superstructures. Some might have slept in the holds.[32] Some pilgrims may have done better in makeshift extra shelters (the anonymous poem's 'many a febylle celle')[33] put up on deck. Many, no doubt, simply had to lie on the open deck. The ships would have been very crowded indeed with pilgrims and crew. The anonymous poem described pilgrims being roughly pushed aside by seamen intent on working the ship, and stories tell of how pilgrims had their purses stolen in the crush.[34] Possibly it was more comfortable, if overall slower, to find a passage on a regular cargo ship. Pilgrims

---

[30] *William Wey, op. cit.* note 2, p. 153.

[31] Only 10% of the licences record the ship's tonnage, so the sample is small.

[32] On Mediterranean galleys areas were chalked on the hold planking for each person, of about one metre by two metres with a little extra room for a travelling box; *William Wey, op. cit.* note 2, pp. 4–7.

[33] *Stacions of Rome, op. cit.* note 9, p. 40.

[34] *An English Chronicle of Richard II, Henry IV, Henry V, and Henry VI*, ed. J. S. Davies, Camden Society Old Series 64 (London, 1855–6), pp. 73–4; Wey also speaks of pilgrims stealing others' water on the journey he made to Jerusalem, *op. cit.* note 2, p. 5.

recorded as going via Bordeaux or Portugal were using ordinary commercial ships,[35] and given England's strong trading connections across the Bay of Biscay, it was easy enough to find a merchant ship going in the right direction, if the pilgrim was prepared to wait a while.

It is still debated whether the licensed pilgrim ships really were just passenger ships or whether they also carried cargo. In the Mediterranean, the Venetians prohibited trading from pilgrim galleys to prevent delay, but there is no similar prohibition recorded in England. Several of the licences issued in 1368 and 1369 specifically allowed the vessels to trade and to carry pilgrims (which might suggest that normally they did not) and, in the early fifteenth century it is possible to trace instances of Southampton ships, licensed to carry pilgrims, also being recorded in the Southampton customs accounts unloading cargoes of wine. The dates of unloading wine are so close to the dates of the pilgrim licences that they suggest they were returning from Galicia with both wine and pilgrims.[36] Some trade seems, therefore, to have been done, particularly in the earlier period.

Realistically, however, many of the large numbers of ships licensed after 1428, were likely to be purely or mainly passenger ships. This is suggested, in the first place, by the amount of direct trade between England and Galicia. This was relatively low compared with the trade between England and the Basque Provinces, or between England and Andalusia, and would probably normally have required no more than two or three ships a year in each direction.[37] An influx of thirty, forty or fifty English ships in Jubilee years was therefore an unusual event and it would be difficult to find cargoes for all of them. Secondly, to judge from Wey's narrative and the existence of multiple licences, the intention of many ship owners was to make a quick journey with a fast turn-round time in Coruña. This would limit the time available for finding cargoes and drawing up contracts, which were time-consuming activities even in places with a system of agents collecting goods on a semi-permanent basis. In the third place, passengers could take up quite a substantial amount of space, especially if make-shift cabins were erected, leaving little dry or covered space for other cargo. By weight, of course, they would bring the ship nowhere near to its full loading capability and light cargo alone could make ship-handling more difficult. However, this was not necessarily a problem. To ease handling the ship could take on more ballast, as happened not infrequently

---

[35] The writer of the anonymous poem of c. 1425 took a boat from Plymouth to Bordeaux; *Two Pilgrim Itineraries, op. cit.* note 14, p. 35.
[36] *Calendar of Patent Rolls 1367–70*, 122, 212 and 226; Ferreira 1988, *op. cit.* note 20, p. 582.
[37] These two areas produced goods particularly useful to England – iron, dried fruit, oil and dyes. Galicia's tallow, hides, skins and wool were of less interest, although her wines (mostly from Betanzos or from Vivero) were attractive. For the preponderance of Basque shipping in the trade see W. R. Childs, *Anglo-Castilian Trade in the Later Middle Ages* (Manchester, 1978), pp. 152–4.

when ships had to sail empty.[38] Finally, it may have been quite profitable to carry pilgrims alone, provided the ship was full and the journey was short. Ship owners were business men and used to assessing possible profits. Assessing medieval profits nowadays is difficult because there are so few figures, and the figures may well be inaccurate, but some suggestions can be made.

It seems that on average pilgrims were carried at the ratio of one pilgrim to one ton portage,[39] and in 1473 the 400 pilgrims aboard the *Mary* of London paid a total of 225 marks (£150) for their passage, presumably there and back. At that time a ton of freight might pay 20 shillings each way between England and Spain; so, if nearly full both ways, the 320 ton *Mary* might earn £600 for a trading voyage, compared with £150 for a passenger voyage. At first sight these figures show pilgrims as far less profitable than cargo. However, the income from pilgrims could be earned over three to four weeks, while the length of a commercial voyage was usually three to four months. In this case the income becomes comparable, at about £40 to £50 per week. Moreover, records show that ships carrying cargo were by no means always full in both directions and so earnings would fall below the maximum. In many cases earnings from a full passenger ship might be higher per week than those for an under-loaded cargo vessel.

This is a simplistic calculation, but it does indicate that pilgrims might be a good proposition, especially if taken at a slack time of year. The licensed voyages should probably be seen as primarily passenger journeys, with no great incentive for the master to look for cargo. Of course, if cargo for England was waiting on the quay and could be accommodated, then the master was highly likely to take it to add to his profits.

A final incentive for taking the sea route to Coruña rather than travelling overland was that, by the late fourteenth and early fifteenth centuries, the safety of the sea voyage was much improved. This is apparent when the sea route taken by the pilgrims is set in the context of England's general commercial activity. For English seamen the Bay of Biscay was well known, and to them, the voyage to Coruña was just one route in a complex network of routes they operated in the Atlantic. English ships sailed the Atlantic from Iceland to the straits of Gibraltar and their links with Gascony and Iberia were particularly strong. They had been sailing to Lisbon and Andalusia since the mid fourteenth century and to Bordeaux since the twelfth. The regularity of the trade is important here. About 120 English ships a year were loading wine in Bordeaux until 1453 (when England lost Bordeaux). Ships came from

---

[38] An enquiry in Devon in 1474 revealed that 25% of outward commercial journeys were without cargo so that ballast of some kind would be necessary; PRO, London, E159/253, Recorda, Trinity, mm. 25–6.

[39] It varied between 1:0.8 and 1:1.25 in the 10% of cases where numbers of pilgrims and the ship's tonnage are both known.

all round England's shores, but those from the south-west, especially Devon and Cornwall, were prominent, just as they were in the transport of pilgrims. For instance, in 1435–1436, 53% of 126 English ships at Bordeaux came from the southwest, and in the Jubilee years of 1428 and 1434 over 60% of pilgrim licences were for south-western ships. Trade between England and Iberia was also well established and, from the mid fourteenth century, English ships sailed with increasing frequency to both southern Spain and Portugal. In the war period of the early fifteenth century letters of safe-conduct were often necessary, but these seem to have been freely granted and probably covered a score of ships in each direction.[40] In more peaceful circumstances, at the end of the fifteenth century, the numbers of ships sailing directly between England and Iberia rose further. Crossing the Bay of Biscay was probably safer then than it had ever been. Seamen were immensely experienced on the route, and navigational skills and ship technology were improving rapidly.

The Bristol customs accounts are particularly useful for demonstrating the regularity of sailings across the Bay of Biscay, because the customs collectors there recorded destinations and last ports of call. In the late fourteenth century, in the seven years 1376–1383, at least sixty-nine ships left for Iberia and 104 for Bordeaux, and in accounts for 1387 and 1390–1391 a further thirty-nine to Iberia, and forty to Bordeaux, were recorded. Sailings took place all the year round.[41] A hundred years later the Bordeaux trade had collapsed, but the pattern of regular sailings across the Bay continued. In the three years of 1485–6, 1486–7 and 1492–3 there were forty-three movements to and from Bordeaux, eighty-four to and from northern Spain, and ninety-two to and from Portugal and Andalusia.[42] The accounts show that the same ships and masters regularly sailed on these routes and came to know them well. For instance, both Bernard Veisy and William Power took Bristol ships to Gascony and Iberia once or twice each year between 1376 and 1383.

---

40 Henry IV of England envisaged granting 60 safe-conducts a year to Spanish ships; 28 Spanish ship masters bought safe-conducts from Henry V in 1413; similar numbers were granted per annum in the 1450s and 1460s. English ships going in the other direction possibly reached similar numbers: the Franco-Castilian treaty of 1454 tried to restrict Spanish safe-conducts to English ships to only 20 a year; Childs 1978, *op. cit.* note 37, pp. 45–9.

41 PRO, London, E122/15/8, 16/2,4, 5, 9, 11, 13, 15, 17, 19–23. For Iberia sailings were as follows: January – 11, February – 8, March – 10, April – 8, May – 10, June – 17, July – 10, August – 9, September – 12, October – 6, November – 2, December – 5. For Bordeaux sailings were as follows: January – 8, February – 13, March – 5, April – 13, May – 6, June – 7, July – 6, August – 9, September – 28, October – 26, November – 12, December – 11. High numbers in September and October reflect the autumn vintage.

42 PRO, London, E122/20/5, 7 and 9. Sailings to Lisbon and Andalusia were as follows: inwards, January – 8, February – 6, March – 5, April – 4, May – 3, June – 7, July – 0, August – 3, September – 5, October – 2, November – 7, December – 3; outwards, January – 1, February – 4, March – 3, April – 9, May – 1, June – 1, July – 1, August – 2, September – 5, October – 8, November – 1, December – 3.

Plate 1 Taking soundings in the mid-fifteenth century, as illustrated in the earliest surviving English treatise on sailing directions. Pierpont Morgan Library, New York. Ms 775, fo. 138v (reproduced with permission).

It is also possible to trace known pilgrim carriers in their other activities, through a variety of records, and this again illustrates the experience of the masters. The *Trinity Courtney*, which was licensed to carry 200 pilgrims to Compostela in January 1445, had been in Bordeaux loading 251 tuns of wine in the previous autumn.[43] Traces of the career of one experienced fifteenth century master, John Lysard, appear in records over nearly twenty years. He commanded ships which regularly carried pilgrims, traded and fought in the

[43] British Library, MS Additional 15524; PRO, London, C76/127 mm. 10, 4.

Perils, or Otherwise, of Maritime Pilgrimage

waters between Lisbon and London.[44] As master of the *Katherine* of Dartmouth, owned by Thomas Gille of Dartmouth, he twice carried forty pilgrims to Coruña in 1434, loaded wine in Bordeaux in 1435, was on war service in the Channel in 1436, and sailed to Portugal in 1439. In the 1440s he moved to Gille's larger ship the *Anthony* and continued similar activities. He loaded wine at Bordeaux in November 1443, was licensed to take fifty pilgrims to Coruña in February 1445, and unloaded wine at Exeter in February 1446. In 1448 he was again working on the Bordeaux route and in 1451 had moved to the 220 ton London ship, *Katherine of the Tower*, owned by the duke of Exeter, in which he was on naval service. In many other cases masters' careers can be traced over decades and show regular, repeated journeys in the Biscay area. This indicates great experience on the routes and suggests relatively safe sailing even in winter months.

To back up the master's experience there were written sailing directions, similar to the modern Admiralty Pilot. The directions provided compass bearings between landfalls, as well as information on tides, currents, harbours, and depth and type of sea-bed. They illustrate the normal trading routes and the practical skills of seamen. Examples survive from the fifteenth century, and it is thought that the practice goes back to the fourteenth century. An English example which is particularly relevant to the pilgrim route includes directions for voyages from the English Channel to Gascony, northern Spain, Andalusia and back to the west coast of England and Ireland.[45] Plotting the given directions on to a chart of the area reveals a complex network of possible routes all round and across the Bay of Biscay. Six landfalls were given for northern Spain: four were of most use for trade with the Basque Provinces, and Capes Ortegal and Finisterre were landfalls for Coruña and onward voyages to Lisbon and Sanlucar. Ortegal, the main landfall for Coruña, was specifically noted by William Wey in 1456, along with Cape Prior and what he called the Tower de la Vale, at the sight of which the sailors lowered a sail.[46] The sailing directions clearly show that direct passages across the bay were made. They provide directions from Cape Ortegal to Poitou, Brittany and Cape Clear in Ireland, and from Cape Finisterre to Gascony, Brittany, the Scilly Isles and

---

44 PRO, London, C76/116 mm. 11, 9, 127 m. 4; E101/192/1, 194/3, 195/19; Devon Record Office, local customs account for 24–25 Henry VI; *Calendar of Patent Rolls 1429–36*, 509; *Calendar of Patent Rolls 1446–52*, 447; PRO, London, E101/54/14.
45 The British Library Lansdowne MS 285 copy is printed in *Sailing Directions for the Circumnavigation of England*, ed. J. Gairdner, Hakluyt Society 79 (London,1889), pp.11–37, and reprinted in D. W. Waters, *The Rutters of the Sea* (New Haven and London, 1967), pp. 181–95. A slightly better text from Pierpont Morgan MS 775 (formerly known as the Hastings MS) is edited by G. A. Lester, 'The earliest English sailing directions', in *Popular and Practical Science of Medieval England*, ed. L. M. Matheson (East Lansing, 1994), pp. 330–67. The main routes across the Bay of Biscay given there are indicated in Figure 1.
46 The Tower, also given as the Tour de Fer or de la Vare in French directions, is the old Roman lighthouse or phare, now the Tower of Hercules, at Coruña.

Cape Clear and Mizen Head in Ireland. They also provide information on soundings for direct crossings of the bay from Finisterre to England. The sailor first set his course north-north-east; then, for the River Severn and Bristol, when he estimated he was 'two parts over' the sea, he should turn north-east until he came within sounding depth; at ninety to a hundred fathoms he should turn north until he reached seventy-eight fathoms with a bottom of grey sand; he should continue north until the bottom became muddy and then turn east-north-east. To go into the English Channel he should wait until 'three parts over' the bay, then go north-north-east by north until he reached a hundred fathoms, then north-east until he reached eighty fathoms. If the bottom was 'stremy', he was then between Ouessant and Scilly at the entrance of the Channel.

Such navigational skills and experience enhanced the safety of sailing in the fifteenth century. The compass was not of course new. It was known from the late twelfth century, certainly used at sea in the thirteenth, spread widely in the fourteenth, and was commonplace by the fifteenth century, allowing regular sailing even in winter months when sun and stars might be invisible. The sailing directions also mention the use of the sand-glass for recording time. These too were not new on board ship and are known in ship inventories in England from 1295. Similarly, the use of the sounding lead was a commonplace of sailing in northern seas, and the sailing directions show the precision with which sailors could 'place' themselves from sampling the sea bed for depth and for bottom. Although the details on particular coasts and harbours given in sailing directions imply that those sailing were in unfamiliar territory, it is important to understand that the directions would have been of little use to a sailor unless he already had considerable general experience of these seas. He needed to understand wind and weather patterns and how the tides and currents acted on his ship. The directions assumed that, watching the way sea and wind interacted, he would know when he was 'two parts over' or 'three parts over' the Bay of Biscay so that he could change course for Bristol or for the Channel. Navigation was securely founded by the early fifteenth century.

It is also probable that ships themselves became safer. Ship technology evolved steadily in the Middle Ages. The steering oar gave way to the fixed rudder in the thirteenth century; the single mast gave way to two, then three, masts early in the fifteenth century. This allowed a variety of square and lateen sails to be tried, which made the ship more manoeuvrable even in head winds. Hulls became stronger and ships became bigger, with a variety of benefits including making them commercially more efficient and safer from attack. Safety is of course a relative matter and the rate of loss in the Middle Ages is difficult to assess. English records certainly show the same men, and ships of the same names, operating for years, but to see how many failed to return we need a long run of very detailed customs accounts, which we generally do not have. However, in two full years of accounts at Bristol, twenty-three voyages to Portugal and Andalusia can be traced and, at most, two ships did not return.

Perils, or Otherwise, of Maritime Pilgrimage

If both were truly losses then the rate of loss was about 8.5%. But if the sample is extended to include voyages across the Bay of Biscay to Bordeaux (from which all ships returned safely) the loss rate was much smaller. It should also be noted that one of the 'missing' masters appears again later, which may indicate that his absence from the earlier record was because he was engaged on a longer, more complex journey, in which a ship could be away from its home port for a year or more.[47]

The question posed at the beginning of this paper was why English pilgrims chose the apparently more dangerous sea route to travel to Compostela. Negative reasons might be that land routes were very harsh and time-consuming and possibly politically difficult for English pilgrims, but more positive reasons might be that the sea route, at its best, was fast and convenient, especially if ship owners organised special passenger voyages. Moreover, the route remained flexible, since, alongside the 'package tours', pilgrims could still form an organised group to charter their own vessel or adapt themselves to the slower rhythms and patterns of regular commerce and join cargo ships to Bordeaux or Spain. Sea transport was becoming safer and might well have been perceived to be so by pilgrims if they enquired about means of transport and were told of regular, all year round sailings to Iberia. This is not to deny the 'perils' of this paper's title. The risk of sea-travel may have been less in the fifteenth century than in earlier ones, but the dangers of storm and wreck were still there. Whether pilgrims travelled on 'package tours', privately chartered ships or cargo ships, for them the voyage was undoubtedly a considerable undertaking. They no doubt gave thanks at the shrine for their safe arrival and prayed for their safe return, but they might have taken comfort from talking to the seamen. For these the voyage to Coruña was no more difficult than one to Bordeaux, Lisbon or Sanlucar to which they sailed as part of their everyday work. While for pilgrims the voyage was still full of discomfort and fear, for ship owners and seamen transporting pilgrims to Coruña was simply an additional opportunity to make money.

---

[47] PRO, London, E122/20/5, 7.

8

Pilgrimage and the Cult of St Katherine of Alexandria in Late Medieval England

KATHERINE J. LEWIS

St Katherine of Alexandria was one of the most popular saints in England between the thirteenth and sixteenth centuries. The importance of her cult to people from a wide range of social backgrounds is shown by the variety of documentary, literary and visual sources which make reference to her. St Katherine's popularity depended to a large extent on the great intercessory and patronal power which she was seen to possess. Visualization, or expression, of the saint and her powers often took the form of a portrayal of the shrine on Mount Sinai, where her body was housed. This famous shrine was a physical goal for wealthy or devout pilgrims. In England, however, representations of Mount Sinai seem also to have become a focus for symbolic pilgrimages. In particular, these symbolic pilgrimages formed part of the devotions of young women, who venerated the saint as a marriage broker. A chapel of St Katherine located on a hill-top in England, containing an image of the saint, could become a substitute Mount Sinai. Pilgrimage to St Katherine thus became a possibility for devotees from all walks of life. This paper examines the role played by Mount Sinai in the dissemination of the cult to Europe and England, and considers the meaning and use of Mount Sinai for St Katherine's followers in late medieval England.

The Beginnings of the Cult of St Katherine

According to the later medieval accounts of her life, St Katherine of Alexandria lived and died in the exotic early fourth-century world of Asia Minor. There are few surviving early accounts of her life. The first extant written or visual reference to the saint, or her passion, dates from the late tenth century; four hundred years after her supposed martyrdom.[1] This is in a Greek text, the

---

1 The most detailed account of the early history of the cult of St Katherine is provided by J. R. Bray, 'The Legend of St Katherine in Later Middle English Literature' (unpublished Ph.D. thesis, University of London, 1984), pp. 6-20.

Menelogion Basilianum, a collection of brief saints' lives arranged in calendar order, written for Basil II (976–1025).[2]

The sparseness of the evidence for her early cult might suggest that St Katherine was little known in the West before the late eighth or early ninth century. It is possible that her cult was only a minor one at this time, perhaps something of a fashionable novelty which inspired few surviving memorials.[3] An early following of some sort is likely to have existed, however, because the basis for the flourishing late medieval cult of St Katherine was her 're-introduction' in the eleventh century.[4] Crusaders probably played an important role in this re-introduction; the cult entered Europe by way of Italy, and became immensely popular all over the continent. It appears that devotion to St Margaret of Antioch filtered into England at about the same time and by much the same means.[5] That St Katherine and St Margaret were the most popular of the virgin martyrs in later medieval England may be connected to these circumstances. No such obvious pattern is apparent for the 'lesser' virgin martyrs, such as Agatha, Agnes or Lucy, who were known in England at an earlier date, but did not subsequently enjoy the same level of popularity.

The focus of St Katherine's cult was Mount Sinai, the mountain where Moses had received the Ten Commandments or Law of God.[6] The emperor Justinian first established a monastery on the mountain, and there was a church built on the site by his death in AD 565.[7] This church was not dedicated to St Katherine but to the Virgin Mary.[8] At some stage in the monastery's history a body was discovered and re-interred in the church. This body was identified as that of a virgin martyr who had died for the faith, namely St Katherine. She was said to have enjoyed limited cult status a few hundred years previously, and was now provided with a feast day (25 November), an exalted pedigree and, most importantly, a legend. The earliest account of this invention is contained in the *Iter ad Terram Sanctam*, or *Journey to the Holy Land*, written by Thietmar in 1217.[9] J. R. Bray has suggested that the historical event

---

[2] Bray, *op cit.* note 1, p. 6.

[3] Bray, *op. cit.* note 1, p. 249. Equally, it is possible that survival of the cult and its growth from the eighth to the eleventh centuries is obscured by the paucity of the evidence.

[4] Bray 1984, *op. cit.* note 1, p. 249; B. A. Beatie, 'Saint Katharine of Alexandria: traditional themes and the development of a medieval German hagiographic narrative', *Speculum* 52 (1977), 785–800.

[5] B. A. Beatie, *op. cit.* note 4, p. 798). For the early cult of St Margaret, see *Seinte Marherete þe Meiden ant Martyr*, ed. F. M. Mack, EETS OS 193 (Oxford and London, 1934; reprinted with corrections, 1958), x–xi.

[6] Exodus 19–20.

[7] A. Kurvinen, 'The Life of St Catharine of Alexandria in Middle English Prose' (unpublished D.Phil. thesis, University of Oxford, 1960), p. 207.

[8] Bray 1984, *op. cit.* note 1, p. 11.

[9] Bray 1984, *op. cit.* note 1, p. 12; Kurvinen, *op. cit.* note 7, p. 209.

of the invention may have happened at the end of the tenth century but, unfortunately, there is no way of knowing exactly when it occurred or under what circumstances.

Thietmar's early thirteenth century record of the event tells of the monks seeing unnatural lights over the peak of the mountain, and following them, until they are led to a body. They take it back to the monastery, where an old hermit is on hand to identify it as the body of St Katherine.[10] The historical event of the discovery of the body led to an addition to St Katherine's legend; in almost all later versions of her life her freshly beheaded body was transferred to Mount Sinai by angels.[11] Mount Sinai therefore provided the initial site and focus for the cult of St Katherine. It was also of intrinsic importance to the wider dissemination of her cult throughout Europe.

Re-Introduction in the Eleventh Century

The most important factor in the successful propagation of the cult of St Katherine in Europe was the removal of her relics from Mount Sinai to Rouen.[12] According to legend, in 1026 one Symeon, monk of Sinai, took three of St Katherine's fingers and brought them to Rouen as a gift to Duke Robert of Normandy, father of the Conqueror.[13] A fifteenth-century collection of sermon exemplars gives the following account of the acquisition:

> Once a monk of Rothomagence came to the monks and abbey on Mt Sinai and there he lived in the service of God and St Katherine for seven years. And he was a very devout man; and he prayed to St Katherine that he might have some relic from among her bones. And suddenly, as he sat in prayer, there was put into his hand, how, he never knew, her little finger; and he thanked

---

[10] Perhaps not surprisingly, in a later version of this account the monks are aware of the legend that the saint's body was brought to their mountain, and they pray for it to be revealed to them. An angel appears and duly carries out their request. See the description of these episodes in the fifteenth-century prose life of St Katherine, *The Life and Martyrdom of St Katherine of Alexandria, Virgin and Martyr*, ed. H. H. Gibbs (London, 1884), pp. 61–3.

[11] See for example *Legenda Aurea*: J. de Voragine, *The Golden Legend: Readings on the Saints 2*, trans. W. G. Ryan (Princeton, 1993), p. 339. Ryan's text is based on the Latin text edited by T. Graesse, *Jacobi a Voragine, Legenda Aurea* (originally published Leipzig, 1850; reprinted Osnabruck, 1969).

[12] Bray 1984, *op. cit.* note 1, p. 9; E. C. Williams, 'Mural paintings of St Catherine in England', *Journal of the British Archaeological Association* 3rd Series 19 (1956), 20–33 (p. 21 n.).

[13] Beatie 1977, *op. cit.* note 4, pp. 785–800 (p. 798). The story of the monk from Sinai and his acquisition of the finger bones is to be found in *Legende Aurea*, *op. cit.* note 11, p. 339.

God for it, and St Katherine, and brought it to his monastery, and there it is worshipped to this day.[14]

The bones were believed to be part of St Katherine's martyred body and were therefore objects of fervent devotion, a direct link to the saint and her power. They provided Katherine's followers with tangible evidence of her legend, which came to exist in many different forms and languages.[15]

Rouen, as a western centre of devotion to St Katherine, and the capital of Normandy, had an important part to play in the dissemination of her cult in the eleventh and twelfth centuries. Probably as a result of the acquisition of her fingers, a monk called Ainard at the monastery of the Holy Trinity in Rouen, wrote a life of St Katherine in Latin in the mid eleventh century.[16] This work provided the source for an Anglo-Norman poem written to establish and propagate the cult in England (ruled by the duke of Normandy in the late eleventh century). It sought to emphasize the central importance of Rouen to the cult of St Katherine.[17] Presumably she was already becoming popular and Rouen wished to remind all English devotees of the part it had played in bringing St Katherine to them.

In addition to their exalted status as parts of the body of St Katherine, the bones at Sinai and Rouen had the additional property of exuding a miraculous, healing oil. Phials of this oil could be taken away by pilgrims. Charlemagne was reputed to have brought back such a phial from Mount Sinai after his legendary pilgrimage to the Holy Land, and a fifteenth-century inventory of Westminster Abbey's relics lists a phial of St Katherine's oil presented by Edward the Confessor.[18] Edward was in exile in Normandy until 1041 and it is not impossible that he could have obtained such a phial from Rouen. Regardless of the authenticity of this relic, the mid eleventh century sees the first recorded appearance of St Katherine's name in England. It occurs in a calendar produced by the scriptorium of the Old Minster at Winchester in

---

[14] *An Alphabet of Tales*, ed. M. M. Banks, EETS OS 126 (London, 1904), 291: 'Som tyme þer come a monk of Rothomagence vnto þe monkes & þe abbay þat is on þe Mownte of Synay, and þer he abade in serves of God & Saynt Katryn vij yere. And he was a passand devoute man: and he prayed evur vnto Saynt Katryn at he mott hafe som relykk of hur bonys. And sodanlie, as he satt at his prayers, þer was putt in his hand, at he wiste nevur how come, hur little fynger; and he thankid God þerof, & Saynt Katryn, & had it home vnto his monasterie, and þer it is wurshuppid vnto þis day.' All translations from Middle English are by the author.

[15] Lives can be found in Latin and Greek, Old Irish, Welsh, Old Polish, Old Czech and Hungarian, English, French, German, Italian and Spanish, see R. W. J. Boykin, 'The Life of St Katherine of Alexandria: A Study in Thematic Morphology Based on Medieval French and English Texts' (unpublished Ph.D. thesis, University of Rochester, 1972), p. 1.

[16] *Seinte Katerine*, ed. S. R. T. O. d'Ardenne and E. J. Dobson, EETS SS 7 (London, 1981), xv.

[17] *Seinte Katerine*, op. cit. note 16, p. xvi.

[18] Bray 1984, op. cit. note 1, p. 10.

about 1050.[19] Winchester was the capital of England at this time and it seems likely that the cult of St Katherine began at the centre of royal government and spread across the country from there. Even if Edward the Confessor did not bring back a phial of St Katherine's oil from Rouen, it is probable that his entourage brought back devotion to her.

St Katherine's Shrine

The earliest extant version of the life of St Katherine copied in England probably also originated from Rouen. This Latin life, known as the Vulgate, was an extremely popular text with over one hundred surviving copies of it in European libraries.[20] It provided the main source for the *Legenda Aurea* life of the saint, and for the lives subsequently written in Middle English.[21] The Vulgate concludes with the information that St Katherine was carried to Mount Sinai and that healing oil still issued from her bones.[22] Mount Sinai subsequently became an important and wealthy shrine, visited by many pilgrims.[23] Nowadays, the best known of these visitors is the German friar Felix Fabri, who left a detailed account of the pilgrimage he undertook in 1483. His description survives in a manuscript preserved in the archives of Ulm cathedral in Germany, his home town.[24] English pilgrims also left accounts of the shrine; for example the fourteenth-century record written by one Thomas Brygg, who visited the Holy Land with his master, Thomas Swinburne.[25] Such accounts were probably known by some of St Katherine's devotees in late medieval England. However the most widely known non-hagiographic source of information about Mount Sinai was the description of it in *Mandeville's Travels*.[26] This later fourteenth century account accords well with descriptions

---

19 Bray 1984, *op. cit.* note 1, pp. 215 and 223.
20 The text of the Vulgate has been edited by d'Ardenne and Dobson, *Seinte Katerine, op. cit.* note 16, pp. 144–203. For a discussion of the text see Bray 1984, *op. cit.* note 1, pp. 23–34.
21 *Legende Aurea, op. cit.* note 11, pp. 334–41. See Bray 1984, *op. cit.* note 1, pp. 87–90.
22 *Seinte Katerine, op. cit.* note 16, pp. 202–3.
23 Some historians have described a military order of Knights of St Katherine, who undertook to guard pilgrims to the shrine. However, as Bray points out, there is very little contemporary evidence to support the existence of such an order in the medieval period; J. R. Bray, 'The Medieval Military Order of St Katherine', *Bulletin of the Institute of Historical Research* 56 (1983), 1–6.
24 See H. F. M. Prescott, *Once to Sinai: The Further Pilgrimage of Friar Felix Fabri* (London, 1957).
25 This account, part of Brygg's *Itinerarium in Terram Sanctam Domini Thomas de Swynburne*, can be found in *Archives de l'Orient Latin* (Paris, 1884), pp. 380–2.
26 The most detailed account of the shrine is provided by the Middle English version preserved in two early fifteenth century manuscripts, and its Latin source, extant in six manuscripts: *The Bodley Version of Mandeville's Travels*, ed. M. C. Seymour, EETS

left by actual pilgrims, and perhaps Mandeville drew on one or more of these for his work. Mandeville describes the focal point of the monastery thus:

> There is the church of St Katherine with many lamps burning ... And beside that high altar are three steps leading up to the alabaster tomb which contains the body of the virgin. The prelate of the monks shows the relics to pilgrims. That same prelate stirs the bones of the martyr with a silver instrument, and out comes a little sweet smelling oil; but it is not like oil or balm because it is blacker in colour, and they give a little of it to pilgrims. And after that they show the head of St Katherine and that cloth it was wound in when the angels brought the body up to Mount Sinai, and there they buried it with that same cloth that is still bloody and evermore shall be.[27]

Apart from visiting the shrine, the pilgrims would also climb to the spot where angels originally left her body.

> And from that mountain men traverse a great valley to reach another mountain where St Katherine was buried by the angels of our Lord.... And afterwards men climb up the mountain of St Katherine that is higher than the mountain of Moses. And there where St Katherine was buried there is neither church nor chapel or other dwelling place, but there is a heap of stones around the place where her body was laid down by the angels. There used to be a chapel but it was cast down and the stones still lie there.[28]

Mandeville exhorts his readers to visit the shrine for the miraculous benefits which such a journey could bring them. It is unlikely that he actually went

---

OS 253 (London, 1963), 38–45. The Middle English version translated from Jean d'Outremeuse's French text includes substantially the same details: *Mandeville's Travels: Translated from the French of Jean d'Outremeuse*, ed. P. Hamelius, EETS OS 153–154 (London, 1919–1923), 37–41. The metrical version describes the monastery, but not the shrine or the relics: *The Metrical Version of Mandeville's Travels*, ed. M. Seymour, EETS OS 269 (London, 1973), 35 and 37–8.

[27] Seymour 1963, *op. cit.* note 26, p. 41: 'Ther is the cherche of Seynt Kateryne with manye lampis brennande ... And besyde that heye auter arn iii. Grecis for to comyn vp to the tombe that is of alabastyr wher the body of the vurgyne is. The prelat of the monkys shewith the relikys to pilgrymmys. That eche prelat steryth the bonys of the martyr with an instrument of syluyr, and thanne comyth a lytil oylw as it were swet; but it is not lik neythir oyle ne baumme for it is more blak, and therof they yeuyn lytil quantite to pilgrymys. And aftyr that they shewyn the hed of Seynt Kateryne and that cloth that it was wondyn in whanne the angel[is] broughte the body vp to the Mon[t] of Synay, and there they grauyd it with that eche cloth that yet is blody and euremor shal be.' See also Hamelius 1919–1923, *op. cit.* note 26, p. 39.

[28] Hamelius 1919–1923, *op. cit.* note 26, p. 41: 'And from þat mountayne men passen a gret valeye for to gon to anoþer mountayn where seynt Kateryne was buryed of the Aungeles of oure lord ... And after men gon vp the mountayne of seynt Kateryne þat is more high þan the mount of Moyses. And þere where seynt Kateryne was buryed is nouther chirche ne chapell ne other duellyng place, But þere is an heep of stones aboute the place where the body of hire was put of the Angeles. þere was wont to ben a chapell but it was casten down + it lyggen the stones þere.'

there himself. The same was probably true of most of those who owned a copy of his *Travels*, or had access to it. The pilgrimage to Mount Sinai entailed a 250 mile journey from Jerusalem across the Sinai desert. It therefore required both fortitude and wealth and was, moreover, only an option for male pilgrims.[29] Thus an account such as Mandeville's could provide valuable details of the shrine and its rituals for devotees who could not visit it themselves.

For the majority of English people the principle source of knowledge about the shrine was provided by the life of St Katherine itself. There are fourteen extant Middle English versions of her life and virtually all of them end with an account of her body being taken to Mount Sinai.[30] The thirteenth-century *Legenda Aurea* life of St Katherine, based on the Vulgate, provided the basic source for the later versions. It simply says 'angels took up the body and carried it from that place a twenty-day journey to Mount Sinai where they gave it an honourable burial. An oil still issues from her bones and mends the limbs of all who are weak.'[31] Some of the Middle English lives expand on this, and may have been influenced by the accounts of those who had actually visited the shrine. The late thirteenth century *South English Legendary* life says:

> An angel came and took the body amid all the people
> And bore it to the hill of Sinai twenty days journeys away
> And buried it there nobly and fittingly
> The bones are still there to this day
> Out of her tomb holy oil still streams
> Through which many a sick man is given relief and life
> Those who obtain the oil take it far abroad
> It is a noble relic of benefit to sick men.[32]

The late fourteenth century Scottish Legendary life says that at the shrine:

> Miracles are performed for her
> As faithful men tell who have sought her

---

[29] The monastery has only been opened to female visitors within the last couple of decades.
[30] Only the shortest life, that in the *Speculum Sacerdotale*, contains no reference to Mount Sinai: see *Speculum Sacerdotale*, ed. E. H. Weatherly, EETS OS 200 (London, 1935), 243–4.
[31] *Legenda Aurea*, op. cit. note 11, p. 339.
[32] *South English Legendary* 2, ed. C. D'Evelyn and A. J. Mill, EETS OS 236 (London 1956), 543:

> An angel com & nom þe bodi among alle þe manne
> & bat hie to þe hul of Synay tuenti iorneyes þanne
> & burede hit þer nobliche & faire ynou also
> þerȝut tu þis dai þe bones beoþ ido
> Of hire tumbe þer vrneþ ȝut holi oylle wel blyue
> Wher þurf meni sik man is ibroȝt to help & to lyue
> Wide alonde his is ilad ho so hit habbe mote
> Noble relik hit is sike men to habbe of bote.

and always will be for the love
Of her and of Christ Heaven's king
And her bones still give out
A very clear oil men say
Which provides hope and healing to all
As they record who have been there.[33]

In his late fourteenth century *Festial*, John Mirk also explains that God has wrought miracles at the shrine, '... and still does to this day'.[34]

Mount Sinai is also to be found in visual representations of St Katherine's life. A portrayal of her body being carried to the shrine seems often to have provided the last scene of wall painting cycles of her life. In 1875 what appeared to be the remains of such a cycle was uncovered in Little Kimble church, Buckinghamshire. It was painted in about 1330 and the only legible portion remaining showed the burial. In a description of it published by E. W. Tristram, two angels, one at her head and one at her feet, with wings outspread, lower her body into the grave. Mount Sinai is represented by some wavy lines.[35] The most extensive extant wall painting cycle of the life of St Katherine, encompassing twenty-five panels, is to be found at Sporle in Norfolk.[36] The cycle dates from *c.* 1400 and the penultimate panel shows the burial of the saint. Mount Sinai is represented by a green hill, dotted with flowers. The hill is surmounted by a brown tomb banded with gold in which can be seen the form of Katherine's body, shrouded in bright red. Two angels hover above the body praying, while two more at the foot of the hill wave censers.

---

[33] *The Legends of the Saints in the Scottish Dialect of the Fourteenth Century* 4, ed. W. M. Metcalf, Scottish Text Society 25 (Edinburgh, 1891), 447:

>   mirakilis ar for hire wrocht
>   as leile men sais þat has hir socht
>   & ay sall be in lowing
>   Of hire & or criste hewynnis kyng
>   & of hire banis but leising
>   Oyle full clere men sais yhet spring
>   þat hope and leile is till all sare
>   as þai record þat has bene þare.

[34] '... and ȝet doþe ynto þis day.' J. Mirk, *Festial*, ed. T. Erbe, EETS ES 96 (London, 1905), 275-7 (p. 277). For other Middle English lives of St Katherine and their descriptions of Mount Sinai see *Altenglische Legenden, Neue Folge*, ed. C. Horstmann (Heilbronn, 1881), pp. 164-71 (p. 171) (*Northern Homily Cycle*), pp. 242-58 (p. 258) (Cambridge, Caius College, MS 175), pp. 260-4 (p. 264) (Oxford, Bodleian Library, MS 14528); O. Bokenham, *Legendys of Hooly Wummen*, ed. M. J. Serjeantson, EETS OS 206 (London, 1938), 172-201 (p. 200); S. Nevalinna and I. Taavitsainen, *St Katherine of Alexandria: The Late Middle English Prose Life in Southwell Minster MS 7* (Cambridge, 1993), pp. 67-95 (p. 95); *The Golden Legend or Lives of the Saints as Englished by William Caxton* 7, ed. F. S. Ellis (London, 1900), pp. 1-30 (pp. 25-7).

[35] E. W. Tristram, *English Wall Painting of the Fourteenth Century* (London, 1955), p. 188.

[36] For a description of Sporle see Tristram 1955, *op. cit.* note 35, pp. 249-50.

Like the words 'still to this day' in the *South English Legendary*, the final panel of this cycle brings the legend of St Katherine into the present. Mount Sinai is shown again, as in the previous panel, but with a tree added to the left of the shrine. The shrine is now closed and decorated more comprehensively with gold. At the foot of the hill kneel three pilgrims, at least one of whom is tonsured. This is the central figure with his back to the audience. He is flanked on either side by two bearded figures, their hands raised in prayer. The man on the left carries a satchel and staff. The man on the right carries a rucksack.

The parishioners of Sporle church, in common with the majority of St Katherine's devotees, were unlikely to be able emulate these figures and visit Mount Sinai themselves. However, this representation of the shrine, combined with other descriptions of it, such as Mandeville's, would at least have allowed them to make a mental pilgrimage. The painting would certainly have reminded the parishioners that although St Katherine had died and gone to her throne in Heaven a thousand years ago, her body remained on earth. Moreover, as tangible proof of her power and of her ability to intervene in earthly matters, her earthly remains still exuded holy oil.

Few saints could boast such an important shrine. Arguably, the identification of the body found on Mount Sinai as that of St Katherine, rather than that of any other virgin martyr, was the single most important factor in the subsequent universal popularity of her cult. John Capgrave's life of St Katherine written in the 1440s shows that accounts of Mount Sinai continued to have currency among her devotees:

> The great miracles which are performed at her grave
> Are not unknown, despite the great distance
> Between it and us; but this knowledge we have.[37]

Concluding the life of St Katherine with a description of her shrine and its miracles demonstrated that prayers offered to her could and would be answered. The shrine on Mount Sinai functioned as a symbol of her power, a reminder that she was able to affect materially people's lives. Thus in the prayer ending one recension of the fifteenth-century prose life, Mount Sinai is presented as proof that St Katherine is able to intervene in the lives of her devotees:

> Eternal almighty God that has provided to the devotees of the blessed virgin St Katherine their desired relief as testimony of pure virginity and as an acknowledgement of special love you made milk flow out for blood when she was beheaded and caused her body to be buried by the service of angels on Mount Sinai, we beseech you grant that we might deserve by her prayers

---

[37] J. Capgrave, *Life of St Katherine*, ed. C. Horstmann, EETS OS 100 (1893), 402:
> The grete myracles whiche ben at hir graue
> Arn ny vnknowe, right for grete distauns
> Be-twyxe that and vs; but this knowleche we haue.

blessedly to get those things that we request and are profitable to our health in this life and to a good passage out of it.³⁸

Having introduced Mount Sinai, Capgrave exhorts his audience thus:

> So, since this hill is as it were a guide,
> Up to that mountain which stands in bliss,
> It is good for us that we swiftly ride
> After this maiden, that she may show us
> A steadfast lore to amend our wrongdoings:
> So shall she be in the manner of a model,
> To bring us to Heaven after our burial.³⁹

Here St Katherine's status as a model of the ideal Christian is used to urge devotees to follow her example and so get to heaven. More literally, the passage refers to the benefits which could be gained by actually travelling across Europe to the Holy Land and Mount Sinai.

The Popular Cult

For many it was, of course, impossible to undertake such a pilgrimage. A way seems, however, to have been found to enable people to make imitative journeys on a more practical scale. There are several medieval chapels dedicated to St Katherine dotted across the English countryside, particularly in Dorset, and significantly many of them are located on hill-tops. This appears to be a deliberate reference to the circumstances of her invention and burial and the existence of her shrine on Mount Sinai. Examples are to be found at Winchester (Hants), Guildford (Surrey) and Christchurch (Dorset).⁴⁰ There were similar chapels at Weymouth, Cerne Abbas, Piddletrenthide, Holworth (all in Dorset) and on the Isle of Wight. The chapels at Milton Abbas (built in the thirteenth century) and Abbotsbury (built in the late fourteenth century), both in Dorset, are perhaps the best preserved. Such chapels would have housed cult images of the saint which formed the focus for prayers directed to her. Contemporary practices of image worship demonstrate that in many

---

³⁸ Gibbs 1884, op. cit. note 10, p. 67: [insert 9]
³⁹ Capgrave 1893, op. cit. note 36, p. 402:
> Thanne, sith this hill is as it were a gyde,
> On-to that mount which þat stant in blysse,
> It is good to us þat we ful hastyly ryde
> After this mayde, þat she may vs wosse
> A stedfast lore for to amende oure mysse:
> Soo shal she been in maner of a fygure,
> To brynge us to heuene after oure sepulture.
⁴⁰ M. D. Anderson, *Looking for History in British Churches* (London, 1951), pp. 14–15 and 189–91.

Pilgrimage and the Cult of St Katherine

instances images of a saint were seen to possess the same power as actual relics.[41] Hill-top chapels of St Katherine could therefore become an accessible alternative to Mount Sinai, perceived as places where similar miracles could be obtained.

One group of devotees who seem to have made particular use of these local, replica shrines were young women of low social status. Their interest is linked to St Katherine's apparent role as a provider of husbands.[42] For women drawn from the ranks of the lesser nobility, gentry and urban elites St Katherine seems to have been seen as a paradigm of ideal femininity. This is indicated by her appearance in courtesy literature directed towards young women.[43] For women of lower rank, however, St Katherine appears to have functioned more directly as a marriage broker.

The perception of St Katherine as a marriage broker seems above all to be predicated on her status as the bride of Christ. This was established by the account of her mystical marriage, an episode which formed part of a narrative describing her birth, early life and conversion, which came to prefix the standard narrative of her passion and martyrdom during the thirteenth and fourteenth centuries.[44] It had become a fairly well established part of the Middle English tradition by the fifteenth century. Capgrave incorporated these episodes into his lengthy version of her life, while the prose life of St Katherine provided the medium by which the description of her mystical marriage was conveyed to a wide audience. It was composed before 1438, when it was incorporated into the *Gilte Legende*.[45] The text survives in four versions in twenty-four manuscripts. It is very difficult to establish which versions of a saint's life lower status people may have had access to, but it is possible that they encountered the mystical marriage in the form of a sermon. Some of the manuscripts of the *Gilte Legende* seem to have been owned and used by priests within parish churches.[46]

The description of the mystical marriage and the events leading up to it provide some insight into why St Katherine came to be seen as a purveyor of husbands. The prose life describes the difficulty the young fourteen-year-old queen has convincing her parliament that she does not need to marry. She has

---

41 M. Aston, *England's Iconoclasts 1: Laws Against Images* (Oxford, 1988), pp. 20–2.
42 K. J. Lewis, 'Rule of lyf alle folk to sewe: lay responses to the cult of St Katherine of Alexandria in England, 1300–1530' (unpublished D.Phil. thesis, University of York, 1996), pp. 218–57.
43 This issue is discussed in K. J. Lewis, 'Model girls? Virgin martyrs and the training of young women in late-medieval England', in *Young Medieval Women*, ed. N. J. Menuge, K. J. Lewis and K. M. Phillips (forthcoming).
44 Kurvinen 1960, *op. cit.* note 7, pp. 90–1.
45 See Kurvinen 1960, *op. cit.* note 7, pp. 1–6 for the textual history of the prose life.
46 For example, Southwell Minster MS 7, contains the prose life of St Katherine (including the mystical marriage), other saints' lives, and a copy of the *Festial*, suggesting that it was used by a cleric for purposes of parochial education. See Nevalinna and Taavitsainen 1993, *op. cit.* note 34, pp. 50–2.

set her sights on the perfect man, Christ, even though she does not yet know his name: 'For he that shall be my lord must be of such noble blood that all kings must worship him. And so great a lord that I shall never dare think that I made him a king. And so rich that he surpasses all others in wealth. And so full of beauty that the angels rejoice to behold him.'[47] Katherine finishes by saying that he must be born of a virgin. In answer to Katherine's tears and sighs as she tries to find this man, the Virgin Mary sends the old hermit Adryan to bring Katherine to his cell, where she shall be wedded to her chosen spouse. Adryan does as he is bidden and persuades Katherine to follow him out into the desert. After becoming hopelessly lost they finally discover the 'glorious minster' where the wedding is to take place.[48]

The following exposition suggests some of the themes and issues which may have been at work in the adoption of St Katherine as a patron for lower status women. It is just one possible reading of the mystical marriage. As with any narrative, the reading of this episode is dependent upon the interests and experiences of its audience. The women concerned did not share Katherine's high secular status, and had no intention of preserving their virginity, but nonetheless regarded her as their special protector. This may have been because they imbued the mystical marriage with a relevance that was not metaphorical but literal. Unlike the continental version of her legend, in which Katherine marries the infant Christ in a dream, Katherine in the English tradition marries the handsome adult Christ in an actual ceremony on earth.[49] Christ seals his vow to Katherine with words which echo contemporary marriage vows. Christ tells Katherine 'Here I take you as my wedded wife, promising you truly never to forsake you as long as you live.'[50] This is reminiscent of the marriage vow, as recorded in the *Use of York*, for example: 'Will you have this woman as your wife and love her . . . and forsake all others for her and be true to her to the end of your life?'[51] After the wedding Christ leaves Katherine and returns to Heaven. She is left with a token proving that the marriage had actually taken place, 'until in the end she saw the ring which our lord had placed on her finger'.[52] This showed that St Katherine experienced an actual marriage with Christ, having created him as the ideal husband in her own words and thoughts. It seems a logical development for young women to have prayed to her for a husband and to regard her as their special patron.

This was a popular aspect of the cult of St Katherine, something which was

---

[47] Kurvinen 1960, *op. cit.* note 7, p. 24.
[48] Kurvinen 1960, *op. cit.* note 7, p. 267.
[49] For an example of the Contintental version, see *Scotichronicon by Walter Bower 1*, ed. J. and W. MacQueen (Aberdeen, 1993), pp. 286–97.
[50] Kurvinen 1960, *op. cit.* note 7, p. 283.
[51] Bray 1984, *op. cit.* note 1, p. 260: 'Wylt thou have this woman to thy wyfe and loue her . . . and all other forsake for her, and hold the only to her to thy lyues end?'
[52] Kurvinen 1960, *op. cit.* note 7, p. 291: '. . . tylle at þe laste she beheld þe rynge þat our lord sette on his fynger'.

not part of the official church rituals and observances of her cult, and therefore not likely to have been formally recorded at the time. Surviving evidence of the custom of young women calling on St Katherine to provide them with a husband depends largely on the records made by antiquarians from the sixteenth century and later. Much of the evidence for this phenomenon, and the customs associated with it, is linked with the medieval hill-top chapels dedicated to the saint, but it can only be suggested that these represent the remaining traces of late medieval practices.

The earliest firm evidence relating to St Katherine's status as a marriage broker is provided by William Camden, one of the founding fathers of antiquarianism.[53] In *Britannia*, first published in 1586, he wrote '... girls keep a fast every Wednesday and Saturday throughout the yeare [sic], and some of them also on St Catherine's day; nor will they omit it. ... The reason given by some for this is, that the girls may get good husbands.'[54] The work of other antiquarians such as John Brand, writing in the 1770s, and W. C. Hazlitt, writing in c. 1900, has established that young girls were accustomed to call on St Katherine to provide them with a husband as recently as the last century.[55] These girls are implicitly of fairly low social status. Most other observations date from the eighteenth and nineteenth centuries.[56] The main indication from the late medieval period that St Katherine was perceived as a provider of husbands is found in a reading of the fifteenth-century prose life of the saint.[57] This at least allows for the strong possibility that her status as marriage broker constitutes a post-Reformation survival of late medieval beliefs and practices. It also elucidates the rituals practised by young women at the hill-top chapels, as recorded by the antiquarians.

The antiquarian sources assert that the hill-top chapels provided a particular focus for the custom of praying to St Katherine for a husband.[58] Most of the extant evidence is related to the chapels at Abbotsbury and Milton Abbas. There is evidence that at least some, if not all, of the other chapels functioned similarly. On St Katherine's day young women would make a pilgrimage to the chapel of St Katherine on foot, sometimes having first drunk from a well dedicated to her. The road at the foot of the hill in Milton Abbas is

---

53 For more on Camden, see R. M. Dorsen, *The British Folklorists: A History* (London, 1968), pp. 2–4.
54 As quoted by J. Brand, *Observations on the Popular Antiquities of Great Britain 1* (New York, 1970), p. 410; also W. C. Hazlitt, *Dictionary of Faiths and Folklore: Beliefs, Superstitions and Popular Customs* (originally published 1905; this edition London, 1995), p. 97.
55 For more on Brand, see Dorsen 1968, *op. cit.* note 53, pp. 13–25.
56 S. Dewar, 'St Catherine of Alexandria and her cult at Abbotsbury', *Proceedings of the Dorset Natural History and Archaeological Society* 90 (1969), 261–3.
57 K. J. Lewis 1996, *op. cit.* note 42, pp. 218–57.
58 Dewar, *op. cit.* note 56; C. Hole, *English Shrines and Sanctuaries* (London, 1954), pp. 159–60; also Anderson 1951, *op. cit.* note 40, p. 15 for the most detailed descriptions of the rituals.

still called Katherine's Well. On reaching the chapel they would recite a prayer to the saint. One version of this is given by Dewar as follows:

> A husband, St Katherine
> A handsome one, St Katherine
> A rich one, St Katherine
> A nice one, St Katherine
> And soon, St Katherine.[59]

At Abbotsbury it was customary for the women to make their prayer while clinging to three holes in the door jamb, their knees in one hole and their hands in the other two. The Dorsetshire folklorist, J. S. Udal, has suggested that the prayer may be an echo of a medieval rhyme.[60] Indeed, it does bear marked similarities to Katherine's description of the perfect husband given above. And, although there is no extant medieval version of this prayer, there is a letter which bears witness that to pray for a husband was a medieval custom. On the 14 September 1465, John Paston III wrote to Margaret Paston, instructing her, 'I pray you to visit the Cross at the Northdoor and St Saviour at Bermondsey while you are staying in London, and let my sister Margery go with you to pray to them that she may have a good husband before she comes home again.'[61]

There is no suggestion of any institutional involvement in these rituals. The women do not appear to go to the chapel to attend a service of any kind. Instead this phenomenon seems to be genuinely popular in nature, a practice that was born of various elements of the life and cult of St Katherine. It was developed in order to respond to the needs of a specific group by that group itself, with reference to the wider cult, but separate from it.[62] As far as lower status people were concerned, the most important and attractive thing about a saint was their ability to perform miracles and affect materially the lives of their devotees on earth. This view was certainly at the forefront of the popular incarnation of the cult of St Katherine.[63]

Perhaps these practices took the form of a large scale ritual involving

[59] Dewar, *op. cit.* note 56, p. 261.
[60] Dewar, *op. cit.* note 56, p. 261.
[61] *Paston Letters and Papers of the Fifteenth Century 1*, ed. N. Davies (London, 1971), p. 529: 'I pray yow vysyt þe Rood of Northedor, and Seynt Sauyour at Barmonsey amonge whyll ye abyd in London, and let my sustyr Margery goo wyth yow to prey to them þat sche may haue a good hosbond or sche com hom ayen.'
[62] R. Hertz, 'St Besse: a study of an Alpine cult', originally published in 1913, translated and republished by S. Wilson in *Saints and their Cults: Studies in Religion, Sociology, Folklore and History* (Cambridge, 1983), pp. 55–100, remains a very useful exploration of the development and dynamics of the official and popular strands in a saint's cult, in particular the ways in which both traditions 'shed a sharp light on the psychology of the profoundly different social groups in which they were elaborated' (p. 79).
[63] A. Gurevich, 'Peasants and saints', in *Medieval Popular Culture: Problems of Belief and Perception*, ed. A. Gurevich (Cambridge, 1988), pp. 39–77.

Pilgrimage and the Cult of St Katherine

groups of women on the feast day itself. At other times women made the pilgrimage on their own initiative as circumstances dictated. The word pilgrimage is used to describe the custom because, despite its small scale, it bears all the hall-marks of such rites; making a special journey on foot to a place at which the saint's power was held to be particularly potent, following prescribed rituals and asking for a specific favour. There was, of course, no relic of the saint to provide a tangible focus, but a cult image of St Katherine housed in these chapels would have performed the same function.

This analysis of the late medieval cult links it back to the life of St Katherine. The late medieval cult is evidently derived from certain aspects of the narrative which would have been very familiar to the young women. The specific rituals associated with St Katherine as marriage broker are predicated on the knowledge of her resting place at Mount Sinai. This popular, informal manifestation of devotion to St Katherine is not to be understood as entirely separate from the more 'official' actions of a Felix Fabri. The young women listening to or looking at representations of this final episode in St Katherine's life could never hope to visit the shrine themselves. By undertaking to climb the hill to their local chapel of St Katherine, an imitation Mt Sinai, they could effect a mimetic pilgrimage and one constructed to suit their specific needs. These women did not have access to the actual body of St Katherine but the hill-top pilgrimage and its associated practices was a way of bringing it within reach. Her presence was simultaneously created and affirmed by the supplicatory actions of these women. They located her both physically and mentally within the map of their lives and experiences.

St Katherine's journey to the Minster perhaps finds its parallel in the walk to the hill-top. Both are undertaken as acts of faith. Katherine trusts in the words of Adryan and the Virgin, the young women trust in the power of St Katherine. The young women seem to have followed some sort of ritual (presumably self-regulated) in order to prepare themselves to petition the saint and improve their chances of success. St Katherine had to be taught Christian doctrine before she arrived at the Minster, and be baptised once she got there, before she was allowed to look upon Christ.[64]

An important aspect of the whole phenomenon must have been the sense of solidarity which it would have engendered. The women who climbed to the chapels were certainly aware that they were participating in a tried and tested ritual. It may have helped them to feel that there was a way in which they could take a hand in determining, or at least influencing, the course of their future. This practice may have been passed down from mother to daughter. The fact that it endured for so long (up until the last century) is testament to its perceived effectiveness.

The power of St Katherine's shrine on Mount Sinai is demonstrated by the creation of the many replica shrines in England, and the replica shrines are a

---

[64] Kurvinen 1960, *op. cit.* note 7, pp. 263 and 279.

testament to the ways in which the cult of St Katherine answered the needs and aspirations of the saint's devotees. Aspects of her cult, such as the pilgrimage to Mt Sinai, could be adapted to fit the capabilities and resources of people drawn from a variety of backgrounds. Capgrave recommended swiftly riding after St Katherine to ensure one's spiritual wellbeing. The hill-top chapels made this a realistic possibility for all of her followers, whatever their status.

This paper is dedicated to my father, John Lewis.

9

Lifting the Veil on Pilgrim Badges

A. M. KOLDEWEIJ

The Sign of the Cross

Conventionally pilgrim badges were used by devout Christians to identify the wearer as a pilgrim, and to protect them from harm. The devil's child Robert le Diable, Robert the Devil, after a lifetime spent robbing, murdering and raping, suddenly repented his sins and resolved to go on a pilgrimage to the Pope in Rome. He made his preparations for the long journey and, according to the Middle Dutch version printed in 1516, '... made the sign of the Holy Cross and rode through the forest straight to Rome'.[1] By crossing himself, Robert the Devil made himself recognisable as a pilgrim, a traveller in God's name.

Recognisability was important, for pilgrims were tolerated as mendicants who could rely on receiving Christian charity, hospitality and generosity from their fellow men. A pilgrim's privileges included exemption from paying tolls, shelter and free board and lodging in monasteries or special hospitals. Pilgrims were not only licensed to beg, but encouraged to do so; indeed, accomplishing the journey in absolute poverty was considered particularly virtuous. It was thus a good deed to give one's fellow men an opportunity to practise Christian charity. The essential point for the pilgrim was that s/he could count on protection from above as a matter of course: anyone who robbed a pilgrim, maltreated them or worse, would instantly incur the wrath of God.

So the sign of the cross placed Robert under special protection as well as identifying him as a pilgrim. We do not know whether his cross was made of cloth and sewn onto his garments, whether it was a badge pinned onto them, whether it was painted, or whether it was simply a gesture sketched by his right hand. In view of the date of the story, the second half of the thirteenth century, the first suggestion seems most likely, but 'crossing' oneself could assume very physical and extreme forms, as for example in a painting of St

---

[1] *Robrecht de Duyvel*, ed. R. Resoort, Populaire Literatuur 2 (Muiderberg, 1980), 85, line 516–18: '... teekende hi metten heylighen cryce ende reedt doer dat foreest den rechten wech na Romen'; p. 123 n.

Roche as a pilgrim in the Austrian Benedictine abbey of Admont (Plate 2).[2] The saint is depicted as having taken the drastic step of incising the sign of the cross in his chest so deeply as to draw blood.

Such a representation, with the cross cut into the flesh, seems excessive, but was closer to reality than might be expected. Seventeenth-century sources mention the considerably older tradition of the tattooed pilgrim's sign. The crusaders are said to have had themselves tattooed as evidence of a visit to the Holy Grave and, in doing so, to have followed a much earlier tradition of tattooed Christian symbols going back as far as the first centuries AD.[3] A copper engraving of 1676 by Hans Martin Winterstein documents the signs which Otto von der Grössen of Hamburg caused to be tattooed on his left and right arms when he visited the Holy Land in 1669. They include the Jerusalem cross, a crucifix, the resurrected Christ and the Chapel of the Holy Grave. Another traveller to Jerusalem, the seventeenth-century Dutch Catholic martyr and Franciscan monk, Hieronymus van Weert (c. 1522–1572), had a tattooed Jerusalem cross on his chest and right arm.[4] Before Hieronymus became one of the nineteen Martyrs of Gorcum, who were hanged by rebel Protestants on 9 July 1572, the eye-witness and hagiographer Rutger van Est (Estius) recorded that the hangmen brutally cut the Jerusalem cross out of his flesh.[5] Travel reports of pilgrims to the Holy Land also mention tattoos, sometimes in minute detail. The chronicle of a town in Holland, for example, described how pilgrims were literally and physically marked with the cross in Bethlehem in the early seventeenth century:

> They have numerous wooden stamps in which the marks are incised and which are then placed on the arms: everybody can pick a stamp of his choice. Coal-dust is rubbed into the incisions in the stamp, which is then placed on the arm so as to transfer the incised mark onto the skin. Then a man holds the arm in his left hand, stretching the skin tight, and in his right hand is a narrow pipe with two needles, which from time to time he dips into ink mixed with oxgall and with which he pricks along the lines left by the wooden stamp. This is painful, and usually leaves a scab for a while; for two or three days the arms are swollen to three times their normal size. After all the lines have been traced with the needle, the arm is washed and examined

---

2 Ute Himmelstoss (ed.), *Kunstschatten uit de Benediktijnerabdij van Admont / Merveilles de l'abbaye Bénédictine d'Admont / Kunstschätze aus dem Benediktinerstift von Admont*, Europalia 87, Oesterreich (Tienen, 1987), pp. 124–5, catalogue no. 30.

3 C. Ruhnke, *Die Tätowierung, eine sozio-kulturelle und medizinische Betrachtung* (Marburg, 1974), pp. 47–9.

4 W. Lampen, 'Hollandsche Jerusalemvaarders in vroeger eeuwen', *Bijdragen voor de Geschiedenis van het Bisdom Haarlem* 45 (1928), 278–80.

5 Estius, *Historia Martyrum Gorcomiensium* (Douai, 1603); reprinted in *Acta Sanctorum Julii II* (Venice, 1747), c. 7, col. 799: '... figuras crucis Hierosolymitanae, quae illi, ut Terrae Sanctae peregrino, erant in pectore et dextro brachio ita certa ratione inscriptae, ut carne integra deleri non possent, adhuc viventi e carne homines inimici, crucis Christi crudeliter exsciderunt'.

for mistakes. If any are found, the procedure is repeated, three times if necessary. When it is finished, the arm is tightly bandaged. The scab which forms on the pricks or the pricked hand drops off after two or three days, but the blue marks remain and will never fade, because the blood mingles with the concoction of oxgall and ink, which penetrates the skin and produces marks.[6]

Metal Badges

For a far greater number of pilgrims in the late Middle Ages (from the twelfth to mid sixteenth century) badges were sewn onto the characteristic cloak, hat or bag. The complete ensemble, plus a staff, identified the wearer as a pilgrim. Usually these badges were either shells or cheap trinkets cast in a lead-tin alloy. In the late fifteenth and sixteenth centuries, examples stamped from wafer-thin brass also became popular. Well-heeled believers could purchase more durable variants in copper or bronze, or costly specimens fashioned from silver, silver-gilt or gold. They were sold, and perhaps in some cases issued as well, as devotional souvenirs in the vicinity of miraculous statues and shrines. The badges showed which holy places had been visited and placed the pilgrim under the protection of specific saints and shrines. Essentially they were Christian amulets or charms, believed to guard the wearer from evil. Each referred in detail to a legend or cult and had its own iconography and meaning.

The cultural references carried by such badges have made them a popular subject for study. Those made of lead-tin were cheap and produced in bulk. This, and their ability to survive in some circumstances, means that they have been found in large numbers by treasure-seekers, amateur archeologists and professional excavators since the middle of the last century. Conditions suitable for the preservation of badges often occur in the Netherlands and here, over the past twenty years, thousands of badges have been located by metal detectors.[7] One remarkable feature of these finds is that assorted secular badges are nearly always discovered among the religious material, under

---

6 Lampen 1928, *op. cit.* note 4, pp. 278–80, quoting from D. B. van Schoorl, *Chronyk van Medenblik* (Hoorn, 1767), p. 120, who obtained this information from a Simon Pietersz Poorter, traveller to Jerusalem in 1614.

7 Metal detectors are used by archaeologists, but also by treasure-seekers and clandestine diggers. It should be pointed out that the large majority of small metal objects discovered by the group euphemistically referred to as 'amateur archaeologists' were found during ground removal (with machines, as in urban renewal projects, or naturally, due to shifting river beds). Once uncovered, these objects are doomed to corrosion within a short space of time. Archaeological facilities are inadequate, unable to cope with the examination of the vast quantities of old habitation layers removed in this way. The activities of the so-called 'grey circuit' are therefore the only means by which these important objects have been preserved.

exactly the same conditions and in exactly the same contexts (Plate 1). It seems that, in the late Middle Ages, people wore not only religious badges but also similar, mass-produced, inexpensive jewellery of a secular nature. The subject matter covered by the secular badges is extremely varied, including representations of utensils, courtly scenes, proverbs and popular stories, as well as what, to the modern eye, are bizarre, erotic fantasies.

The State of the Investigation[8]

Although both religious and secular badges have been found together, they have largely been studied in isolation, or else segregated in some other way, for example with expensive badges being treated as jewellery. The earliest publication on pilgrim signs dates from 1848 and concerns a few badges in the British Museum.[9] However, the first wide-ranging research into badges was undertaken by the collector Arthur Forgeais, prompted by the numerous items found in the Seine.[10] Forgeais' work was published privately and initially was only followed up on a small scale, with work on new material appearing sporadically in local and regional publications. Almost a century later an even more ambitious investigation was undertaken by Kurt Köster, who concentrated on investigating specific case studies and establishing well-founded classifications. Regrettably, work on the comprehensive catalogue of pilgrim badges (*Pilgerzeichenkartei*) which Köster had initiated, and which was supported by the Deutsche Forschungsgemeinschaft, ended with his death in 1986. The German bell specialist, Jörg Poettgen, continues to publish fairly regularly on badges, specifically those which were cast onto bells[11] and, in

---

[8] An earlier version of this survey was presented at a symposium in the Boijmans Van Beuningen Museum, Rotterdam, 1994: A. M. Koldeweij, 'Laatmiddeleeuwse insignes: Verzamelgeschiedenis en stand van onderzoek, cultuurhistorische aspecten', in *Heilig en Profaan: Laatmiddeleeuwse insignes in cultuurhistorisch perspectief*, ed. A. M. Koldeweij and A. M. Willemsen (Amsterdam, 1995), pp. 14–16. For the more extensive literature on which this survey is based, see H. J. E. Beuningen and A. M. Koldeweij, *Heilig en Profaan: 1000 laatmiddeleeuwse insignes uit de collectie H. J. E. van Beuningen*, Rotterdam Papers 8 (Cothen, 1993); R. M. van Heeringen, A. M. Koldeweij and A. A. G. Gaalman, *Heiligen uit de modder: In Zeeland gevonden pelgrimstekens*, Clavis Kunsthistorische Monografieën 4 (Utrecht/Zutphen, 1987), 143–8.

[9] R. Smith, 'Religious signs or tokens of the Middle Ages', *Collectanea Antiqua* 1 (1848), 81–91.

[10] A. Forgeais, *Notice sur des plombs historiés trouvés dans la Seine*, 5 vols. (Paris, 1863–1866).

[11] Most recently, and for references to earlier work, see J. Poettgen, 'Europäische Pilgerzeichenforschung: Die Zentrale Pilgerzeichenkartei (PZK) Kurt Kösters († 1986) in Nürnberg und der Forschungsstand nach 1986', *Jahrbuch für Glockenkunde* 7–8 (1995–1996), 195–206.

1995, Andreas Haasis Berner obtained an MA degree with a dissertation on pilgrim badges to c. 1350.[12]

In England, pioneering work similar to that of Kurt Köster has been carried out by Brian Spencer at the Museum of London, albeit solely on English material. His published work includes some twenty-five relevant articles, plus books on the collections of badges in Salisbury Museum, Wiltshire, and on material from Norfolk.[13] Spencer is now retired but continues to work and has completed his magnum opus on badges from London, particularly those found in the Thames.[14] Unfortunately, institutional continuity seems unlikely.

In France, Colette Lamy-Lasalle, also now retired, researched badges after the war. Her work, and indirectly also that of Arthur Forgeais, has been continued by Denis Bruna, who wrote his dissertation on religious and secular badges at the Université de Paris I. Valuable publications on diverse aspects of the field have followed, including the comprehensive catalogue of badges in the Musée de Cluny.[15] Valuable work has also been carried out on Scandinavian badges by Niels-Knud Liebgott of the Nationalmuseum in Copenhagen and Lars Andersson of the Nationalmuseum in Stockholm.[16]

In the Netherlands, the spectacular finds made in the Zeeland delta area were first highlighted in an exhibition in Utrecht, 1981. A wider range of medieval and post-medieval material, including both religious and secular badges found in the East Schelde river, was subsequently exhibited in *Treasures from the Schelde* in Bergen-op-Zoom, 1987. The lewd and erotic subject matter of some of the profane badges caused a commotion, triggering a revival of interest in this material, much of which had actually been published in the nineteenth century.[17] In 1986/1987 the author of this article, in collaboration

---

[12] A. Haasis Berner, *Pilgerzeichen des Hochmittelalters: Untersuchung zu ihrer Entstehung und Bedeutung*, MA thesis, Albert-Ludwigs-Universität, Freiburg im Breisgau (privately printed, 1995).

[13] B. Spencer, *Pilgrim Souvenirs and secular Badges*, Salisbury Museum Medieval Catalogue Part 2 (Salisbury, 1990); B. Spencer, *Medieval Pilgrim Badges from Norfolk* (Norfolk Museum Service, 1980).

[14] In a letter of 25 November 1994, Brian Spencer told me that he had finished his catalogue of pilgrim signs and similar badges from medieval sites at London. This extensive work has been availabe in typescript for some time and was published in the last weeks of 1998.

[15] D. Bruna, 'Les Enseignes de pèlerinage et les enseignes profanes au moyen âge, Paris, 1995' (unpublished doctoral thesis, l'Université de Paris I, 1995); D. Bruna, *Enseignes de pèlerinage et enseignes profanes*, Musée National du Moyen Age, Thermes de Cluny (Paris, 1996).

[16] N.-K. Liebgott, 'Frøslevklokkens relieffer', *Historisk Samfund for Praesto Ambt: Ärbog 1971–1972*, 291–315; N.-K. Liebgott, 'Dobefonten i Varde Jacobi Kirke', *Nationalmuseets Arbejdsmark* (1973), 31–44; L. Andersson, *Pilgrimsmärken och vallfart* (Lunds Universitet, 1989).

[17] A. Forgeais, *Priapées* (no place, no date, probably Paris 1858; I am indebted to D. Bruna for sending me a photocopy of this extremely rare booklet); T. Wright, *The Worship of the Generative Powers during the Middle Ages of Western Europe* (1866),

with R. M. van Heeringen, by then the Provincial Archaeologist of Zeeland, and the art historian, A. A. Gaalman, compiled a register of religious badges found up to that point in Zeeland.[18] The material was exhibited at the Zeeuws Museum, Middelburg, and the Museum voor Religieuze Kunst, Uden. The Zeeland finds have continued to be documented by R. M. van Heeringen (those of 1998 to 1991 are published in the *Archeologische Kroniek van Zeeland*). In 1993 some of the private collection of badges amassed by H. J. E. van Beuningen, which demonstrate the spectacular nature of the Dutch discoveries, were exhibited in the Boijmans Van Beuningen Museum, Rotterdam. The exhibition was combined with a conference, the proceedings of which were subsequently published.[19] A sequel to the 1993 publication, recording about 1200 further badges unearthed in the Netherlands, is now in preparation and will again be accompanied by an exhibition at the Boijmans Van Beuningen Museum in Rotterdam. The large number of finds in the Netherlands in recent decades has also prompted an ambitious research project at the Catholic University of Nijmegen, where an international database of both religious and secular badges is being set up as a modern successor to Köster's *Pilgerzeichenkartei*.[20]

Most of the studies which have breached national boundaries concentrate on badges as jewellery, and tend to include only the finest and most costly examples. This approach was taken by Joan Evans, whose first study, *Magical Jewels of the Middle Ages and the Renaissance particularly in England*, was published in Oxford in 1922. The tradition is continued by Yvonne Hackenbroch[21] and by Ronald W. Lightbown, whose catalogue of the collection of European jewellery in the Victoria and Albert Museum, London, has been published recently.[22] While Hackenbroch concentrates on precious badges and order enseignes, Lightbown also draws attention to cheap religious and secular badges.

The study of badges from an anthropological, rather than art historical viewpoint, was pioneered by the Frenchman, Lionel Bonnemère (1843–1905), who researched aspects of folklore, and included them in his discussion of charms. Bonnemère left his collection, mainly of French material, to the Musée National des Arts et Traditions Populaires in Paris, and both the assemblage

---

reprinted in *A History of Phallic Worship*, 2 vols. (New York, 1992), II, pp. 59–65 and plates IX–X.

[18] Van Heeringen, Koldeweij and Gaalman 1987, *op. cit.* note 8.
[19] Van Beuningen and Koldeweij 1993, *op. cit.* note 8; Koldeweij and Willemsen 1995, *op. cit.* note 8, pp. 14–16.
[20] Work on the database started early in 1998. For further information contact Prof. Dr A. M. Koldeweij, Department of Art History, Catholic University of Nijmegen, Postbus 9103, 6500 HD Nijmegen, Netherlands. E-mail: a.koldeweij@let.kun.nl
[21] Y. Hackenbroch, *Renaissance Jewellery* (New York and Munich, 1979); Y. Hackenbroch, *Enseignes: Renaissance Hat Jewels* (Florence, 1996).
[22] R. W. Lightbown, *Mediaeval European Jewellery – with a catalogue of the collection in the Victoria and Albert Museum* (London, 1992).

and his notes were made accessible quite recently.²³ A wider field is covered in the German standard work by Liselotte Hansmann and Lenz Kriss-Rettenbeck, with a survey of all kinds of amulet forms from prehistoric, medieval and modern times. The late medieval secular and religious badges form only a modest part of this work, but it does present a wealth of material that is closely related in form, subject matter, function and meaning.²⁴ The apotropaic aspects of both secular and religious badges – that of bringing good luck and warding off evil – have also been stressed in various articles by the Dutch art historian, Jan Baptist Bedaux.²⁵ Finally, a catalogue and exhibition held in London in 1991, *Treasures and Trinkets*, has documented the jewellery collection of the Museum of London, including late medieval badges, with an emphasis on the symbolism and associations of jewellery.²⁶

For academics the great value of religious and secular badges is that they were cheap, mass-produced items, worn by ordinary people. The surviving examples represent aspects of those ordinary people's thoughts and beliefs. The badges as objects therefore provide a point of departure for broader discussions. As this survey of the literature shows, much work has now been done on describing and recording the badges and identifying their associations, particularly in the case of the religious material. Some of the other relevant visual and written sources have also now been identified. None the less, research has as yet lifted only a corner of the veil. These late medieval gewgaws and devotionalia can only be understood if defined in anthropological terms and studied within their original contexts. There is an incredible abundance of religious badges, and new types and variants are constantly being found. Moreover, the seemingly inexhaustible supply of other source material, providing explanation or identification, can only gradually be digested.

The situation is more problematic in the case of profane, secular material. The badges themselves survive in an amazingly rich and intriguing assortment of subjects and themes, with numerous variants and an ever-widening range of representations. However, unlike their religious counterparts, there

---

23 L. Bonnemère, *Amulettes et talismans: La collection Lionel Bonnemère*, ed. M. Bouteiller, Notes et Documents des Musées de France 23 (Paris, 1991). Bonnemère was co-founder in 1886 of the *Revue des Traditions Populaires* and published some thirty articles in this periodical between 1886 and 1898.

24 L. Hansmann and L. Kriss-Rettenbeck, *Amulett und Talisman: Erscheinungsform und Geschichte* (Munich, 1977).

25 J. B. Bedaux, 'Laatmiddeleeuwse sexuele amuletten: Een sociobiologische benadering', in *Annus Quadriga Mundi: Opstellen over middeleeuwse kunst opgedragen aan prof. dr. Anna C. Esmeijer*, Clavis Kunsthistorische Monografieën 8 (Utrecht, 1989), 16–30; J. B. Bedaux, 'Functie en betekenis van randdecoratie in middeleeuwse handschriften', *Kunstlicht* 14 (1993), 28–33; J. B. Bedaux, 'Profane en sacrale amuletten', in Koldeweij and Willemsen 1995, *op. cit.* note 8, pp. 26–35.

26 T. Murdoch (ed.), *Treasures and Trinkets: Jewellery in London from Pre-Roman Times to the 1930s* (Museum of London, 1991).

are far fewer other sources which relate to these badges. Although we have the actual objects, we have no illustrations or descriptions of them, little or no information about who produced them, what inspired them, who bought them or why. One way of overcoming these difficulties and furthering this field of study is to take the view that both religious and secular lead-tin badges would be better understood if seen as similar and closely related objects, rather than as artefacts which belonged to quite separate spheres.[27]

Under the Guise of a Pilgrim

It was probably around 1470 or 1480 that Hieronymus Bosch drew the two surviving sheets covered with sketches of beggars, cripples and street musicians, now in Brussels and Vienna respectively.[28] In these jottings Bosch drew the ragtag and bobtail elements of society, equipping them with a variety of props, such as a lute or pair of bellows. A few of the beggars, lame or otherwise, also sport badges, three of which are identical. Plate 3 shows one of these figures wearing a badge identifiable as the pilgrim sign associated with the town of Wilsnack, northern Germany. This badge is a representation of the Three Miraculous Hosts of Wilsnack, as shown in Plate 18 (top).[29]

In the context of these sketches, Hieronymus Bosch surely intended this badge to denote something other than the conventional view of the devout, respectable pilgrim. Rather he shows how the attire of the pilgrim was a convenient cloak for social outcasts. The three linked circles on the Wilsnack badge represent the three hosts, a sign which could be quickly drawn and which would be immediately recognisable. The Wilsnack badge was appropriate to the questionable atmosphere in which Bosch places it here, for there was severe theological criticism of the devotional aspects of this shrine and the badge itself. The miracle was not considered all that credible and the wearing of the Host – the body of Christ – as a badge was regarded by some as intolerable.[30] Despite such criticism, however, people continued to flock there and

[27] A. M. Koldeweij, 'The wearing of significative badges, religious and secular: the social meaning of a behavioural pattern', in *Representation of Social Positions*, ed. W. Blockmans and A. Janse (Turnhout, in press); A. M. Koldeweij, 'Sacred and profane: medieval mass-produced badges', in *Art and Symbolism in Medieval Europe*, ed. G. de Boe and F. Verhaeghe, Instituut voor het Archeologisch Patrimonium 5 (Zellik, 1997), pp. 135–7.

[28] Brussels, Royal Library, Print Room; Vienna, Albertina, no. 43.154. Opinions differ as to the dating of these two sheets. See T. Frenken (ed.), *Jheronymus Bosch* (Noordbrabants Museum, 's-Hertogenbosch, 1967), catalogue nos. 49–50.

[29] For Wilsnack, see Van Beuningen and Koldeweij 1993, *op. cit.* note 8, pp. 145–6 and figs. 130–7.

[30] O.-F. Gandert, 'Das Heilige Blut von Wilsnack und seine Pilgerzeichen', in *Brandenburgische Jahrhunderte: Festgabe für Johannes Schultze zum 90. Geburtstag* (Berlin, 1971), pp. 73–90.

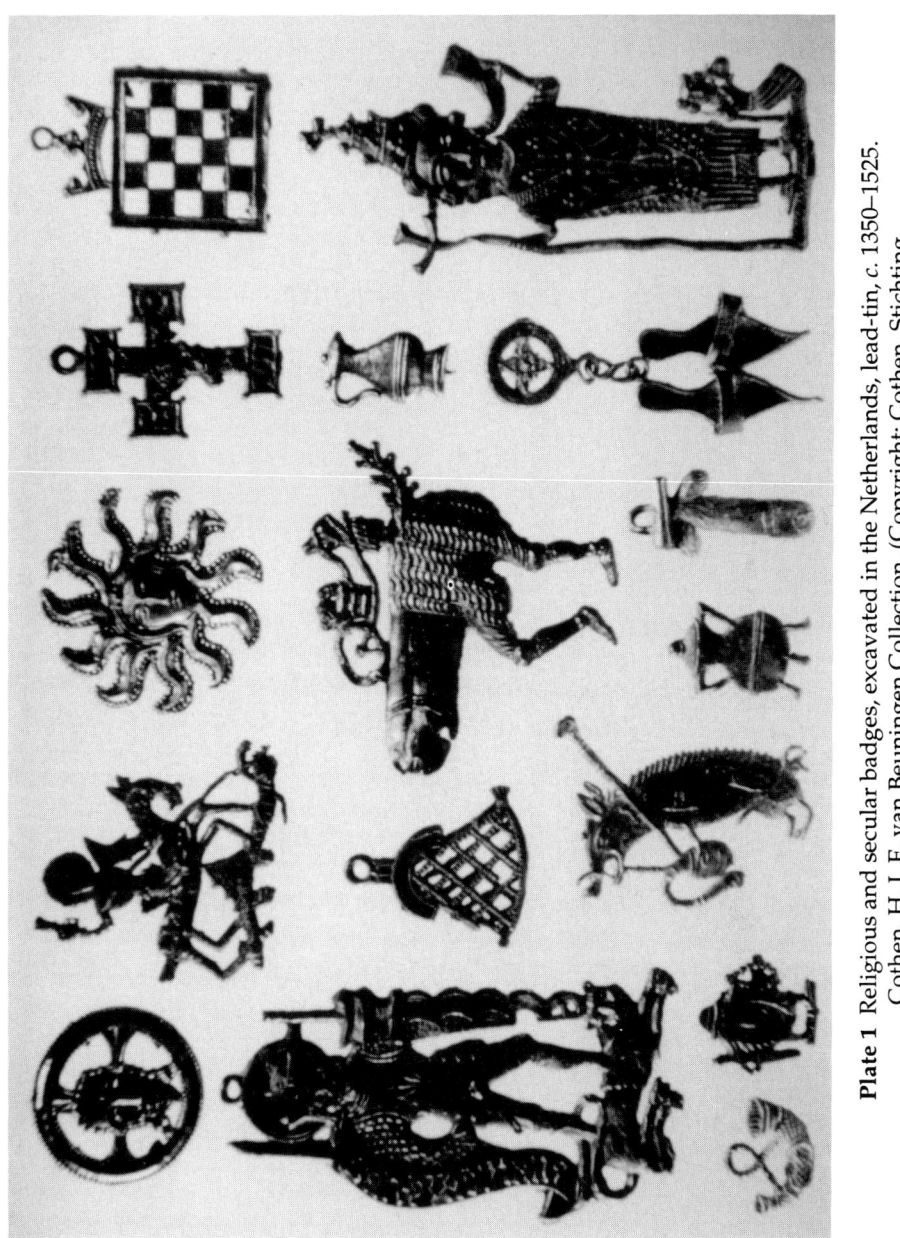

Plate 1 Religious and secular badges, excavated in the Netherlands, lead-tin, c. 1350–1525. Cothen, H. J. E. van Beuningen Collection. (Copyright: Cothen, Stichting Religieuze en Profane Insignes; photograph Tom Haartsen).

Plate 4 Pieter Bruegel the Younger, Flemish proverb: a burgher handing an arrow to a young lady, oil on panel, diameter 16.5 cm, Christie's Amsterdam, summer 1987. (From *Christie's International Magazine* 1987, *op. cit.* note 73).

Plate 2 St Roche with the angel, detail of a Calvary, tempera on pine, 70 x 57.4 cm, Styria or Carinthia, *c.* 1460. Admont Abbey, Styria. (From Himmelstoss 1987, *op. cit.* note 2, p. 125).

Plate 3 Hieronymus Bosch, lame beggar with a pilgrim sign of the three miraculous Hosts of Wilsnack, detail from a sheet with thirty-one beggars, pen in grey-brown, 28.5 x 20.6 cm, Vienna, Albertina, inv. no. 43.154. (From Frenken 1967, *op. cit.* note 28, p. 50).

Plate 5 Badge: crowned vulva as an archer on horseback, her crossbow taut. Lead-tin, 1375–1425, found in Amsterdam, h. 31 mm, w. 21 mm. H. J. E. van Beuningen Collection, Cothen, inv. I, 1323. (Copyright: Cothen, Stichting Religieuze en Profane Insignes; photograph Tom Haartsen).

Plate 6 Phallus glass, dark blue-green glass, found at Mainz, first half of sixteenth century. Krefeld, Karl Amendt Collection. (From Baumgartner 1987, *op. cit.* note 67, p. 104).

Plate 7 Phallus glass, blue-green and blue glass, first half of sixteenth century. Rheinisches Landesmuseum, Trier, inv. no. GG 735. (From Baumgartner and Krueger 1988, *op. cit.* note 67, p. 422).

Plate 8 A young woman's arrow strikes a winged phallic beast with a bell tied round its 'neck'. Margin illustration in a 1392 copy of Johannis Andrea, *Novella in librum tertium Decretalium Gregorii IX*, Paris, Bibliothèque Nationale, MS Lat. 4014, fol. 1. (From Bedaux 1995, *op. cit.* note 25, p. 29).

Plate 9 Badge: female smith forging a phallus. Lead-tin, fourteenth century, found at Konstanz, Fischmarkt. (From Flüeler 1992, *op. cit.* note 70, p. 435).

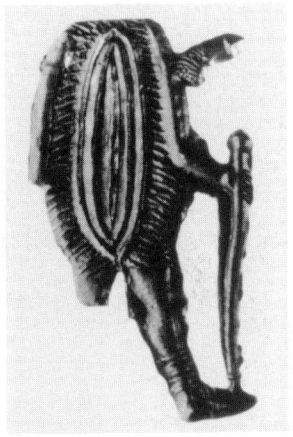

Plate 10 Badge: vulva-pilgrim with phallus staff and rosary, wearing a pilgrim's hat and wooden pattens. Lead tin, 1375–1425, found at Reimerswaal, h. 33 mm, w. 19 mm. H. J. E. van Beuningen Collection, Cothen, inv. I, 2184. (Copyright: Cothen, Stichting Religieuze en Profane Insignes; photograph Tom Haartsen).

Plate 11 Fragment of a badge: vulva-pilgrim wearing a phallus badge. Lead-tin, 1375–1425, found at Rotterdam, h. 36 mm, w. 21 mm. H. J. E. van Beuningen Collection, Cothen, inv. I, 2056. (Copyright: Cothen, Stichting Religieuze en Profane Insignes; photograph Tom Haartsen).

Plate 12 Itinerant beggars. Woodcut, title-page of the first edition of the 'Liber Vagatorum', 1510. (From Boehnke and Johannsmeier 1987, *op. cit.* note 31, p. 78).

Plate 13 Cockle-shell, 1400–1450, pilgrim badge from Santiago de Compostela, excavated at Nieuwlande, flooded land of Zuid-Beveland, h. 65 mm, w. 71 mm. H. J. E. van Beuningen Collection, Cothen, inv. I, 1652. (Copyright: Cothen, Stichting Religieuze en Profane Insignes; photograph Tom Haartsen).

Plate 14 Vera Icon badge from Rome. Stamped brass, 1475–1525, excavated at Rotterdam, h. 31 mm, w. 31 mm. H. J. E. van Beuningen Collection, Cothen, inv. I, 2364. (Copyright: Cothen, Stichting Religieuze en Profane Insignes; photograph Tom Haartsen).

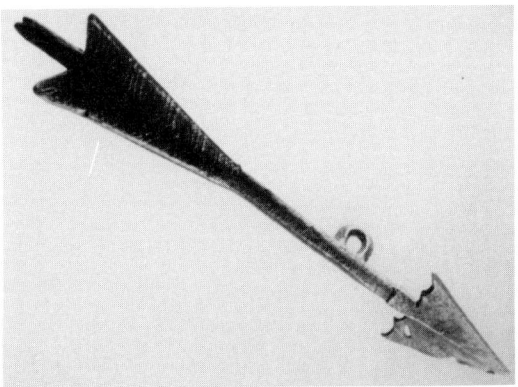

Plate 15 Badge: arrow. Lead-tin, 1375–1425, excavated at Nieuwlande, flooded land of Zuid-Beveland, h. 71 mm, w. 15 mm. H. J. E. van Beuningen Collection, Cothen, inv. I 1622. (Copyright: Cothen, Stichting Religieuze en Profane Insignes; photograph Tom Haartsen).

Plate 16 Pilgrim badge of the 'Engelweihe' at Einsiedeln. Lead-tin, 1400–1500, excavated at Nieuwlande, flooded land of Zuid-Beveland, h. 76 mm, w. 63 mm. H. J. E. van Beuningen Collection, Cothen, inv. I, 1392 (the cross at the top is a replacement). (Copyright: Cothen, Stichting Religieuze en Profane Insignes; photograph Tom Haartsen).

Plate 17 St Anne pilgrim badge from Düren. Lead-tin, 1475–1525, excavated at Dordrecht, h. 36 mm, w. 18 mm. H. J. E. van Beuningen Collection, Cothen, inv. I, 1669. (Copyright: Cothen, Stichting Religieuze en Profane Insignes; photograph Tom Haartsen).

Plate 18 Fir-wood support with a pilgrim's sign from Wilsnack and one from Blomberg. Tin-lead badges, 1450–1500, excavated at Amsterdam in 1973, h. 14 cm, w. 7.9 cm. Amsterdams Historisch Museum. (Photograph: Buren, A. M. Koldeweij).

Plate 19 St Odilia pilgrim sign from Odilienberg (Alsace). Lead-tin, 1400–1450, excavated at Nieuwlande, flooded land of Zuid-Beveland, h. 65 mm, w. 46 mm. H. J. E. van Beuningen Collection, Cothen, inv. I, 0848. (Copyright: Cothen, Stichting Religieuze en Profane Insignes; photograph Tom Haartsen).

des pauls der Werckes die
zu brettich meß des land
bescheinus/

Hanßo to Ingstatt als er jung
was, macht zu and verkauft ein
klauspr and ein Creuz abdry/

Frantz mispult and yeig macht
ein andrem kapp

Jorg von Bassirrem, macht ein
kruglen hafnen, and ein + abding

Albrecht der Baboring macht ein handt
pistfell and ij hundt rot Creuz west
abdruck

Hanns der [Oxxxx] macht ein
[Gexxxx] [xxxx] als [xxxx] [xxx] und
ein [xxxx] [xxxx]

[figure]

[xxx] der [xxxx] macht ein [xxx]
[xxxx] und ein [xxxx] [xxx]

[figure]

[xxx] der [xxxx] macht [xxx] [xxx]
[xxxx] und ein [xxxx] [xxx] als [xxx]
[xxx]

[figure]

Hanns [xxx] der [xxxx] macht ein
[xxxx] [xxxx] und ein [xxxx] [xxx]

[figure]

Plate 20c

Plates 20a, b and c Records of trial, 'Verzeichnis der Bettler, die zum Bundschuh gehören', 9 September 1517. Karlsruhe, Generallandesarchiv Karlsruhe, Breisgau, Generalia, Aktenband 79/3384.

Plate 21 Pilgrim's horn, pipe-clay, partly glazed, 1300–1400, excavated at Utrecht, w. 355 mm. H. J. E. van Beuningen Collection, Cothen, inv. 379/F.99. (Copyright: Cothen, Stichting Religieuze en Profane Insignes; photograph Tom Haartsen).

Plate 22 Beggar's badge of the city of Antwerp, 1565, stamped brass, h. 62 mm, w. 62 mm. Antwerp, Museum Mayer van den Bergh, inv. 1756. (Photograph: Brussels, IRPA-KIK).

Lifting the Veil on Pilgrim Badges

Wilsnack remained a tremendously popular pilgrimage goal until the Reformation.

The misuse of pilgrims' garb and badges is documented elsewhere, for example in the description of spurious pilgrims in the *Liber vagatorum*, or *Book of Vagabonds*, printed around 1510 in Lower Germany (Plate 12). Under the heading 'Christians and Swindlers' the book says: 'These are beggars who pin badges to their hats, especially Veronica of Rome, shells and other signs. And each of them sells these signs to the other, so that people believe they have been to all the places whose signs they wear, although they have never been there. And because they deceive the people in this way, they are called swindlers.'[31] The book was a success and was reprinted, revised and translated several times. A slightly longer version in Dutch appeared in Antwerp in 1563[32] and the book was emulated in England.[33] In addition to the swindlers or *Calmieren*, twenty-seven other kinds of beggars and charlatans were listed. Pilgrims occupied a prominent place among them. People defined as of the first type of beggar, the *Bregern*, were described as either not wearing pilgrim badges at all, or wearing only a few. They approached people with a modest, simple mien, asking only for alms for the sake of God and Our Lady. They were seen as genuine in that they begged out of necessity and abandoned the practice as soon as some means of subsistence offered itself.[34] The second group, the *Stabüler*, were deemed less honest. They were not really criminals, but 'half bad and half good; not all of them are bad, but most are'.[35] These were itinerant beggars who took their wives, children and their possessions on their peregrinations from one place to another. They were professional pilgrims, begging their way through life, able but unwilling to work. Their cloaks are patched together and, like their hats, studded with pilgrim badges.[36]

The only two pilgrim badges mentioned specifically in the *Liber vagatorum*

31 '... Christianern und *Calmieren*. Das sind Bettler, die Zeichen an den Hüten tragen, besonders römisch Veronika und Muscheln und andere Zeichen. Und gibt jeweils einer dem andern Zeichen zu kaufen, dass man glauben soll, sie seien an den Stätten und Enden gewesen, wovon sie die Zeichen tragen, obwohl sie doch niemals dorthin kommen. Und sie betrügen die Leute damit, die heissen *Calmierer*.' 'Liber vagatorum', in *Das Buch der Vaganten: Spieler, Huren, Leutbetrüger*, ed. and trans. H. Boehnke and R. Johannsmeier (Cologne, 1987), p. 93.
32 *Der Fielen, Rabauwen oft der Schalken Vocabular* (Jan de Laet, Antwerp, 1563); modern Dutch translation in *Van Schelmen en schavuiten: Laatmiddeleeuwse vagabondteksten*, ed. H. Pleij (Amsterdam, 1985). Also on this genre, see W. L. Braekman, 'Organisatie en beroepsgeheimen van bedelaars: een heel bijzondere "ordonnantie" ', *Volkskunde* 96 (1995), 1–19.
33 J. Awdeley, *The Fraternity of Vagabonds* (London, 1561); T. Harman, *A Caveat for Common Cursitors, Vulgarly called Vagabonds* (London, 1566); both reprinted in A. V. Judges, *The Elizabethan Underworld* (London, 1930), pp. 50–60 and 61–118.
34 Boehnke and Johannsmeier 1987, *op. cit.* note 31, pp. 80–1.
35 '... halb böse und halb gut, nicht alle sind bös, aber der grössere Teil'. Boehnke and Johannsmeier 1987, *op. cit.* note 31, pp. 80–1.
36 Boehnke and Johannsmeier 1987, *op. cit.* note 31, pp. 80–1.

were the 'Veronica of Rome and shells'.[37] These were two of the best known pilgrim signs; the cockle-shell being strongly associated with pilgrimage to the shrine of St James at Compostela, and the veronica (the representation of Christ's face on Veronica's sudarium) with the journey to Rome (Plates 13 and 14). They were much more widely used, however, being made and sold in a great many other places, using a variety of materials and techniques. Carved jet badges in the form of a shell were probably not produced specifically as Santiago souvenirs[38] while eight unused specimens of St Veronica's sudarium, not even cut out of the parchment on which they were painted, were found in the monastery at Wienhausen, north Germany, where they may have been made for sale.[39] A slate mould dating from the late fifteenth century, used to make pilgrim badges with a representation of the True Image or Vera Icon, is also thought to be of German origin, perhaps from the Upper Rhine.[40]

The associations between badges and pilgrims had long since become generalised and, by the time the *Liber vagatorum* was written at the beginning of the sixteenth century, pilgrim badges were associated to some extent with cheats and frauds. As time went by and the metal pilgrim badges were gradually replaced by little paper pennants, medals and other souvenirs, figures portrayed as the wearers of badges acquired an increasingly negative image. Remarkably accurate information about three fake pilgrims and their identifying badges is preserved in the record of evidence given by a prisoner called Michel von Dinkelsbühl in 1517.[41] Michel was part of the *Bundschuh* of 1517. *Der Bundschuh* were the four revolutionary plots or conspiracies of 1493, 1502, 1513 and 1517, which were followed by the peasant uprising of 1524–1525 in south-west Germany. The plots of 1513 and 1517 employed a wide network of informants, some of whom operated as itinerant beggars. Michel was taken prisoner and interrogated. He described the appearance and clothing of the conspirators with whom he had been in contact in astounding detail. He had evidently been familiar with the activities of tramps and vagabonds for a considerable time. Many of them could be recognised by their clothes, their genuine or counterfeit disabilities and their habits. Michel's interrogators obviously attached importance to the tiniest details of his account. One of the ringleaders, he said, wore a white cloak edged with black velvet and

---

[37] '... römisch Veronika und Muscheln'. Boehnke and Johannsmeier 1987, *op. cit.* note 31, p. 93.

[38] K. Köster, *Pilgerzeichen und Pilgermuscheln von mittelalterlichen Santiago-Strassen*, Ausgrabungen in Schleswig: Berichte und Studien 2 (Neumünster, 1983), 141–55; Van Heeringen, Koldeweij and Gaalman 1987, *op. cit.* note 8, especially pp. 59–63.

[39] Horst Appuhn, *Kloster Wienhausen, Band IV: Der Fund vom Nonnenchor* (Wienhausen, 1973), pp. 19–21 (with additional literature).

[40] J. De Coo, *Museum Mayer van den Bergh, Catalogus 2: Beeldhouwkunst, Plaketten, Antiek* (Antwerp, 1969), p. 272 catalogue no. 2347.

[41] Albert Rosenkranz, *Der Bundschuh, die Erhebungen des südwestdeutschen Bauernstandes in den Jahren 1493–1517*, 2 vols. (Heidelberg, 1927).

could be recognised by a silver arrow on his cap.⁴² Among his many followers were a man called Kilian Ratz whose identifying sign was a white feather in his cap, and another man called Allexander, who always wore a black cap with a gilt medal.⁴³ Three of the beggars who worked for the *Bundschuh* pretended to be pilgrims. One of them had two bad legs, wore a tattered black cloak, a black hat and had two pilgrim badges on two boards, one of Our Lady of Einsiedeln, the other of St Anne.⁴⁴ Another, with a long red beard, wore the large, grey smock of a carter and 'vil heiligen' (many saints). According to another transcript of the same text 'wol acht zeichen' (as many as eight signs) were on his hat, including badges of St Odilia and of the fourteen auxiliary saints (Plate 19).⁴⁵ And finally there was a man with a long coat the colour of iron, with 'das kindlin von Trient' (the Christ Child of Trento) on his red cap.⁴⁶

The first three, more secular, cap ornaments – the arrow, the feather and the gilt medal – cannot be precisely identified, but contemporary illustrations show figures from humbler walks of life with similar ornaments, and some examples have been found in excavations (Plate 15).⁴⁷ The form of the pilgrim badges described by Michel can be identified with greater precision. Einsiedeln was a popular pilgrimage goal, especially in the fifteenth century, and several variants are known of the badges showing the dedication by Christ and angels of the chapel with the miraculous statue of the Virgin Mary (Plate 16).⁴⁸ Badges of St Anne were particularly associated with Düren (Plate 17).⁴⁹ The badge of the fourteen auxiliary saints probably refers to the Vierzehnheiligen monastery in Franconia, but Jena in Thuringia is another possibility since badges representing all fourteen auxiliary saints plus the Infant Jesus, with or without his mother, were sold at both places.⁵⁰ The Odilia badge was probably from Sankt-Odilienberg in Alsace (Plate 19).⁵¹ The custom of fixing the extremely fragile lead-tin badges to a piece of wood, mentioned by Michel in relation to Einsiedeln and St Anne, has been archaeologically documented. A fir-wood panel measuring 14.3 by 7.9 cm, discovered in Amsterdam, had the

---

42 Rosenkranz 1927, *op. cit.* note 41, II, p. 269: '. . . ein silberin pfil im baret'.
43 Rosenkranz 1927, *op. cit.* note 41, II, p. 279: '. . . ein swarz biret und ein vergulten pfenning daran'.
44 Rosenkranz 1927, *op. cit.* note 41, II, p. 280: '. . . zwei zeichen uf zweien brittlin, das ein unser frauw von Eynsidel, das ander sanct Ann'.
45 Rosenkranz 1927, *op. cit.* note 41, II, p. 281: '. . . nemlich die 14 nothelfer und unser Frauwen, sanct Otilien'.
46 Rosenkranz 1927, *op. cit.* note 41, II, p. 282.
47 Van Heeringen, Koldeweij and Gaalman 1987, *op. cit.* note 8, pp. 119–20, no. 42.
48 Van Heeringen, Koldeweij and Gaalman 1987, *op. cit.* note 8, pp. 119–20, no. 42.
49 Van Beuningen and Koldeweij 1993, *op. cit.* note 8, p. 123, no. 23.
50 Kurt Köster, 'Mittelalterliche Pilgerzeichen', in *Wallfahrt kennt keine Grenzen*, ed. L. Kriss-Rettenbeck and G. Möhler (Munich/Zurich, 1984), p. 219, fig. 97 a–b.
51 Van Beuningen and Koldeweij 1993, *op. cit.* note 8, p. 182, no. 296; E. van Loon-van de Moosdijk, 'St Odilia auf westeuropäischen Glocken: Pilgerzeichen aus dem Elsass', *Jahrbuch für Glockenkunde* 7–8 (1995/1996), 185–94.

A. M. Koldeweij

badges of the north German eucharist pilgrimage destinations, Wilsnack and Blomberg, nailed onto it (Plate 18).[52] Similar boards have been found elsewhere.[53]

Michel's remarkable testimony suggests that badges of all types were frequently worn by ordinary people, including the more subversive elements of late medieval society, and were used as personal identifiers. The marks of nine beggars who were members of the *Bundschuh* were recorded in a short paper titled 'Dangerous Beggars can be recognised by their Marks' (Plates 20a, b and c).[54] This document, now in the Generallandesarchiv in Karlsruhe, was probably written as an appendix to a report on members of the *Bundschuh* which was sent by the municipal authorities of Freiburg to the town of Villingen.[55] The nine marks used as signatures by the conspirators were described and drawn in this record, and six of them referred to pilgrims and pilgrimages. The traitors were said to 'visit the country like beggars'. One wore a cockle-shell with two crossed pilgrim staffs, while the sign of another was a butcher's chopper stamped with a cockle-shell.[56] The other four included Michael's or Aachen horns; a long sword and a Michael's horn, a scythe and an Aachen horn, a Michael's or Aachen horn with an owl and another with a dung fork.[57] In the late Middle Ages these horns, along with the bag, hat, staff and cape, were part of a pilgrim's standard equipment. They were small, trumpet-like instruments, made of either earthenware or metal, sold at pilgrimage places and blown by the faithful at reliquary processions and the like (Plate 21).[58] This custom was particularly well known in Aachen, and in other towns in the area. Presumably they were also popular at destinations which venerated St Michael. A pilgrim blowing his horn is represented on one of the romanesque capitals in the abbey at Mont-St-Michel, Normandy, and pilgrim horns, albeit of a much later date, have been found there.[59] The drawings of the marks show the two types of horn that were used: one of them short and only

---

[52] J. Baart, W. Krook, A. Lagerweij, N. Ockers, H. van Regteren Altena, T. Stam, H. Stoepker, G. Stouthart, M. van der Zwan, *Opgravingen in Amsterdam: 20 jaar stadskernonderzoek* (Haarlem, 1977), pp. 392–3.

[53] U. Müller, *Holzfunde aus Freiburg / Augustinerkloster und Konstanz* (Stuttgart, 1996), p. 180.

[54] Rosenkranz 1927, *op. cit.* note 41, pp. 292–4, no. 33.

[55] Rosenkranz 1927, *op. cit.* note 41, p. 291, no. 32.

[56] Rosenkranz 1927, *op. cit.* note 41, pp. 292–94: '... in betllers wis das lant besuchen'; '... ein jacobsmuschel und 2 jacobssteb crutz wis dodurch'; '... ein fleischmesser und ein muschel dorin'.

[57] Rosenkranz 1927, *op. cit.* note 41, pp. 292–94: '... ein michels- oder acherhorn und ein ulen doruf'; '... ein lang schwert und ein michelshorn'; '... ein misthacken und ein michels- oder acherhorn'; '... ein senessen und ein acherhorn'.

[58] Van Heeringen, Koldeweij and Gaalman 1987, *op. cit.* note 8, p. 140; Van Beuningen and Koldeweij 1993, *op. cit.* note 8, pp. 305–7, nos. 931–8.

[59] Fragments of red clay horns (seventeenth or eighteenth century) are in the Musée de Normandie, Caen; C. Quétel, *Le Mont-Saint-Michel* (Paris, 1991), p. 106.

slightly curving, imitating ivory hunting horns, the other long and narrow, with one or more coils, copied from metal horns.

In these cases both pilgrim badges and secular insignia were adopted as identifiers for nefarious purposes. Pilgrim badges may have been particularly popular among the lame or deformed. In any case they had the advantage of making the trappings of poverty respectable and might encourage donations. All these badges were probably also seen as lucky charms and, in this sense, at least, they differed little from the examples which were adopted by the devout.

The lead-tin badges which cause most surprise in modern times, and most interpretative difficulty, are those known as the erotic badges. They include what would nowadays be seen as deeply offensive parodies of pilgrims and their signs. One popular theme is a vulva – the female sexual organ – disguised as a pilgrim with the characteristic staff, hat and rosary. The staff is sometimes surmounted by a phallus (Plate 1, bottom left; Plate 10).[60] The visual game is taken furthest in the variant in which the vulva-pilgrim has pinned on her own badge, which is in the form of a phallus (Plate 11). Excavations in both France and the Netherlands have yielded some ten variants on these lines.

Many of the erotic badges have been found alongside their more strictly religious fellows.[61] They have, also, been found in large numbers and cannot be regarded as isolated, late-medieval curiosities. Because they are so alien to modern European life they need to be placed within their own, now extinct, tradition, and seen in a broad anthropological context. For this reason the medieval phallic badges were displayed side by side with a number of Roman phallic charms in the *Sacred and Profane* exhibition at the Boijmans Van Beuningen Museum in 1993–4. This juxtaposition also served to demonstrate the high degree of abstraction among Roman erotica, compared with the almost absurdly realistic medieval fantasies. Parallels for the decorative use of phalluses and phallic animals are best known in antiquity, for instance in the Greek vase decorations of the sixth and fifth centuries BC which include winged phalluses, phallic bipeds and quadrupeds and unattached phalluses.[62] Such representations are generally thought to have been intended to bring luck and ward off evil. Of course this much older material may not be seen as a direct precursor of the medieval tradition. However studies of erotic illustrations in the margin of a Roman de la Rose manuscript of c.1350 have also interpreted them as apotropaic.[63]

---

[60] E. Poche and J. Pesina (ed.), *Katalog Sbirky Stredovekeho Umeleckeho Remesla* (Prosinec, 1986/ Únor, 1987), p. 24, catalogue no. 176; Van Beuningen and Koldeweij 1993, *op. cit.* note 8, p. 264, catalogue no. 663–6.

[61] Van Beuningen and Koldeweij 1993, *op. cit.* note 8, pp. 254–64, figs. 610–68.

[62] In addition to the literature cited by Jones (M. Jones, 'Een andere kijk op profane insignes', in Koldeweij and Willemsen 1995, *op. cit.* note 8, pp. 73–4), see for example E. C. Keuls, *The Reign of the Phallus: Sexual Politics in Ancient Athens* (Berkeley/Los Angeles/London, 1985).

[63] A. M. Koldeweij, 'A Barefaced Roman de la Rose (Paris, BN MS français 25526) and

Illustrations like these as well as some later medieval texts, notably in the Old French *fabliaux*, show that erotic representations were not restricted to the form of badges.[64] There are direct parallels between some margin illustrations and badges. In the margin of a page from a copy of Johannis Andrea, *Novella in librum tertium Decretalium Gregorii IX*, for instance, there is a winged phallic beast, a bell tied round the shaft, being struck from behind by an arrow shot by a huntress; a theme which is also known on badges (Plate 8).[65] Other parallels are found on everyday items such as utensils, for example a late fourteenth century earthernware plate (a waster) from Aardenburg in Zeeland, Flanders, is decorated in white and yellow slip with a large phallus.[66] Of slightly later date, the late fifteenth and sixteenth centuries, are the phallus drinking glasses made in Germany and probably also in the Netherlands *à la façon de Venise* (Plates 6 and 7).[67] There are countless other late medieval parallels for sexual badges to be found in both literary and visual sources.

On the whole it seems that it is still quite difficult for us, and especially for the wider public, to realise that this material has a place in our immediate past, in the Christian, late medieval Western world. That is why medieval erotica

some Late Medieval Mass-Produced Badges of Sexual Content', in *Flanders in a European Perspective: Manuscript Illumination around 1400 in Flanders and Abroad*, ed. M. Smeyers and B. Cardon (Leuven, 1995), pp. 499–516. On the same margin illustrations see also M. Camille, *Image on the Edge: The Margins of Medieval Art* (London, 1992), pp. 147–9; G. Bartz, A. Karnein and C. Lange, *Liebesfreude im Mittelalter* (Stuttgart/Zurich, 1994), pp. 54–55; M. Müller, *Minnebilder: Französische Minnedarstellungen des 13. und 14. Jahrhunderts*, Pictura et Poesis 7 (Cologne/Weimar/Vienna 1996), 53–6 and 161.

[64] Examples of studies in which such analogies are drawn, but without establishing correspondences so obvious as to permit a detailed interpretation or to demonstrate truly identical representations, are: Bedaux 1995, *op. cit.* note 25, pp. 26–35; Jones 1995, *op. cit.* note 62, pp. 64–74; J. van Os, 'Seks in de 13de-eeuwse fabliaux: literaire voorlopers van de erotische insignes?', in Koldeweij and Willemsen 1995, *op. cit.* note 8, pp. 36–43. For the *fabliaux* see, among others, R. Howard Bloch, *The Scandal of the Fabliaux* (Chicago, 1986), who explicitly states (p. 63): 'Detached sexual organs are an integral part of the representation of the body in the fabliaux and more the rule than the exception.'

[65] Paris, Bibliothèque Nationale, MS Lat. 4014, fol. 1. Bedaux 1993, *op. cit.* note 25, p. 31; Bedaux 1995 *op. cit.* note 25, pp. 28–9; Malcolm Jones, 'Sex and Sexuality in Late Medieval and Early Modern Art', in *Privatisierung der Triebe: Sexualität in der frühen Neuzeit*, ed. D. Erlach, M. Reisenleitner and K. Vocelka (Frankfurt am Main, 1994), pp. 187–304.

[66] Now in the collection of the Municipal Archeological Museum at Aardenburg. J. A. Trimpe Burger, 'Aardenburgse potterbakkerswaar', *Mededelingenblad Nederlandse Vereniging van Vrienden van de Ceramiek* 72 (1974), 2–12, fig. 5; A. van Dongen, 'Het gebruiksvoorwerp als draagteken', in Koldeweij and Willemsen 1995, *op. cit.* note 8, p. 83.

[67] E. Baumgartner, *Glas des späten Mittelalters: Die Sammlung Karl Amendt* (Dusseldorf, 1987), p. 104, catalogue no. 126; E. Baumgartner and I. Krueger, *Phönix aus Sand und Asche: Glas des Mittelalters* (Munich, 1988), pp. 421–2, catalogue no. 530; Koldeweij 1995, *op. cit.* note 8, pp. 18–20.

are frequently unrecognised or misunderstood, or dubbed 'antique', 'Roman' or 'pagan'. A late medieval wooden phallus dug up on the Norwegian coast near Bergen is a case in point, being published as a toy, amulet or votive gift.[68] Reactions to badges are similar. A striking example is found in the 1976 pewter catalogue of the Kunstgewerbemuseum in Cologne, in which two badges in the form of winged phallic beasts, one of them with a bell, are classified as late antique, while an ummistakably medieval phallus of gigantic proportions, beside a man with a small dog and surrounded by an illegible banderole, is described as an unidentifiable object.[69] Another medieval erotic badge remained unrecognised in both print runs of the exhibition catalogue *Stadtluft, Hirsebrei und Bettelmönch*.[70] This unusual find from Konstanz was described in the catalogue as 'unclear' and as a 'nude, female figure, evidently a blacksmith, seeing that she is forging a piece of iron on an anvil in front of a blazing fire'. What the unclothed female smith is shaping from the incandescent metal is a winged phallus (Plate 9).

In some cases the subject matter is ambiguous. Should a pin shaped into an arrow[71] or a bow and arrow[72] be associated with marksmen's guilds and such like, or should they be seen – and in my opinion this is more likely – as amorous or erotic allusions? Is there, for instance, a parallel among erotic badges with a late sixteenth century tondo by, or in the manner of, Pieter Bruegel the Younger showing an archer, his bow stretched taut, offering a gaily plumed arrow to a lady leaning against a tree (Plates 4 and 15)?[73] Can this be compared to a badge like the crowned vulva on horseback with a taut crossbow shown in Plate 5?[74]

This and other erotic badges seem a far cry from the pilgrim signs and other devotional badges. Nevertheless, they all belong to the same large and extremely varied group of late medieval mass-produced popular jewellery. Where archeological conditions were conducive to the preservation of late medieval small metal objects, badges of every category have been found in close proximity to one another and often in amazing concentrations. Badges or brooches which in our eyes have very different themes were worn in the same society, perhaps even simultaneously by the same people, or by different

---

68 A. E. Herteig, *Kongers havn og handels sete: Fra de arkeologiske undersøkelser på Bryggen i Bergen 1955–68* (Oslo, 1969), fig. 18.
69 H.-U. Haedeke, *Zinn* (Cologne, 1976), p. 56, catalogue nos. 9a–b and p. 74, catalogue no. 67.
70 M. and N. Flüeler, *Stadtluft, Hirsebrei und Bettelmönch: Die Stadt um 1300* (Zurich/Stuttgart, 1992), pp. 434–5.
71 Van Beuningen and Koldeweij 1993, *op. cit.* note 8, p. 315, fig. 989.
72 Van Beuningen and Koldeweij 1993, *op. cit.* note 8, p. 280, fig. 771 and p. 310, figs. 959–61.
73 Auctioned at Christie's, Amsterdam, in the summer of 1987: oil on panel, tondo, diameter 16.5 cm *Christie's International Magazine*, May/June 1987.
74 Van Beuningen and Koldeweij 1993, *op. cit.* note 8, p. 262, fig. 656.

people in the same context. All types of badges were incredibly popular and they must all surely have held their place in the late medieval imagination as lucky charms. In general, it seems, badges were objects with a magical charge, whether religious or profane.

In the late fifteenth century and especially in the sixteenth, the practice of indulgences and the indissolubly connected phenomenon of the itinerant pilgrim were severely frowned upon. The unfavourable light this shed on the pilgrim was not entirely due to malpractices within the Roman church. Another cause were the social developments which culminated in groups of beggars and vagabonds, like those described above, being accorded the status of pilgrims. On the one hand society excluded the impoverished, labelling the poor as such by obliging them to wear badges very similar to pilgrim badges (Plate 22); on the other hand the poor opportunistically exploited the image and concomitant advantages of the pilgrim.

Translated from the Dutch by Ruth Koenig.

10

Pilgrimage to Walsingham and the Re-Invention the Middle Ages

SIMON COLEMAN and JOHN ELSNER

Constructing Pilgrimage

Recent scholarship has become increasingly self-aware that the images we propagate about the medieval world are themselves highly contemporary constructions. For example, in his contentious, judgmental but eminently readable 1991 book, *Inventing the Middle Ages*, Norman Cantor told 'the story of the founding era of medieval studies from 1895 to about 1965' as a series of constructions by 'the great medievalists' in which their 'lives, works and ideas' are presented as mutually intertwined.[1] Whatever the merits of Cantor's argument may be, there is no doubt that any vision of an ancestral past is always accompanied by a certain amount of self-projection.

The specifically academic variety of self-fashioned history is far from being the only example of fabricating the past in the image of various concerns of the present. Taking a very particular case, this essay suggests that the Anglican revival of pilgrimage to Walsingham in the early twentieth century – which was in theological terms a reaction against some of the effects of religious reform in the early modern period – created a ritualised medievalism in order to valorise its authenticity as an ancient form of Christian worship. It is also intended to demonstrate that, even in the present, the Norfolk pilgrimage has retained its ability to evoke the Middle Ages in a powerful and resonant way. The revival of modern Walsingham as a recreated medieval site has given it a particular relationship to pre-Reformation Christianity that is both appealing and controversial to many members of the Anglican communion. The sacred, set-apart space and time created by pilgrimage to the village are not merely a means to escape from the everyday world; they also provide the ideological resources to engage with, and comment on, rather more mundane forms of ecclesiastical politics.

There are many kinds of medievalism to be detected today amongst the thousands of pilgrims as well as tourists who visit the site. In addition, the

---

1 N. F. Cantor, *Inventing the Middle Ages: The Lives, Works, and Ideas of the Great Medievalists of the Twentieth Century* (Cambridge, 1992), quotes from the preface, p. 7.

image of Walsingham as an authentic medieval site of pilgrimage has changed over the last century, not only as ideas about the medieval have shifted, but also as notions of what it is that constitutes authenticity have undergone something of a sea-change. This paper is therefore concerned to examine the various ways of dealing with history that are revealed by different participants in the revived pilgrimage.

The approach taken here incorporates a wide range of sources of data; those which deal with the medieval past as revealed by archaeology and architecture, as well as twentieth century reconstructions of such a past. One of the authors (Coleman) is a social anthropologist, while the other (Elsner) is an art historian, and both disciplines were drawn upon for this piece of research. Analysis of written material from the Anglican archives (incorporating historical and archaeological surveys, fictional works and a regular newsletter)[2] has been combined with data derived from around thirty interviews with officials of the Anglican shrine and lay pilgrims.[3] A number of field trips undertaken since 1994 have allowed attendance of pilgrimage services at Walsingham, examination of the vernacular and ecclesiastical architecture of the village and observation of the movements of pilgrims and tourists throughout the village.

At the centre of the argument presented here is a concern with varied perceptions of history and (the passage of) time in relation to pilgrimage practices, texts and material culture. The anthropologist Victor Turner famously compared pilgrimage in the world religions to initiation rites of tribal societies in which participants enter sacred time and space in order temporarily to transcend mundane social structures.[4] The central, liminal period of such rites of passage ideally provides a consecrated time out of time: a period, as Turner put it, when 'one ceases to keep one's eye on the clock' and when 'social groups . . . may be thought of as periodically coming to a realisation of how their present state relates to their mythical and quasi-historical past'.[5]

At Walsingham, the medieval period has provided a specific and sacred reference point for pilgrims and keepers of the shrine, a form of temporal

---

[2] These texts will be quoted throughout the essay. Of particular interest is the Anglican newsletter, started as *Our Lady's Mirror* in 1926.

[3] Officials were interviewed at Walsingham itself. Pilgrims have been interviewed either at Walsingham or in their home parishes. All interviewees were asked questions concerning their own religious background, level of involvement in the shrine, knowledge of its historical past and views regarding the present significance (on personal and denominational levels) of the pilgrimage to Walsingham.

[4] V. Turner, *Blazing the Trail: Way Marks in the Exploration of Symbols*, ed. E. Turner (Tucson, Arizona, 1992), p. 29. Turner was also aware of some of the problems associated with comparing large-scale pilgrimages to initiation rites: he notes for instance that (modern) pilgrimage tends to be voluntary, whereas initiation is founded in obligatoriness, p. 36.

[5] V. Turner 1992, *op. cit.* note 4, p. 136.

orientation that enables devotees to engage, however briefly, in a liminal period of escape from everyday life. Yet the means of evoking such a transcendent world have been contested since the revival of the cult, when the Anglican shrine was built in 1931 and enlarged later in the decade. The medieval roots, explicitly claimed by the revivalists to relate to the modern institution's origin, were controversially 'demonstrated' by the use of relics and archaeological discoveries incorporated in the shrine. Nowadays, some pilgrims still maintain that such an intrinsic, metonymic contact with the past is both evident and a key factor in establishing the shrine's sacred quality. To many others, however, the link to be established is more symbolic, metaphoric, and depends on a very different, rather more self-consciously playful, notion of what it means to engage 'authentically' with the medieval world. Both attitudes nevertheless depend on creating, as an essential aspect of the pilgrimage experience, the sense of being in touch with a world that is remote from normal experience, located within both a biblical and a mythico-historical narrative.

Of course, pilgrimages, like rites of passage, involve spatial as well as temporal separation from the everyday. According to the classic (but now much criticised) anthropological account of Christian pilgrimage made by Victor and Edith Turner in the 1970s,[6] on reaching his or her goal, the pilgrim is exposed to and increasingly circumscribed by powerful religious sacra and symbolic structures; shrines, images, liturgies, and topography. It is contended here that the material culture of Walsingham is vital in evoking the sacralised medievalism of the pilgrimage experience. The sense many visitors have of the place as a site that has been treated as sacred over the centuries is initially created, in many cases, by viewing buildings, objects and liturgies that appear to be ancient.

Anthropological studies of pilgrimage generally, focusing on pilgrims' accounts and on the interrelations between local communities and wider social consciousness, have tended to give insufficient emphasis to the potential effects on pilgrims of the material culture of the pilgrimage site.[7] For instance, in a recent collection of papers on contemporary Christian pilgrimage, the sacred centre has been characterised as 'a religious void' and 'a vessel into which pilgrims devoutly pour their hopes, prayers, and aspirations'.[8] It is

---

6   V. Turner and E. Turner, *Image and Pilgrimage in Christian Culture: Anthropological Perspectives* (Oxford, 1978), pp. 8–11. For a summary of critiques of the Turners' work, see J. Eade and M. J. Sallnow (ed.), *Contesting the Sacred: The Anthropology of Christian Pilgrimage* (London, 1991), pp. 4–5.
7   Further on this issue, see S. Coleman and J. Elsner, 'Contesting Pilgrimage: Current Views and Future Directions', *Cambridge Anthropology* 15.3 (1991), 63–73 (especially pp. 69–73); and for a specific example, see S. Coleman and J. Elsner, 'The Pilgrim's Progress: Art, Architecture and Ritual Movement at Sinai', *World Archaeology* 26/1 (1994), 73–89.
8   See Eade and Sallnow 1991, *op. cit.* note 6, p. 15.

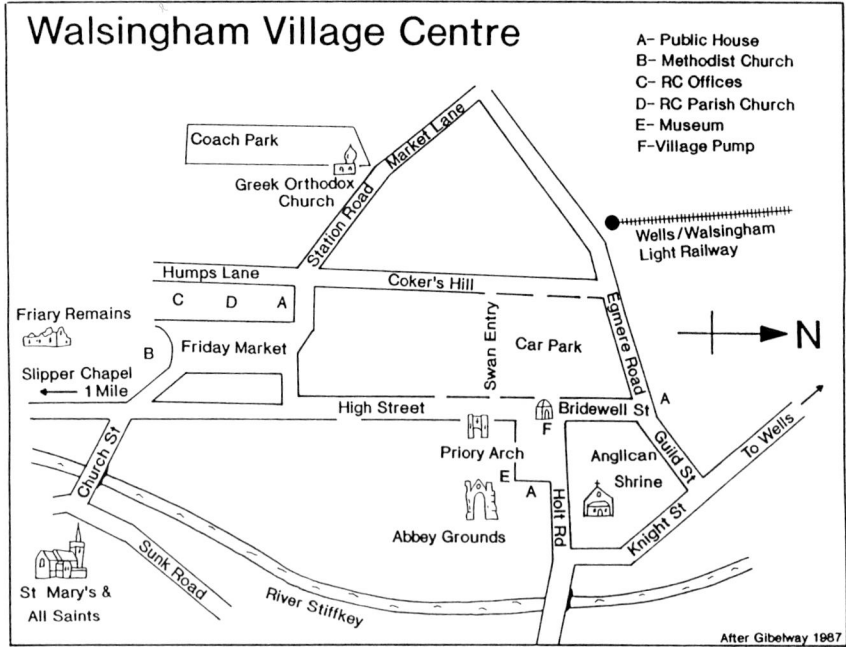

Figure 1 Map of Walsingham village centre (Willmott, 1997, after Gibelway, 1987). The length of the High Street from Common Place to Church Place is c. 250 m.

certainly the case, as we discuss below, that pilgrimage centres tend to be polyvalent symbolic spaces, able to accommodate, reflect and absorb multiple responses (often from pilgrims of diverse social, ethnic, even religious origin). Nonetheless, the architectural and visual structure of a site – its lay-out, its liturgical and theatrical potential, its specific placing of altars, relics and shrines – is an important if limited modulator of pilgrims' experience. The material aspects of the shrines and their environs, just as much as the recitations of local guides, provide resources that may prompt pilgrims to take certain paths in their reactions to or experience of the holy (see Figure 1 for a map of the village).

While the study of pilgrimage by the Turners is by far the most careful anthropological attempt to evaluate the material culture of pilgrimage centres,[9] their account does not sufficiently allow for the role of some participants – pilgrims – in using objects to construct their own pathways, to create their own meanings (both private and communal), to perform their own rituals at a site. The material culture of a pilgrimage centre, quite apart from its

[9] See V. and E. Turner 1978, *op. cit.* note 6, especially pp. 243–55 for 'notes on a processual symbolic analysis' which is effectively a taxonomy of symbols (including objects of material culture) in ritual and their meanings.

Pilgrimage to Walsingham

use by the hierarchy controlling the shrine to set out an establishment view, is also available as a prompt for private, sometimes ironic, even subversive, narratives by visiting groups or individuals.[10] Just as the viewers of an exhibition may be expected to wander round in different orders and to come out with different responses (in what has recently been elegantly analysed as a modern form of secular ritual),[11] so we can hardly expect visitors wandering through the space of a major pilgrimage centre (simultaneously exhibition hall and liturgical theatre) to emerge with anything like a single view.

The specific and complex ways in which the architecture and material structure of pilgrimage sites work to modulate experience are manifold. Recent studies of relics and reliquaries displayed in pilgrimage centres have explored their power to provoke imaginative memory, whereby narratives and legends – oscillating between a prized physical object and the memories it evokes – are constructed to produce (and to transform) the meanings of the shrine as a whole.[12] The importance of memory as a process of constructing pilgrims' identity through real or imagined historical genealogies should not be underestimated: the very sanctity of a pilgrimage site is in part dependent on its focusing and symbolising the identity of a community, be it very local, regional, national or even international and interdenominational.[13] Like souvenirs, relics bring to life (or trace a path back to) an origin or a founding event, and thus for the believer they make present the full, holy effect of the past. (This process of re-invoking the past inevitably involves influence from the imagination and motivations of the pilgrim.[14]) Similarly, the collections of other objects often found at sacred centres help to assimilate pilgrimage sites into the club of holy places. Each holy place is represented by, indeed embodied in, the physical remains of the past. These remains are often carefully labelled so as to preserve the link between them and the saint, or

---

[10] See S. Coleman and J. Elsner, 'Performing Pilgrimage: Walsingham and the Ritual Construction of Irony', in *Ritual, Performance, Media*, ed. F. Hughes-Freeland (London, 1998), pp. 46–65.

[11] See C. Duncan, *Civilizing Rituals: Inside Public Art Museums* (London, 1995), pp. 7–20.

[12] See the excellent discussion by A. G. Remensnyder, 'Legendary Treasure at Conques: Reliquaries and Imaginative Memory', *Speculum* 71 (1996), 884–906; also on the concept of 'imaginative memory' in relation to material artefacts A. G. Remensnyder, *Remembering Kings Past: Monastic Foundation Legends in Medieval Southern France* (Ithaca, 1995), pp. 1–3.

[13] A good account of the regional diversity of saints' cults during a single period is R. Van Dam, *Saints and their Miracles in Late Antique Gaul* (Princeton, 1993), pp. 11–49. For an attempt to measure the relative importance of shrines in contemporary Europe according to the criteria of the size of 'the catchment basin' and the number of annual visitations, see M. L. Nolan and S. Nolan, *Christian Pilgrimage in Modern Western Europe* (Chapel Hill, 1989), pp. 19–35.

[14] On this in relation to souvenirs, see S. Stewart, *On Longing: Narratives of the Miniature, the Gigantic, the Souvenir, the Collection* (Baltimore and London, 1984), pp. 132–51 (pp. 134–5).

sacred place, they came from.[15] Thus visiting one shrine may vicariously put the pilgrim in touch with the entire tradition to which that shrine claims to belong.

This examination of Walsingham as a revived shrine, and as a means of re-invoking the past, demonstrates how the Middle Ages are conjured up in a wide variety of media; in texts, oral narratives, liturgies and architecture. It attempts to illustrate how images of the past blend with present concerns in the creation of powerful religious experiences within pilgrimage. The 'medievalism' of the shrine at Walsingham to many Anglican pilgrims is key to their perception of the place as holy, but, as this paper will also show, there are as many ways to invoke the medieval as there are ways to relate to the sacred.

Walsingham and the 'Feel' of the Medieval

The theme, then, is not the Middle Ages as they (really) were, but as they are – as they are used today and as they were constructed in the early twentieth century, to create mythologies which authenticate modern traditions and activities. One might look at numerous areas where medievalism is used in this way, from the culture of the theme park lending a historical identity to a particular place, to advertising and the media's penchant for re-enacting and dramatising history even as it tells stories. But pilgrimage is a special case of such medievalism, because many of its practitioners – at least those at Walsingham – show a high level of awareness that they are following, indeed that they are involved in reviving, an extremely ancient tradition. To be a pilgrim to Walsingham is to walk along the roads trodden by pilgrims since the Saxon era (at least, so goes the myth) including kings, bishops and even (subsequent) sceptics like Erasmus.

In late medieval times, the shrine of Our Lady of Walsingham in Norfolk had become England's most popular pilgrimage centre.[16] According to legend, the shrine was founded in 1061 after the Virgin appeared to a local lady called Richeldis and instructed her to build at Walsingham a model of the Holy House at Nazareth (where the Virgin had received the vision of the Angel Gabriel during the Annunciation).[17] By the later Middle Ages, the shrine at Walsingham had come to be regarded as 'England's Nazareth'. What was

---

[15] Further on this aspect of relics at pilgrimage centres, see J. Elsner, 'Replicating Palestine and Reversing the Reformation: Pilgrimage and Collecting at Bobbio, Monza and Walsingham', *Journal of the History of Collections* 9 (1997), 117–30.

[16] See J. C. Dickinson, *The Shrine of Our Lady of Walsingham* (Cambridge, 1956), pp. 24–47, and for a comparison with medieval Loreto, see V. and E. Turner 1978, *op. cit.* note 6, pp. 175–202.

[17] For a discussion of the problematic dating of the origins of pilgrimage to Walsingham, see M. Clayton, *The Cult of the Virgin in Anglo-Saxon England* (Cambridge, 1990), pp. 139–41.

claimed to be Richeldis' original building, in which the statue of Our Lady was kept, was enclosed in a sumptuous fourteenth-century chapel off the north side of a grand twelfth-century priory church.[18]

This bald narrative, told with various elaborations by modern pilgrims since the site's revival in the early years of the twentieth century, is inextricably linked with a series of fantasies about, and appropriations of, the Middle Ages.[19] Along with the Holy House, the main attraction of the site before the Reformation had been a medieval statue of the Virgin.[20] The original image was burnt by the Reformers in 1538, when the Walsingham shrine was suppressed. In 1922, Alfred Hope Patten, vicar of St Mary's church, Little Walsingham, re-dedicated a replica of the medieval statue. This, and his revival of pilgrimage to Walsingham, were highly controversial in the Church of England of the 1920s, when the book of Common Prayer was still in everyday liturgical use, and when anything even faintly tinted with Roman Catholicism was seen as deeply suspect. The defection to Rome of such distinguished Anglican luminaries as John Henry Newman in the previous century had heightened antipathy to the Roman Catholic Church. Hope Patten, however, belonged to that faction of the Anglo-Catholic movement which aimed to reverse the Protestant impetus of the Reformation by creating a self-consciously 'Catholic' tradition within the Church of England.[21] In conflict with the Anglican hierarchy, and in particular with his direct superior the bishop of Norwich, Patten decided in 1931 to move his shrine and statue out of the parish church onto land privately owned by the Anglo-Catholic Society of Our Lady of Walsingham.[22]

Patten and his supporters saw themselves as reviving the lost medieval Catholic tradition in England, which they did not see as synonymous with the contemporary Church of Rome.[23] Despite their affirmation of Catholicism, the

---

[18] On the Holy House (its siting, archaeology and medieval context), see J. C. Dickinson 1956, *op. cit.* note 16, pp. 95–104; on the Marian vision, see for example C. Stephenson, *Walsingham Way* (London, 1970), pp. 18–23.

[19] On the revival of Anglican pilgrimage to Walsingham in the twentieth century, see Stephenson 1970, *op. cit.* note 18, pp. 123–68, and P. G. Cobb (ed.), *Walsingham* (Bristol, 1990) for a convenient collection of some primary sources. A brief account of the site and its revival is U. King, 'England's Nazareth: Pilgrimages to Walsingham during the Middle Ages and Today', in *Wallfahrt Kennt Keine Grenzen*, ed. L. Kriss-Rettenbeck and G. Mühler (Munich and Zurich, 1984), pp. 527–41.

[20] On the statue, which was copied from a seal of the medieval priory preserved in the British Museum, see C. Stephenson 1970, *op. cit.* note 18, pp. 123–7.

[21] On Patten's connections with the Oxford Movement as well as his romantic medievalism, see C. Stephenson 1970, *op. cit.* note 18, pp. 73–91.

[22] For an account of the conflict between the Walsingham shrine and the Diocese of Norwich, see C. Stephenson 1970, *op. cit.* note 18, pp. 146–54, 159–66 and 194–200.

[23] With its celebration of a Marian site, not least as a bastion against secularism, Walsingham parallels developments in other European pilgrimage centres such as Lourdes and Fatima. Unlike these sites, however, it was presented as a revival rather

Anglo-Catholics were archetypally sectarian – indeed Protestant – in their resistance to the authority of the ecclesiastical hierarchy. As Patten wrote in the spring number of *Our Lady's Mirror* of 1931, the private newsletter of the Society of Our Lady of Walsingham:

> The Bishop of the Diocese demanded that the images should be taken away and that many other matters should be 'reformed'.... But the removal does not mean the end of the revived devotion or suppression of the Shrine. We are going to build a Chapel to which Our Lady of Walsingham will be translated.[24]

By the summer number of *Our Lady's Mirror*, the 'sad ... news' of removing the images had given way to the mounting rhetoric of revival:[25]

> We are living in historic days again. New beginnings, new prospects, new hopes. One wonders how people felt and talked and thought in Walsingham eight hundred and seventy years ago when they saw the walls of the little chapel in the meads of the Stiffkey river rising; and when among the trees they found the Holy House completed. What did these people, just like ourselves, but long-haired be-tunicked Saxons, think when they looked into that new little building for the first time?[26]

However quaint the language may seem now, it combined a myth of medieval fellowship, simple spirituality and contemporary resonance with the little Englander's appeal to the landscape of rivers and country lanes.

On October 15, 1931, Patten led a procession of about three thousand pilgrims in a special pilgrimage which translated the image to the new shrine (Plate 1). In the autumn number of 1931, he proclaimed that the Holy House was:

> ... as far as we know, the first Chapel built by English Catholics from all over the country, since the Dissolution, for the express purpose of raising a Sanctuary for the housing of a Shrine, in the real sense of the word. In ancient days, it was the foremost Holy place in England; the National Shrine. It is fitting in the steady course of Catholic revival in this land, that it should be the first re-erected.[27]

In making such claims, Patten comes close to giving the shrine a civil religious importance, as a national symbol, which went beyond religious

---

than a new apparition of Our Lady; in addition, the message of Walsingham is more one of restoration than the apocalyptic visions of newer shrines, especially Fatima. For a brief summary of apparitional shrines in Western Europe, see M. L. and S. Nolan 1989, *op. cit.* note 13, pp. 275–90.

24 *Our Lady's Mirror* (Spring 1931), p. 2.
25 On the moving of the shrine from the parish church as 'a very sad piece of news', see *Our Lady's Mirror* (Spring, 1931), p. 2.
26 *Our Lady's Mirror* (Summer, 1931), p. 1.
27 *Our Lady's Mirror* (Autumn, 1931), p. 1.

Plate 1 The statue of the Virgin and Child, located in Patten's restored Holy House. (S. Coleman and J. Elsner).

denominationalism. In this sense, only, parallels can be drawn with the pilgrimage shrine at Guadaloupe, discussed by some scholars as a national symbol.[28] Yet, even more than the Mexican shrine, Walsingham's place within its own church was deeply ambiguous and far from mainstream. The reactions to Walsingham and to its medievalism were (and still are) numerous. In the *Evening Standard* on 1 September 1926, Herbert Hensley Henson, bishop of Durham, wrote a furious attack on the revival of Marian pilgrimage to Walsingham:

> The attempt to revive pilgrimages can only succeed if it carry the religious Englishman back to the spiritual level of the Middle Ages.... The revived pilgrimages ... are rather 'pageants' than religious acts. The pitiable rubbish of the Walsingham processional hymn could only be intelligible as part of a 'pageant'. As an act of religion, it would be profane.[29]

Bishop Henson's distaste for Walsingham's 'pageantry' involves an aesthetic but also a moral resistance to the ritual theatre of pre-Reformed Christianity. His article consistently casts a familiar Protestant doubt on the immoral character of pilgrimage as a 'scandal (which) persisted throughout the Middle Ages and has survived the Reformation'.[30] The fact of the site's recent invention is for Henson a further indication of its inauthenticity, merely indicating, as he put it, 'the illusion of medievalism'. The pilgrim's reponse to Walsingham, whether positive or negative, thus turns fundamentally not just on what the site offers in the present, but on whether s/he has a romantic or a dismissive view of the medieval piety which the site claims to revive. In the context of Anglican spirituality in the early twentieth century, the concept of pilgrimage could not be divorced from contested attitudes to the Middle Ages. Pilgrimage was seen as the crucible of a Christianity which was either the faithful florescence of the tradition of the Fathers or a decadent accumulation of extra-scriptural clutter and corruption which needed reforming.

The view of Walsingham as a paradigm for a romantic medieval piety was sketched in Henson's time with great vigour by Hope Patten, and by his small but vociferous body of Anglo-Catholic supporters, in a variety of pamphlets and fiction. An early example of the genre, written before Patten became involved with Walsingham, is *The Pilgrims of Walsingham or Tales of the Middle*

---

[28] See for example, E. Wolf, 'The Virgin of Guadalupe: Mexican National Symbol', *Journal of American Folklore* 71 (1958), 34–9.

[29] Henson's *Evening Standard* article was republished and attacked in the October 1926 issue of *Our Lady's Mirror*. On Henson (1863–1947), see O. Chadwick, *Hensley Henson: A Study in the Friction between Church and State* (Oxford, 1983).

[30] For a sustained attack on the Protestant historical assumptions about pre-Reformation English Catholicism implicit in the kind of history professed by Henson, see E. Duffy, *The Stripping of the Altars: Traditional Religion in England 1400–1580* (New Haven and London, 1992).

Ages: An Historical Romance by Agnes Strickland, published in 1885.[31] This followed Geoffrey Chaucer 'the Walter Scott of the thirteenth century'[32] in taking a medieval pilgrimage as its co-ordinating theme, as well as employing a Chaucerian narrative strategy:

> Each of the votaries to the shrine of our Lady of Walsingham, in this work, like Chaucer's Canterbury Pilgrims, is pledged to relate a tale. The present volumes contain those of Cardinal Wolsey, King Henry, the Abbot of Glastonbury, Queen Catherine, the Emperor Charles, and the Abbess of Ely. Those of Mary of France, Charles Brandon, Duke of Suffolk, Anna Boleyn, Sir Thomas Wyatt, &c., &c., are necessarily deferred till a Second Series of the Pilgrims of Walsingham.[33]

Other literary gestures, more directly connected with Patten, include *A Maid of Walsingham: A Story of the Fifteenth Century* by the Rev. H. J. T. Bennetts MA (the Walsingham library has a copy signed 'A. Hope Patten, 1924'),[34] and *The Legende of Our Ladye of Walsingham: For Little Childer* 'by a Benedictine, Saint Mary's Abbey, Bergholt, 1938'.

The revival of the medieval site by the Anglicans was carried out in the context of a parallel Roman Catholic revival of an alternative shrine nearby. The Roman Catholic revival was based at the Slipper Chapel in the village of Houghton St Giles, about a mile from the centre of the Walsingham, down a road called the 'Holy Mile'. The chapel is a fourteenth-century building which was probably the last stopping point on the medieval pilgrims' road to Walsingham before reaching the shrine. It had been bought in the mid-1890s by a wealthy woman called Charlotte Boyd, who converted to Roman Catholicism soon after the purchase.[35] The first formal pilgrimage to Walsingham since the Reformation took place on 20 August 1897, and was led by Father Wrigglesworth, prior of Downside.[36] Although the chapel did not come into active use until the 1930s, it then provided Roman Catholics with a genuinely medieval building with impeccable credentials given its role as part of the original pilgrimage route to Walsingham.

Two centres of pilgrimage were thus being created out of a single medieval

---

31 A. Strickland, *The Pilgrims of Walsingham or Tales of the Middle Ages: An Historical Romance* (London, 1885).
32 Strickland 1885, *op. cit.* note 31, p. i.
33 Strickland 1885, *op. cit.* note 31, pp. iii–iv.
34 H. J. T. Bennetts, *A Maid of Walsingham: A Story of the Fifteenth Century* (London, 1924).
35 Boyd paid for the restoration of the Chapel from its former function as a cow shed to a replica of its medieval glory. She died in 1906 and relatively little happened at the Slipper Chapel until 1934, when a Mass was said there after its authorisation for worship. For (a somewhat partial but instructive view of) the Roman Catholic revival, see H. M. Gillett, *Walsingham: the History of a Famous Shrine* (London, 1946), pp. 69–80.
36 See, for instance, R. W. Connelly, *Walsingham is for Today* (London, Catholic Truth Society, 1987), p. 8.

origin. These restitutions were competitive appropriations of tradition articulated not only in theology, but also liturgy, archaeology, and architecture. Both sides claimed to have established connections with a real historical past. Both came to house figures of the Virgin based on the medieval Priory seal. Nobody disputed that the Slipper Chapel provided a genuine link to the original pre-Reformation pilgrimage, but (as discussed below) it did have the disadvantage of ceding the more central part of the village to neutral or Anglican influence (see Figure 1).[37]

Modern pilgrimage to Walsingham must therefore be seen as a dual phenomenon. Relations between the two main religious groups that occupy the village are now described as ecumenical, but there is no doubt that intense and overt rivalries existed in the first half of this century. The Roman Catholic purchase on the authenticity evoked by the Middle Ages was through metonymy – the actual use and possession of an authentic fragment of the original pilgrimage tradition. In response, the Anglicans could initially only offer access through replication – through a copy of the statue and a copy of the Holy House. Fortunately, 'archaeology', in the process of excavating the foundations of the new shrine, would provide the Anglo-Catholic establishment with their own metonym, more authentic still than the fourteenth-century Slipper Chapel, since it would be considered contemporary with the 'Saxon' foundation of the site.

Prompted by Patten (and in part in response to the Roman Catholic appropriation of the Slipper Chapel), some Anglicans made a contentious and ambitious claim: to have found the very site of the original Holy House, that built following the Virgin's appearance to Richeldis in 1061, in the course, ironically, of constructing its replica. The claim was based upon the discovery of a well when the foundations of the Holy House were being excavated. In the words of Hope Patten:

> From excavations made during the preparation of the site it was discovered that this garden once formed part of a courtyard, and it is considered by the architect and other experts to have been part of the original Chapel yard of the ancient Shrine. After the position of the new buildings had been determined a thirteenth century well was unearthed on a level with the court,

---

[37] Roman Catholic pilgrimage has continued to flourish in the environs of Walsingham, particularly since the 1930s. Nowadays Catholics frequently start their pilgrimages in the centre of Walsingham before processing down the Holy Mile to the Slipper Chapel. On more important pilgrimage days, however, Roman Catholics, like Anglicans, hold services in the grounds of the ruined Priory, and sometimes ecumenical pilgrimages are arranged. While our comments on medievalism do apply to many Roman Catholics, Anglicans (not least through the activities of Patten) have generally been more concerned both with the physical reconstruction of the Holy House at Walsingham and with the evocation of the medieval period as a counterbalance to a post-Reformation Church.

some four feet below the surface. As it was cleaned a fresh and cold spring bubbled into the old well.[38]

Patten decided that this was the holy well of Richeldis' original site.[39] Sir William Milner (who both funded the building and provided its architect from his own architectural practice)[40] wrote:

> The structure of the well was, at the bottom few courses, oak logs; and higher up circular, of rough flint-work; quite consistent with a late Saxon date: and near at hand was a large masonry foundation, square, and with a square socket in it, which was undoubtedly the base of a great cross. It was found that the well dropped into the place exactly between two piers of the new arcade of the covering church; and we none of us have any doubts that what was discovered was the original Holy Well.[41]

Milner, who was both the 'architect' and the 'expert' Patten had mentioned, relied largely on faith to prove the well's authenticity (note the two-fold denial of 'doubt' in his account).

This combination of archaeology, faith and good fortune (not only in the finding of the well but in its fitting perfectly into the already planned arcade of the new shrine) provided more than a direct metonymic link to Walsingham's 'Saxon' origins on a historical level. It was also significant in terms of the spatial and liturgical dynamics of the village. The well was much closer to the village than the Roman Catholic Slipper Chapel; indeed, it was within sight of the Augustinian Priory, which had been the centre-point of medieval Walsingham. Furthermore the discovery was taken by Patten as a sign, a vindication of his own standpoint in opposition both to Roman Catholics and the many sceptics located in the Church of England. There is an extraordinary passage in a eulogy written by Sir William Milner on Patten's death (see Plate 2), in 1958, describing what supposedly happened the night before the installation of the image in the restored Holy House in 1931:

> A strange thing happened the night before, when Fr. Patten was in the new building, and was conscious of the presence of several figures, in the dress of the Augustinian Canons, visiting the various altars, consulting a paper which one of them held in his hands, and then nodding their heads at evident pleasure at each altar, newly consecrated that day.[42]

---

38 A. Hope Patten, *Sactuary of Our Lady of Walsingham described by Erasmus* (pamphlet published in Walsingham, 1931), p. 14, excerpted in Cobb 1990, *op. cit.* note 19, p. 28.
39 See Stephenson 1970, *op. cit.* note 18, p. 156.
40 See Cobb 1990, *op. cit.* note 19, pp. 102–4. Milner was one of Patten's principal associates. He provided the land, finance and architect (Romily Craze) for the shrine and subsequently served in its College of Guardians.
41 *Our Lady's Mirror* (Autumn, 1958), p. 21.
42 *Our Lady's Mirror* (Autumn, 1958), p. 20.

Plate 2 Patten's tomb in the south-west portion of the Anglican shrine church. His feet rest on a small copy of the Holy House (S. Coleman and J. Elsner).

What is significant here is not merely the appropriation of the past in a building, but the way in which the process of restoration provides its own legitimacy on spiritual as well as archaeological grounds. Patten is not only claiming to have identified a site of medieval miracles, he is also locating his modern restoration within the quasi-mythical tradition of the original foundation of the shrine. Richeldis had a dream or vision of the Virgin Mary, while Patten himself appears to have had a vision of those who guarded the medieval shrine, approving the historical accuracy of his reconstruction. In addition, the discovery of the well was taken by Patten to be an exact equivalent to a sign given to Richeldis – holy water.

Of course, Patten (and before him, Richeldis) are by no means the only figures in the Christian world to have appropriated the power of the Holy House. The famous medieval shrine at Loreto in Italy is said to be the original building, transported by angels (via a circuitous route) from Nazareth.[43] In turn, Notre Dame in the United States has a replica of Loreto, completed in

---

[43] On Loreto, see F. Grimaldi, *La Historia della Chiesa di Santa Maria di Loreto* (Loreto, 1993) and F. Grimaldi (ed.), *Il Santuario di Loreto* (Rome, 1994).

1859. For McDannell,[44] such exercises in religious replication are also exercises in the production of authenticity. The religious object is, for believers, easily located within both conventional religious narrative and the spiritual desire of the spectator or pilgrim. At Walsingham, multiple narratives reinforce each other: the biblical story of Virgin and Child is augmented by that of the Virgin and Richeldis a millennium later. After the passage of almost another thousand years, Patten's revival produces its own links with the mythico-historical tales of the medieval as well as biblical past.

It seems appropriate that a site centrally concerned with incarnation (involving the Virgin's motherhood and the early life of Jesus) should have become the centre of disputes over the 'authentic' restoration of pilgrimage tradition in material shape. Both the incarnation and the revival of the tradition are concerned with the immanence of the sacred, the degree to which spiritual meaning can be derived from earthly action and physical form. Given the stakes involved, it is perhaps not surprising that Roman Catholics certainly did not take Patten's claims to be the Gospel Truth. For instance, a book by a Catholic archaeologist H. M. Gillett, published in 1946, expresses views held by many contemporaries with similar religious beliefs. His work is remarkable not least because he talks about the restoration of the pilgrimage tradition without making any direct mention of the Anglican presence at the site.[45] The message would have been clear enough to the initiated. Discussing a nineteenth-century excavation in the village, he asserts that 'nothing since discovered has the remotest claim to authenticity', and that 'one does not wish to pour scorn on other peoples' findings and feelings; but latterly statements have been made of such an extreme and final nature that some kind of warning is called for lest an utterly false tradition be perpetrated and perpetuated'.[46] Still more pungent is the following:

> Any number of sects and denominations may come along and out of devotion to the Blessed Mother erect chapels and shrines at Walsingham. But be they set up, even on the very spot of Our Lady's choosing, they may never become The Shrine of Our lady of Walsingham. It is a hard fact, but a true one, that just as the Desolation came through repudiation of the Holy See, Restoration can be made only in union with the Holy See.[47]

In these claims for the pilgrimage site there are a series of subtle (and sometime not so subtle) attempts at positioning a revived Walsingham within national and ecclesiastical consciousness. The site is seen in various contexts as a rival to, and equivalent of, medieval Canterbury; as a means of contact with

---

44 C. McDannell, *Material Christianity. Religion and Popular Culture in America* (New Haven, 1995), pp. 155–61.
45 Gillett 1946, *op. cit.* note 35, pp. 67–80.
46 Gillett 1946, *op. cit.* note 35, p. 22.
47 Gillett 1946, *op. cit.* note 35, p. 72.

pre-Reformation Christianity; as representative of the nation's past and present and its potential for spiritual revival; and as a battle-ground for the supremacy of Anglo- or Roman Catholic versions of the faith. In these ways, Walsingham's revival comes close to echoing John Eade and Mike Sallnow's depiction of great pilgrimage sites as being fetishised yet empty vessels, able to reflect back to the interpreter a vision of his or her aspirations.[48] At Walsingham such aspirations have often been expressed specifically through a claim to represent medieval forms of piety. The modern day, recreated, pilgrimage functions as a focal point for wider disputes concerning the right to represent and reclaim the spirituality of the medieval Church.

Patten's Stones

We have seen how the process of restoration, physical as well as theological, became central to both Patten and his Roman Catholic rivals. In Patten's case the revival involved the creation of a replica of Richeldis' Holy House which would again be located within a chapel. Although it was obviously a modern version of the building supposedly put up by Richeldis, the construction was based on measurements derived from medieval sources. Patten ensured a further, tangible and direct connection with the Middle Ages by incorporating as many medieval remnants as possible not only in its decor but in its very structure.

A large part of the fabric of the Holy House as well as the main structure of the principal altars of the Anglican shrine at Walsingham were constructed from a collection of medieval stones gathered together in or after 1931 (Plate 3).[49] Each stone proclaims its origin in the Middle Ages, either by means of some medieval carving or through careful labelling with their provenance, such as 'Lincoln Cath', 'Clare Priory' or 'Burnham A'. (Of course a significant number of stones came from the Priory ruins at Walsingham.) Most of the sites represented were monasteries destroyed during the English Reformation; the stones are therefore fragments, or relics, of an event in the medieval past which Patten's revival of pilgrimage was attempting to reverse. The stones relate Patten's revived Walsingham not only to its medieval predecessor but also to the entire monastic tradition eradicated by Henry VIII's reformers.

While there are many medievalising objects in the Anglican shrine at Walsingham – including reliquaries (one purporting to be of the True Cross), statues for veneration, votive dedications, banners and paintings – the collection of stones is special. Not only was it embedded in the very fabric of the new shrine, but it was used to authenticate the foundations and genealogy of

---

[48] Eade and Sallnow 1991, *op. cit.* note 6, pp. 9–16.
[49] On the collection of stones, see at greater length J. Elsner 1997, *op. cit.* note 15, pp. 44–5.

Plate 3 The view pilgrims have as they enter the main door of the Anglican shrine church. A relief depicting the Annunciation is placed in front of the western wall of the Holy House. Above and to the side of the relief can be seen some of Patten's stones, taken from pre-Reformation ruins (S. Coleman and J. Elsner).

Anglican pilgrimage to Walsingham in the medieval tradition of English spirituality which the Reformation had truncated (or so Walsingham's revivers believed). On the exterior faces of the Holy House, there are over 170 stones whose provenances are virtually a catalogue of the monasteries dissolved by Henry VIII. More stones, some inscribed, are located in the interior of the Holy House. Very few of these relics are not English, for instance one from Chartres on the south side and one from Patmos in the interior. Describing their use in *Our Lady's Mirror* in 1932, Patten wrote:

> The altar [inside the Holy House] is built of stones, chiefly from the ruined Priory of our Lady of Walsingham, but among them are others from Binham Abbey, a cell of the great Benedictine Abbey of St Alban's, the Pilgrim Chapel of Our Lady of the Red Mount at Lynn, Rievaulx Abbey, the first Cistercian house in Yorkshire, colonised directly from St Bernard's own Clairvaux, Dunwich priory, near the site of the submerged East Anglian Cathedral, Netley Abbey, Barking Abbey, founded by St Erkenwald for his sister S. Ethelberga, Byland Priory, another Cisterian monastery colonised from Sabigney and Furnes, and Mileham Priory.[50]

This text gives more than the identities of the monasteries. It affirms their genealogical relations to still greater foundations (like St Alban's or Clairvaux) or to saints (St Bernard, St Erkenwald and St Ethelberga). The fragments from Binham, Lynn and Dunwich – a local group following 'the ruined Priory of our Lady of Walsingham' – evoke the medieval spirituality of East Anglia, where Walsingham was the principal pilgrimage site in the Middle Ages.

Patten's most explicit and remarkable effacement of the temporal and religious gap between the Church of England and the ideal Catholic Church of the Middle Ages lay in the one inscribed stone of the Holy House which was not medieval. This was the foundation stone which announced in Latin that the building had been restored when Pius XI was pope, when Bertram was bishop of Norwich and when Hope Patten was parish priest of Walsingham.[51] Such a suppression of the historical distinctions and disagreements between the churches of Rome and England provoked a strong protest not only from the Roman Catholics but also from the Anglican bishop Bertram Pollock of Norwich.[52] Patten's justification is instructive. The foundation stone, he wrote:

> ... has been inserted in the wall as a witness to the claim of Anglicans, a claim our English Roman 'friends' will not allow, namely that we (the donors) believe that in this year of grace 1931 the rightful parish priest of Walsingham is Hope Patten, not Fr Grey of Fakenham [the nearby Roman Catholic priest] – and that the true bishop of the diocese is Dr Pollock and not the [Roman Catholic] Bishop of Northampton. But while maintaining these

---

[50] *Our Lady's Mirror* (Winter, 1932), p. 3.
[51] See Stephenson 1970, *op. cit.* note 18, pp. 159–61.
[52] See Stephenson's discussion, 1970, *op. cit.* note 18, pp. 159–61.

facts we also record our belief and affirm that we are not members of a separate body, cut off from the rest of Christendom, and to emphasise this fact we state that in this year 1931 Pius XI was Chief Bishop.[53]

Patten's extraordinary Anglo-Catholic position was this: the English Church was part of the traditional and ancient Catholic Communion led by Rome, but not of the modern Roman Catholic Church. It belonged to an ideal, medieval Church, the church of the monasteries and of medieval pilgrimage. It was into this pseudo-medieval wonderland of traditions (albeit re-invented) and fragments (some of them possibly fakes), of pilgrimage shrines and monastic rituals, that Patten's collection of stones attempted to propel the Walsingham shrine.

The stones evoked an ideal, medieval, past. They were romanticised as ruined remains, fetishised as pseudo-relics, and now restored by incorporation into the revived shrine. Patten's new Walsingham was not only the authentic site of medieval Walsingham, itself the result of Richeldis' supernatural vision, but was also a modern act of atonement for the error of the Reformation (which was the historical moment when, in Patten's view, original medieval spirituality came to an end). After the completion of the Holy House in 1931, Patten repeated the strategy of using the medieval to fabricate the present: more ancient stones were collected, to build the altar in the chantry of Edward I, dedicated in September 1936, and to construct the High Altar. The enlarged church was dedicated in June 1938. Again most of the stones for these two altars came from the demolished medieval abbeys and priories of England.[54] Thus, in the substantially complete version of Patten's pilgrimage church, the most sacred elements in the building – the altars and the model of the Holy House – as well as much of the fabric of the church itself, were fragments of pre-Reformation English monasticism. No gesture could more visibly, rhetorically or liturgically pronounce Walsingham's purpose as an expiation of the sins of Reformation and a reconstruction of the sanctity of a medieval church which Patten idealised and romanticised in equal measure. It also provided pilgrims of the Anglo-Catholic faith with the possibility of encountering, during the sacred time of an often annual visit and renewal of commitment, the literal as well as metaphorical touchstones of their faith.

Quite how the stones were acquired remains something of a mystery. Patten's biographer, and successor as administrator of the Walsingham shrine, speculates that 'some had been removed by "cloak and dagger" methods'.[55] Thus Patten's stones may resemble the medieval age in another sense: they may be modern-day equivalents of the *furta sacra*, the stolen relics used to adorn or even help establish sacred sites in the Middle Ages. Whatever the

---

53 Quoted in Stephenson 1970, *op. cit.* note 18, pp. 159–61.
54 On the two altars, with a diagram of the stones of the High Altar, see Cobb 1990, *op. cit.* note 19, pp. 44–5.
55 See Stephenson 1970, *op. cit.* note 18, p. 163.

truth may be, the shrine's appropriation of the past through its very fabric works on many levels. It has a characteristically material referent, evoking history and archaeology in the most direct manner possible, in a sense effacing the fact that the Holy House is a mere replica of the original. Walter Benjamin has commented on the necessity of the presence of an original in art, as a guarantor of authenticity and sacred aura.[56] The new Holy House, although a copy of a copy of an original, clothed itself in fragments of 'real' medieval buildings. Moreover, it rapidly acquired its own sacred aura. The devotion and testimonies of pilgrims were inscribed in *ex voto* plaques and placed opposite the western end of the Holy House around the interior of the shrine church's west door. Offerings of candles from associated parishes were placed alongside the Holy House's outer walls.

The material culture of Anglican Walsingham thereby came to reconstitute a sense of the medieval past in the act, apparently, of merely reviving it. The Holy House with its stones provides relics not merely symbolic of the past, but actually consubstantial with it.[57] The stones, moreover, are not merely piled up in a corner: they contribute to a building that itself commemorates simultaneously the incarnation of Christ and the incarnation of the historical/mythical tradition of Richeldis. In bringing the stones together in this way, the shrine manages both to celebrate multiple places destroyed by the ravages of the past and to bolster the spiritual authenticity of a single place, Walsingham, as the sacred centre in which such places are unified in the present. The historical and religious legitimacy of fallen monasteries is thereby both restored and appropriated. In the process, the dispersed sacredness of multiple shrines is said to be brought together and focused on a single, all-encompassing site.

Pilgrims in the Present

In the early part of this century, during the re-establishment of the Anglican shrine, pilgrimage to Walsingham was, on the whole, carried out by a relatively restricted constituency of committed Anglo-Catholics. Given the somewhat sectarian position of the shrine in relation to the rest of the Church of England, such pilgrimage implied a particular statement of one's identity within the contemporary church as well as a desire to connect with the quasi-medieval world created by Patten and his associates. Today, the shrine's position has changed within the Church as a whole as well as in relation to wider cultural spheres. Walsingham is now a prime tourist site, with its medieval buildings open to the uncommitted public as well as the many thousands of Christians who come each year. The Anglican shrine now

---

[56] W. Benjamin, 'The Work of Art in the Age of Mechanical Reproduction', in *Illuminations*, ed. H. Ahrendt (London, 1970), pp. 219–53 (pp. 222–7).
[57] P. Connerton, *How Societies Remember* (Cambridge, 1989) p. 43.

co-operates with the Roman Catholics in a spirit of explicit ecumenism. The general population's involvement with Anglicanism has lessened since Patten's day, at least in terms of ritual attendance, while the Church of England itself has become an increasingly heterogeneous liturgical and theological institution.

In these new contexts, Walsingham remains something of a bastion of conservatism, and has won few friends within the liberal wing of the Church as a result of its refusal to approve the ordination of women. Yet there is no doubt that the appeal of pilgrimage to the village has broadened. The core of parish-pilgrims to the Anglican shrine, those who come every year on annual weekends, remain self-identified Anglo-Catholics who see their visits primarily as a means to meet others of like mind and spirituality. However, many of the other pilgrims interviewed over the past two years regard a visit to Walsingham less as a statement of religious identity than as a 'fun-day-out', an occasion to experiment with unfamiliar liturgy, even to 'camp-it-up' with sprinkling at the well, or the smells and bells of mass, away from the constraints of their everyday liturgical lives. In this sense, they continue the attitude, so common to pilgrimage in general, of revelling in escape from mundane existence, yet do this in a way that involves a rather playful embrace of the medievalising traditions available at Walsingham. The boundaries between sacred travel and tourism have become less distinct, and are even consciously breached by some. More than one pilgrim, including clergy, has actually described the experience as akin to going to a funfair.

The broadening out of pilgrimage to Walsingham in recent times has had some important influences on the contemporary re-inventions of the site. In effect, a number of different 'medievalisms' now exist, each reflecting distinct forms of attachment to pilgrimage. Undoubtedly, some pilgrims, particularly those committed to Anglo-Catholicism, retain something of Patten's desire to establish direct links with the past through both the liturgy and the material culture of the shrine. Here, for instance, is a pilgrim who takes parishioners to the village every year:

> You come here and it begins to fall into place. . . . After a while you realise that what you do back [home] in say a church that was built at the end of the last century has been going on in some of these churches for seven or eight centuries, and it makes you feel that you are part of something which is more than . . . just local, just the way we do it, just the way people have been doing it in my lifetime.

Here, pilgrimage is seen as an opportunity not only to establish a link with the past but also a connection with a place that provides national validation for parochial practices. Rather more colourfully, we observed a priest describing the practice of permitting multiple groups to worship simultaneously at different altars as 'splendidly medieval'; just, it was implied, what he expected and required of the place.

This sense of re-invoking the past is evident, also, in some of the official presentations of the site for tourists. For instance, a guide on one of the tours of the village encourages her listeners to stand in the High Street, with their backs to the so-called Martyrs' House, and to look with half-closed eyes to their right and left during processions by Anglo- or Roman Catholics. Her claim is that from this position it becomes impossible to tell whether one is observing a modern or a medieval pilgrimage, and indeed some pilgrims have made similar comments when describing processions they have witnessed or participated in.

If these represent a notion of medievalism that might be described as 'unironic', implying that reaching back into the true past exists as a possibility, other forms of viewing the history and archaeology of Walsingham can also be identified. Here, for instance, are the words of a priest at the Anglican shrine, discussing the importance or otherwise of Walsingham's founding narrative:

> Whether it actually happened like that . . . I mean the endless controversies over where the medieval shrine actually was, at the end of the day doesn't really mean very much to me, I have to say. I mean it's not essential to the place . . . If we were to discover that Richeldis never existed or something, obviously there was something that happened or else this would not have been such an important place of pilgrimage. And I think it's that continuity with the past which is more important – you know, not the evidence of 1061, or 1068, or 1242.

What is expressed here is a common theme in some of our interviews; that the specifics of the medieval period, and implicitly the authentic piety of Richeldis' Walsingham, are inherently unrecoverable. But at the same time the pilgrim can be sure that in the very act of pilgrimage s/he maintains an essential continuity with an admittedly ill-defined past. The site comes to represent 'true' tradition, but not in a way that permits dogmatic claims to accurate historical knowledge. Such an attitude is perhaps especially appropriate to Walsingham, where for many years the original site of the Holy House was not known, and where even today there is some dispute among pilgrims as to whether archaeological evidence pointing to a spot adjacent to the Priory is reliable (Plate 4).

Most striking, however, are those pilgrims (devoted Anglicans, if not Anglo-Catholics) who view even the idea of asserting continuity with the medieval past as problematic. For these visitors, the site represents the opportunity to play with notions of the medieval that can shift, be variously appropriated, precisely because they can be seen as mere inventions of the present.[58] Thus, a deaconess states:

---

[58] On invented traditions, see E. Hobsbawm and T. Ranger (ed.), *The Invention of Tradition* (Cambridge, 1983), pp. 1–14.

Plate 4 A picture of the Augustinian Priory grounds during an important Roman Catholic pilgrimage. The spot marking the assumed original site of the Holy House is marked by the statue of the Virgin and Child (S. Coleman and J. Elsner).

> I have a sneaking suspicion that Walsingham is probably like Scottish culture and Celtic Christianity. They're both inventions of the nineteenth century.... I don't think it matters. I think it expresses something we want to express and can express through that place.... It would be false to say this is something we've inherited unchanged from the medieval period. Actually, we've invented it for ourselves ...

Walsingham is indeed a place where some pilgrims bypass conventional liturgies, setting up stations of the cross, for instance, which derive much of their meaning for the participants because they evoke self-consciously constructed views of an imagined past, not because they construct historically accurate enactments of medieval ritual. As one pilgrim, who described himself as a socially liberal Anglo-Catholic, put it, pilgrimage allows him and those in his group to 'medievalise in a social sense'. Thus, for him and his fellow pilgrims, to drink in the pub, revel in the feel of the place and mix religious business with pleasure, was a sufficient and probably more 'authentic' link at least with Chaucerian medieval pilgrimage than any solemn liturgy would have been. Or again, a young Roman Catholic woman, who had been on Anglican pilgrimages, described her liking of Walsingham thus: 'I like all these things like marquees and pennants and medieval romances, and it was a part of all that I suppose!' Some parallels may be evident here with another ancient English pilgrimage site, Glastonbury, described by Marion Bowman.[59] As in Walsingham, the polyvalent attractions of the place involve the juxtaposition of location and legend, fact and faith, the present and the past, with visitors prompted to arrive at syntheses of whatever they find most meaningful.

In a sense, the more playful visitors to Walsingham are 'post-pilgrims', self-conscious in their adoption of pilgrimage ritual, aware of alternatives and even of the constructed nature of the place.[60] Yet, in their evocation of the medieval, they are just as true to pilgrimage tradition as the shrine's revivers led by Hope Patten. Turner's point about the liminal nature of rites of passage is, of course, that they often give participants the space to experiment, to play, or at least present to themselves and others alternatives to the taken-for-granted.

For Patten, Walsingham provided a means to re-enter and revive a world of the past, to be accepted into an 'authentic' Church of his choosing and, in effect, creation. In this sense, the re-incarnated medieval period provided both the *fons et origo* of correct faith, and a critique of the contemporary Church. Among many newer pilgrims, however, engagement with Walsingham and its traditions takes on a more distanced form, one that is aware of the historical contingency of the original foundation as well as of the revival of the shrine.

Talking of pilgrimage in the contemporary and, indeed, post-modern, world, Pace notes the need for a subjective sense of individual identity, and how: 'Religion, to use a metaphor, having been chased out of the window of the crystal palace of modernity, comes back through the front door.'[61] He means by this that collective religious belief and practice need not be abandoned in a climate of scepticism, but rather change their function: they may lose the authority of absolute truth, but find a role in providing symbolic resources through which people reflect upon their own potentialities. In a similar vein, talking of contemporary tourist practices, Urry refers to the ways in which the self and its structuring over time have become increasingly privatised.[62] As a result, the time-space paths of individuals are 'de-synchronised' and moved away from sites of mass consumption. Certainly, Pace's and Urry's points have resonance with the activities of many pilgrims to Walsingham, for

---

[59] M. Bowman, 'Drawn to Glastonbury', in *Pilgrimage in Popular Culture*, ed. I. Reader and T. Walter (London, 1993), pp. 29–62.
[60] J. Urry, *Consuming Places* (London, 1995), p. 140.
[61] E. Pace, 'Pilgrimage as Spiritual Journey: An Analysis of Pilgrimage Using the Theory of V. Turner and the Resource Mobilization Approach', *Social Compass* 36/2 (1980), pp. 229–44 (p. 240).
[62] Urry 1995, *op. cit.* note 60, pp. 217–18.

whom the place is a means to create an experience that uses a theatrical sense of the past in order to cultivate highly personalised spiritual experiences. The deaconess quoted above spent much of one of her visits to Walsingham alone, in the Holy House, almost unaware that she had come with a large party of pilgrims and a clergyman who was supposed to guide them through the site. In her decision to remove herself from the official pathways of the shrine, she echoes the actions of many other contemporary visitors; those who regard themselves as strongly committed to the Anglican faith yet also in need of a revitalised and partially distanced relationship to its institutions.

Final Remarks

This paper should not be read as an attempt to deny Walsingham's medieval credentials, but rather to show how the site has incorporated a number of different notions of the medieval, within its material culture, liturgies and symbols. This ability to incorporate a wide range of ideas and practices is, of course, characteristic of the great pilgrimage sites of Christianity and other world religions, whose continued success often relies on their ability to absorb and even sanctify the religious and cultural assumptions of a huge range of pilgrims. Bowman, for instance, has described the co-existence of Greek Orthodox, Roman Catholic and Protestant pilgrimage to Jerusalem and notes: 'The holy city is . . . a place where pilgrims who have inherited or developed certain images of a "Jerusalem" . . . can embody these images and engage them as aspects of the material world.'[63] We have argued that Walsingham provides lay pilgrims and some clergy with the means to engage imaginatively as well as liturgically with images of the past, and through the workings of the imagination to construct a pilgrimage site and a vision of the Middle Ages partially of their own devising.

An important part of our argument has been that Walsingham, as a site designed specifically for pilgrimage, engages its visitors with the temporal and spatial characteristics of the 'liminal'. In its capacity to act as a stage for the construction of a variety of medievalised and sacralised experiences, Walsingham has the potential to provide temporary release from mundane existence and everyday ritual forms. Those who visit the Anglican shrine as pilgrims expect it to be no ordinary place; although they may be with familiar companions, they often feel that their journey has a special purpose or meaning. The symbolically-charged worlds of the past and of the sacred

---

63 See G. Bowman, 'Christian Ideology and the Image of a Holy Land: The Place of Jerusalem Pilgrimage in the Various Christianities', in Eade and Sallnow 1991, *op. cit.* note 6, pp. 98–121 (p. 99). Idem, 'Contemporary Christian Pilgrimage to the Holy Land', in *The Christian Heritage in the Holy Land*, ed. A. O. Mahony, G. Gunner and K. Hintlian (London, 1997), pp. 288–310.

reinforce each other in ways that both Hope Patten and many Christians today would recognize as being central to their experience of the place's spirituality. Whether the pilgrimage provides a 'fun day out' in rural England or the opportunity to visit a site where everything 'falls into place', the special character of Walsingham derives from its ability to suggest a world divorced from the commonplace.

In these regards, Walsingham may be fortunate in the particular time period to which it refers. The Middle Ages are associated in the minds of many pilgrims, even among those professing little historical knowledge, with a Chaucerian world of picturesque carnival. The time period is also valued because of its credentials in referring to a pre-Reformation England. It has already been noted that this aspect of the place's history was hugely important to Patten. It is also mentioned by others who work at or visit the shrine (both Anglo- and Roman Catholics), who wish to see Walsingham as a place where the historic cleavage in the Church can be healed, either through union or appropriation of one side by the other. For many, the medieval period evoked by Walsingham is not that of a museum, nor that of distant and dry history, but rather a past that has an urgent and living role to play in the present.